ANKARA
CITY GUIDE

ANKARA
CITY GUIDE

Ilse Naves Scheidel • Hein-Jan Keijzer

AKILÇELEN
kitaplar

AKILÇELEN KİTAPLAR
Yuva Mahallesi 3702. Sokak No: 4 Yenimahalle / Ankara
Tel:+90-312 396 01 11 (pbx) Faks: +90-312 396 01 41
www.akılcelenkitaplar.com
bilgi@akilcelenkitaplar.com
Yayıncı Sertifika No: 12382
Matbaa Sertifika No: 13987

ISBN: 978-605-5069-31-5

ANKARA, 2014

Yayına Hazırlık : Boğaç Erkan
Sayfa Düzeni : Belgin Tuna
Kapak Tasarımı : Lodos Grup
Kapak Fotoğrafı : Boğaç Erkan
Baskı : Ayrıntı Basım Yayım ve Matbaacılık Ltd. Şti.
28. Cadde, 770. Sokak No: 105/A
İvedik Organize Sanayi
Yenimahalle/Ankara

Table of Contents

Introduction to Ankara

Ankara is located in central Turkey on the Anatolian peninsula, the Asian side of this continent-spanning nation. The city sits at an altitude of 850 metres (2800 feet and has existed as a settlement for several thousand years. For many centuries it was an important trading post on the Silk Route connecting Europe with the riches of Asia and Africa. In 1923 the city was became the capital of the new Republic of Turkey and a tremendous growth spurt began. With around 5 million inhabitants today, it is the second largest city, after İstanbul, in modern Turkey.

It's not just grey suits

Ankara has a reputation as a boring, bureaucratic city. A city void of culture or entertainment. But Ankara's biggest problem is that everyone compares her constantly with İstanbul, a city with centuries of culture and history, as well as the lion's share of recent investment. İstanbul's inhabitants, the *İstanbullu*, are particularly scathing of the capital. In their eyes, Ankara is a dull place missing all the excitement and intrigue of İstanbul. They commonly joke that *"The best thing in Ankara is the train back to İstanbul"*.

Although less well known than her more popular sister, Ankara actually has a rich history of ancient civilisations. It can be hard to find the traces in-between the concrete apartment blocks and crowded streets. But they do exist, and with this guide we intend to help you find them.

Another plus-point for Ankara, and one of the reasons for its being chosen as capital, is its central location. From Ankara you can set off to explore this diverse country which has things to offer every kind of tourist; whether you are looking for cultural exploration, culinary experiences, or a lazy summer on the beach, Turkey has a corner for you. The capital's central location makes stop-overs common on many package tours. Don't just treat it as a rest, take at least a day to get out and explore the city!

What does Ankara have to offer?

The 5 million people living here include a significant body of expats from around the world. Ankara is the home of all the foreign embassies, meaning a great number of diplomats live here, as well as international business people, international students and the few pioneering tourists. Add to these the large body of students from the several universities in the city, as well as all the locals, and you realise there must be something for all these people to do!

This is what we had in mind when we arrived in Ankara. Instead of listening to all the warnings that it would be "boring" we started to explore the city. And guess what, we liked it! We found a modern art scene, decent bars, fashionable restaurants, vibrant neighbourhoods, interesting museums, and lively bazaars selling typical Anatolian products and food. What's more, through our exploration we learned about the interesting and rich history of the city.

We fell in love with Ankara, with its hidden gems and unknown destinations. Ankara is a bustling centre of art (opera, jazz, art galleries, film festivals, modern dance, theatre), education (eight universities within city limits), politics (all of the government institutions and military headquarters) and international diplomacy (the embassies mentioned earlier). It's just that, unlike İstanbul, Ankara is a fruit you have to peel to get to the goodness inside. Its culture is not out in the open, but it is there. There are so few travel books about Ankara, pointing at the things it has to offer, but you will find out that the more you get to know about Ankara, the more interesting it gets.

How to use this guide?

We divided the city into segments and highlighted the best of each of them. At the beginning of a chapter you'll find a map on which these highlights are marked. Practical information, some history, and a few of our favourite restaurants can be found in separate chapters. Pick out what interests you and do not be afraid to switch between the chapters at random.

Use this book as a guide but do discover the city by yourself.

We're confident that you'll agree that the city has much more to offer than the train back to İstanbul. *Enjoy Ankara!*

Ilse and Hein-Jan

Disclaimer

At all times we did our very best to include accurate information. It's entirely possible, unfortunately, that between the time of writing and your reading the book things may have changed. We can't accept any liability for any issues arising from this. In general, Turkish people are extremely helpful and even take joy from assisting others. Don't hesitate to ask them if you need help, no matter how broken (or non-existent) your Turkish might be. University students, if you think you can identify them, will be more likely to have some knowledge of English or other European languages.

Asking for help in a shop or café might even get you an offer of a glass of tea, which is (unlike more touristic İstanbul) not always designed to extract money from you.

If you have anything to add or just want to get in touch, please free to email us at guideankara@gmail.com.

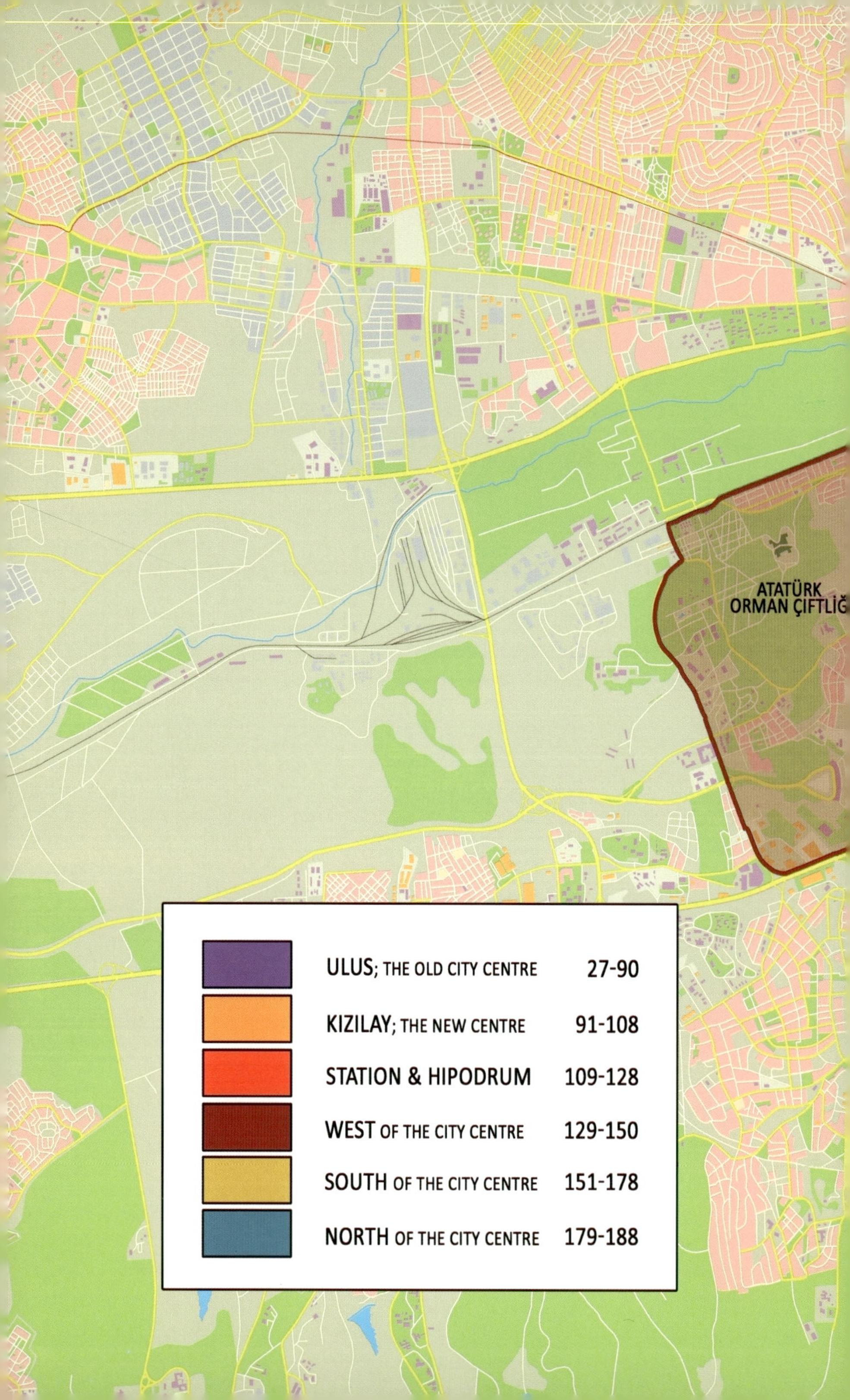
ATATÜRK ORMAN ÇIFTLIĞ
ULUS; THE OLD CITY CENTRE 27-90
KIZILAY; THE NEW CENTRE 91-108
STATION & HIPODRUM 109-128
WEST OF THE CITY CENTRE 129-150
SOUTH OF THE CITY CENTRE 151-178
NORTH OF THE CITY CENTRE 179-188

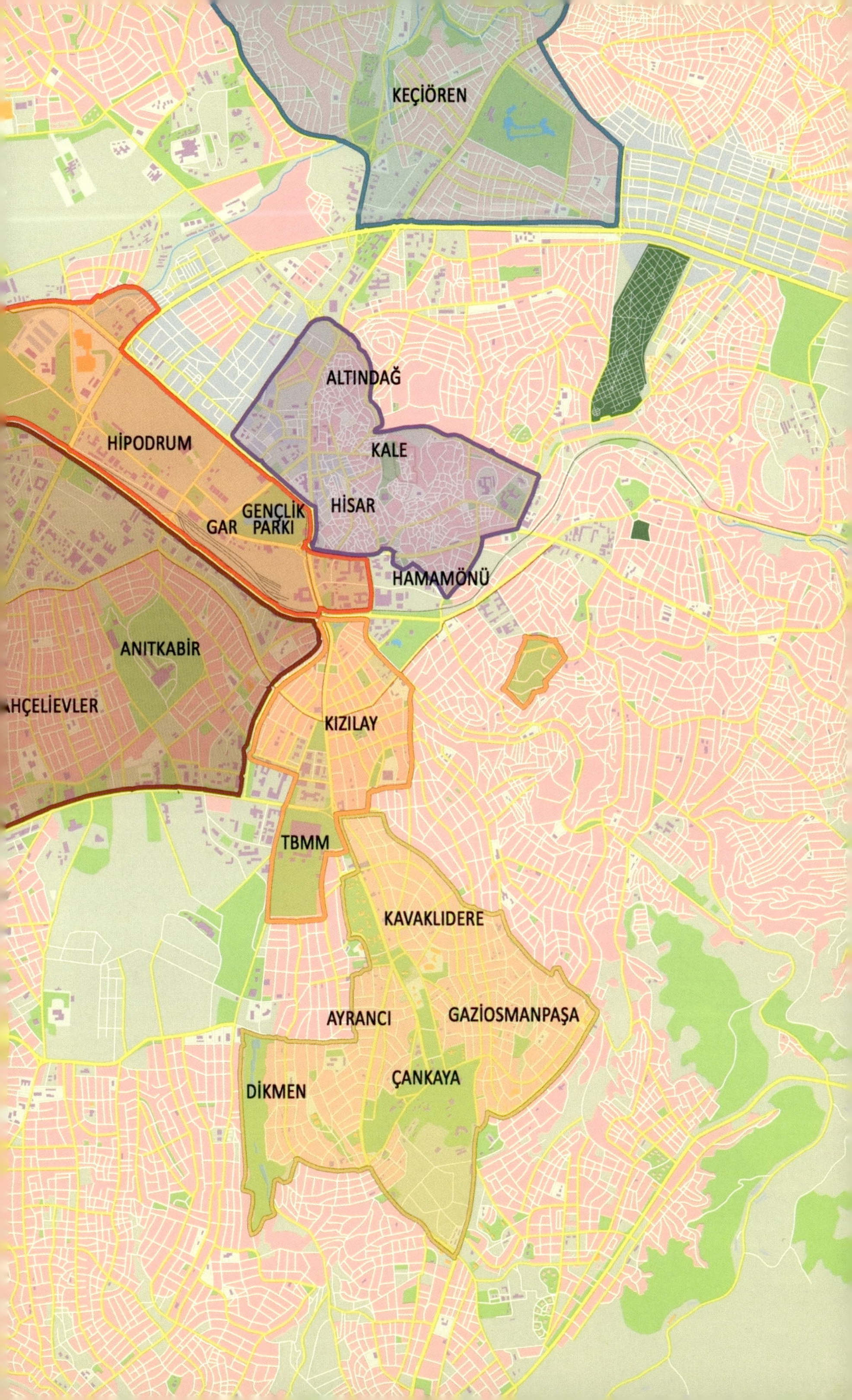
KEÇİÖREN
ALTINDAĞ
KALE
HİSAR
HAMAMÖNÜ
HİPODRUM
GENÇLİK
PARKI
GAR
ANITKABİR
AHÇELİEVLER
KIZILAY
TBMM
KAVAKLIDERE
AYRANCI
GAZİOSMANPAŞA
DİKMEN
ÇANKAYA

History

History

In 1923, Ankara became the capital of the newly founded Republic of Turkey. After the War of Independence, the era of the Ottoman Empire ended. The government, ministries and many embassies and financial and public institutions moved from İstanbul to Ankara, the capital of the new republic. This move changed the little dusty and dilapidated provincial city into a modern metropolis and the centre of political power and international diplomacy in Turkey.

Mustafa Kemal Atatürk, the leader of the Turkish nationalist movement, had chosen Ankara three years previously (1920) as the headquarters of his resistance movement. The city was situated at a crossroads of important north to south and east to west roads and was located on a strategic railway line through Anatolia. But more importantly, the city lay in the centre of the independent piece of land in central Anatolia, the part of land that the Allies (*Russians, Britain, France, Greece* and *Italy*) left to the Turks after World War I. In 1920,

Parliament building (1920). Photo: Vekam

the rest of the Ottoman Empire was still occupied by the Allies, including the Ottoman capital İstanbul. From Ankara, *Atatürk* started his independence movement and war against the Greeks and the Sultan of the old Ottoman power. And he succeeded. The Turkish nationalists won the War of Independence. On 29 October 1923 they replaced the Ottoman Empire and founded the Republic of Turkey and chose Ankara as the new capital city.

Before this capital shift and the founding of the Turkish Republic, Ankara had already had a very long and interesting history. Many different civilisations, with various cultures and beliefs, left their mark on Ankara. Some of their artefacts are visible in the museum of Anatolian Civilisations. The remains of more recent civilisations and history are also visible on the streets. Especially in the old city centre of Ankara, *Ulus*, you will find a number of sites of historical interest. Most of them are for free.

Ancient History

The oldest traces of civilisation go back to the Bronze Age. Around 2000 BC the Hittites, an Indo-European civilisation, were a dominant power in the Anatolia region. In its heyday the empire encompassed a large part of modern Turkey and north-western Syria and, to the

Gavurkale

east, upper Mesopotamia (Iraq and Iran). The centre of this mighty ancient empire was Hattuşa, an ancient city near modern Boğazkale, 200 km west of Ankara (see chapter *Outside Ankara*). There you will find the remains of this impressive civilisation. Anadolu Medeniyetleri Müzesi *(The Museum of Anatolian Civilisations)* in Ankara also shows an impressive collection of artefacts from Hittite times, such as jewellery, utensils, cuneiform tablets and religious objects. This ancient civilisation's settlements were found in and around Ankara. Some of them are still visible, like Gavurkale (60 km southwest of Ankara) (see chapter *Outside Ankara*). At this place, where there was once a Hittite castle or fortress, you can see Hittite reliefs carved on a cliff.

Greek texts in the walls of the citadel

After the Hittites, the Phrygians, Lydians, Persians and the Greeks ruled over Anatolia. Ankara grew under these successive powers and the city became more and more important as a trading centre in the region. This was because of its interesting location in the middle of Anatolia, at the junction of north to south and east to west trade routes. Situated on a strategic hill in the middle of a plateau between the mountains, Ankara was a perfect spot for trading caravans from the surrounding areas to meet each other. The city developed as an important trading centre, especially under the Greeks, who came to Ankara around 300 BC. It was the Greeks who called the city *Άγκυρα* (Ankyra), which means "anchor" in Greek. Later this name changed into *Ancyre, Engüriye, Angara, Angora* and finally *Ankara*. But the origin of the city name can be traced back to this Greek period. In 278 BC, Central Anatolia, including the city, was occupied by the Galatians, a Celtic race. They made *Ancyra*, as they called the city, the headquarters of the "*Tectosage*" tribe. So the city became an important tribal centre for the Galatians.

Roman Era

In 25 BC, the Roman emperor Augustus conquered *Ancyra* and the city became part of the Roman Empire. The Romans first made *Ancyra* one of the three main administrative centres of Anatolia. But when Augustus decided to upgrade *Ancyra* into a major provincial capital of the province of Galatia, the city became a grand metropolis in the Roman Empire.

The city was located on and around the hill where Ulus is situated nowadays. The centre of Roman Ankara was situated around a sacred precinct, where the Temple of Augustus was housed. Around

▶ Roman coins

▶ The excavations of the Roman theatre

Temple of Augustus. Photo: Vekam

this area were Roman baths and a theatre. The bath complex in the Çankırıkapı district was one of the largest of its kind in the Roman world. Archaeologists assume that the city was supplied with water by an aqueduct. This probably brought fresh water from Elmadağ, a mountain 20 km southeast of the city. Now the area of the Roman bath is an open air museum, where the ruins of buildings and temples from Ancyra are displayed. The remains of the Roman theatre have become more and more visible, since archaeologists re-started excavations in 2009.

The ruins of Roman *Ancyra* tell us that the boundary of the ancient Roman city to the north was a small river, the Hatıp Çayı, which flowed along *Ancyra.* This river does not exist anymore, but it was a tributary of the Ankara Çayı. Ankara Çayı still exists and flows from the east to the west through Ankara. But in a lot of places it is covered, diverted from the original stream and sometimes hardly visible. To the west, the Roman city was situated in the area of Gençlik Parkı, as far as Ankara Garı (the main railway station). The southern boundary of the city was at the site where you now find the Hacettepe University. Also

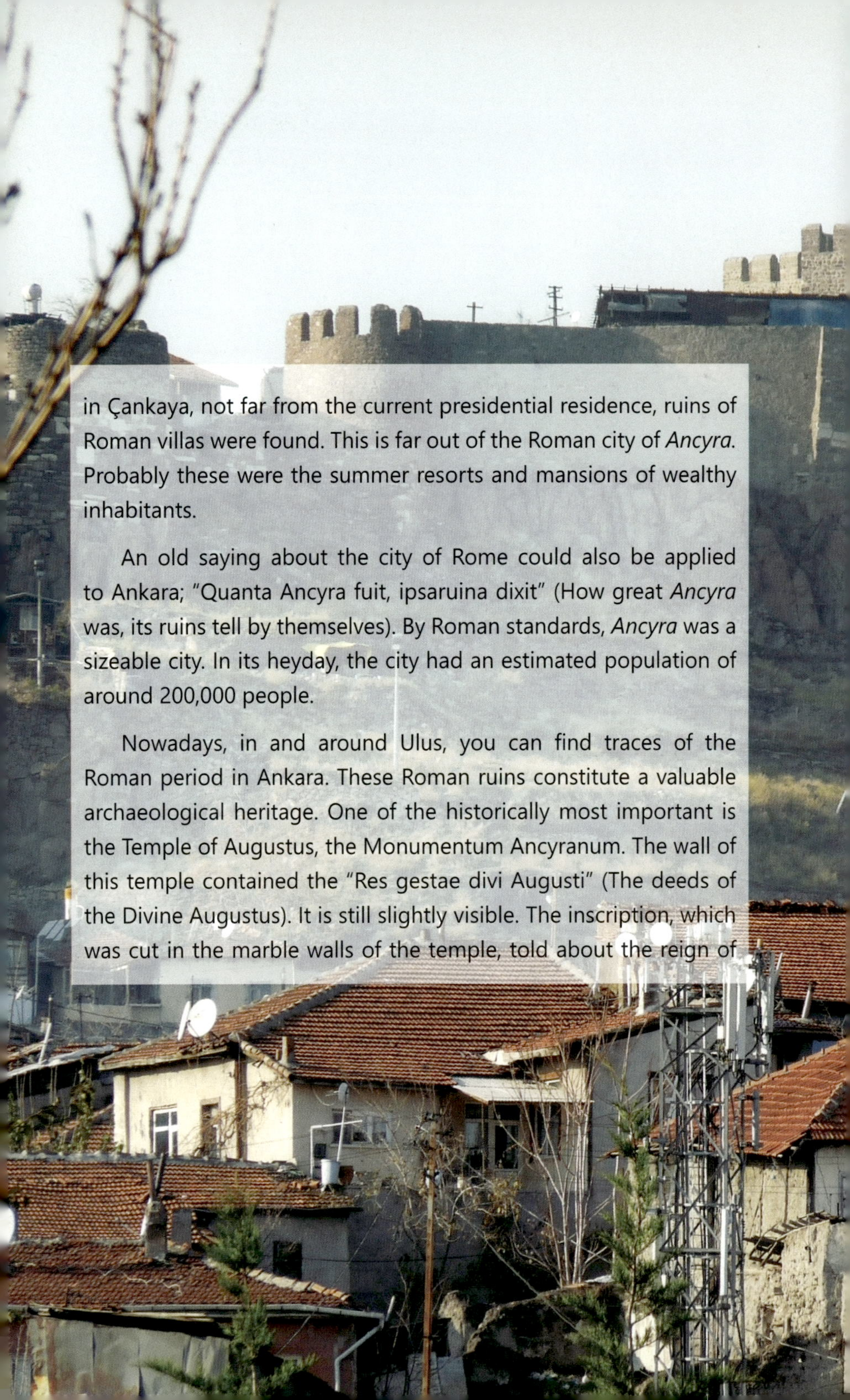

in Çankaya, not far from the current presidential residence, ruins of Roman villas were found. This is far out of the Roman city of *Ancyra*. Probably these were the summer resorts and mansions of wealthy inhabitants.

An old saying about the city of Rome could also be applied to Ankara; "Quanta Ancyra fuit, ipsaruina dixit" (How great *Ancyra* was, its ruins tell by themselves). By Roman standards, *Ancyra* was a sizeable city. In its heyday, the city had an estimated population of around 200,000 people.

Nowadays, in and around Ulus, you can find traces of the Roman period in Ankara. These Roman ruins constitute a valuable archaeological heritage. One of the historically most important is the Temple of Augustus, the Monumentum Ancyranum. The wall of this temple contained the "Res gestae divi Augusti" (The deeds of the Divine Augustus). It is still slightly visible. The inscription, which was cut in the marble walls of the temple, told about the reign of

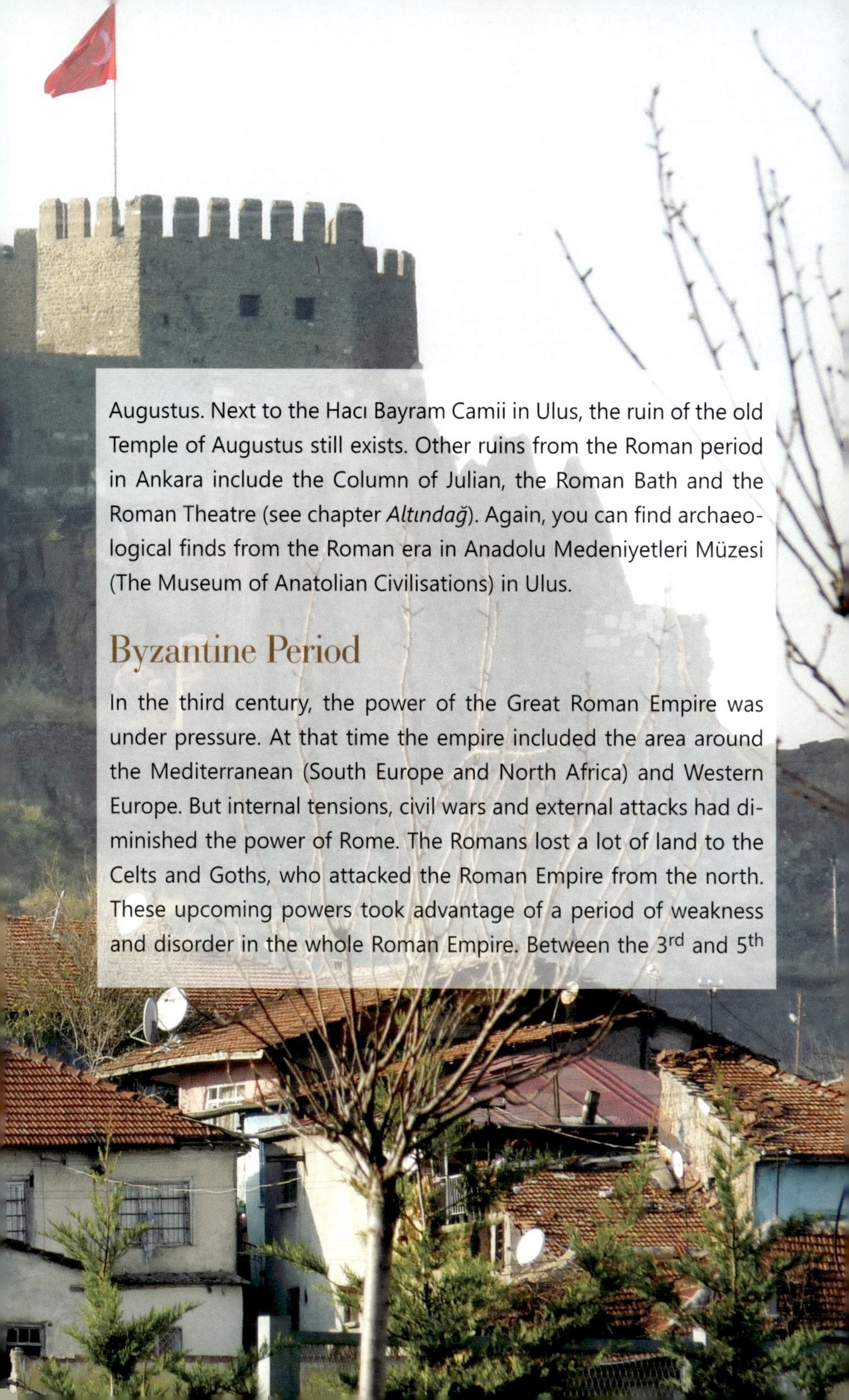

Augustus. Next to the Hacı Bayram Camii in Ulus, the ruin of the old Temple of Augustus still exists. Other ruins from the Roman period in Ankara include the Column of Julian, the Roman Bath and the Roman Theatre (see chapter *Altındağ*). Again, you can find archaeological finds from the Roman era in Anadolu Medeniyetleri Müzesi (The Museum of Anatolian Civilisations) in Ulus.

Byzantine Period

In the third century, the power of the Great Roman Empire was under pressure. At that time the empire included the area around the Mediterranean (South Europe and North Africa) and Western Europe. But internal tensions, civil wars and external attacks had diminished the power of Rome. The Romans lost a lot of land to the Celts and Goths, who attacked the Roman Empire from the north. These upcoming powers took advantage of a period of weakness and disorder in the whole Roman Empire. Between the 3rd and 5th century AD Rome´s power was declining more and more in Western Europe. When Rome fell, the southeastern part of the former empire still existed. Emperor Constantine I left Rome in the year 330 AD and moved to the city Byzantium. This was a site astride the seaway from the Black Sea to the Mediterranean and the land route from Europe to Asia. Byzantium was located in the centre of his remaining empire and he made this the new capital of the East Roman or Byzantine Empire. He named the city after himself, Constantinople.

In the first centuries of the Byzantine Empire, Ancyra became a kind of holiday resort for the emperors. In the 4th and 5th centuries the emperors would retire from the humid summer weather in Constantinople. They preferred the dry mountain atmosphere of *Ancyra.*

During the Byzantine era, the city continued to be a trading centre on the crossroads of trade routes through Anatolia and an important military, logistical and ecclesiastical centre. But the city lost some importance and influence, because Constantinople, the new capital of the empire, was so close by.

Because of the many attacks of several Arab Muslim armies between the 6th and late 11th century, the ruling powers changed frequently in *Ancyra.* But most of the time the Byzantines ruled in the city. Ankara's symbol, the tower of the citadel (Ankara Kalesi), was built in the 7th century. Its current form was made during a comprehensive restoration in the 900 AD.

Seljuks and Mongols

After the Byzantium era, *Ancyra* had several successive rulers. Firstly, in 1073, the Seljuks came from Central Asia and conquered parts of Anatolia, including the city of Ankara. Some interesting remains of the Seljuk period in Ankara are the masterpiece of Seljuk woodcarving in the Alaaddin Camii. This mosque, at the foot of the Ankara castle in the citadel, was built in 1178. It is one of the oldest mosques in Turkey (see chapter *Ulus-Hisar*). Another interesting Seljuk remain is Arslanhane Camii in Ulus.

Arslanhane Camii. Photo: Vekam

In 1243, the city was conquered by a strong and pugnacious folk from Central Asia, with cruel fighters on horseback: The Mongols. Under the leadership of Batu Khan, they conquered almost the whole of Central and Western Asia and parts of Eastern Europe, as far as Hungary. The Mongol conquest of Anatolia was a quick process. It only took them from 1241 to 1243 to take power in Anatolia from the Seljuks. They remained in power until the mid-14th century. In and near Ankara an *Ilkhanate* garrison was stationed. The city became an important military base for the Mongols.

Ottoman Era

As quickly as the Mongols came, they withdrew again. Probably because they had to choose a new Great Khan in Mongolia or were needed in other, more central parts of the empire. What remained in Anatolia was a land divided into a patchwork of independent Byzantine states. One of these Ghazi emirates was led by Osman I (1258-1326).

Ottoman Sultan Bayezid prisoned by Timur, after The Battle of Ankara.
Painting: Stanisław Chlebowski

He wanted to create one big empire again, like the Byzantine Empire once was. An empire on three continents: Europe, Asia and Africa. He began to conquer, to expand his territory and with success. The empire of *Osman*, the Ottoman Empire, started to grow firstly under the leadership of *Osman* I, and then, after his death, under his progeny. The empire extended across Anatolia, Eastern Mediterranean, Balkans, the Black Sea region, the Middle East and Northern Africa. Probably one of the most crucial victories was the conquest of Constantinople in 1453, which marked the end of the Byzantine era.

Return of the Mongols

Ankara had already become part of the Ottoman Empire in 1356. However, in 1402, the Mongols returned. Their new leader sought to rebuild the Mongol Empire of his predecessors. With long and relentless fighting, the Mongols returned in Anatolia, defeating the Ottoman Empire. In 1402 they conquered the important city of Ankara again, after "*The Battle of Ankara*". But this only lasted a year. In 1403 the Ottomans retook the city. After that time, the city remained under Ottoman rule for over 500 years.

Thriving Business

In the Ottoman Era, Ancyra, or Angora as the city was called in these days, continued to be a commercial centre. Angora was famous for the *sof* (mohair). This cloth was made from the wool of the *Ankara Keçisi*, a breed goat from Ankara with long hair. The *sof* from Ankara was sold in İstanbul, Bursa, Aleppo and exported to Venice, Poland and England. The city became well known for its *sof* and the Angora goat. This breed of goats gave the city not only wool, but also leather. So, beside the *sof* production, Ankara also had prosperous tanneries and was famous for its shoe manufacturing. In addition to the thriving leather and cloth industry, Angora also had a military importance because of its location and its citadel.

As Angora became more prosperous, it expanded and old districts were renewed or replaced with new quarters. Between 1427-1428 the old Roman sacred precinct, with the Temple of Augustus, was replaced with the Hacı Bayram Camii. The stones of the old Roman building were, in that time and also in later periods, reused in new buildings and objects. You still can see this, in the wall of the Hacı Bayram Camii and the walls of the citadel and the castle.

In 1440 the Karacabey quarter was built, consisting of a mosque, a tomb, a fountain and baths. Nowadays this district is better known as Hamamönü. There the old bath, Karacabey Hamamı (1440), still exists and is still in use. It can be visited for an authentic Turkish bath and massage (see chapter *Hamamönü*).

Angora was a sizeable city, with a mixed community of Muslims, Christians and Jews, all living in their own quarters. At the beginning of the 17th century the citadel had 9 and the whole city 85 of these quarters. In those days Angora had an estimated population of around 30,000 inhabitants. Due to the economic growth of Angora, the city kept on growing and expanding. Business was thriving. Big market halls and trading complexes were built in Ulus between the 15th and 17th century for the trade in wool, cloth, leather and related articles.

Some of these hans still exist, like the Kurşunlu Han and Mahmut Paşa Bedesteni (1464-1471), nowadays the Museum of Anatolian Civilisations, the Çengel Han (1522), nowadays the Rahmi Koç Museum, the Çukur Han, nowadays Divan Hotel and the Sulu Han (1511), nowadays a bazaar with handicraft supplies, beads and necklaces on the Şehit Teğmen Kalmaz Caddesi (see chapter *Ulus-Hisar* and *In and Around the Citadel*).

Little Ice Age

For two centuries, Ankara was a prosperous trading city but all this prosperity came to an end around the end of the 16th century. The climate fluctuations of the Little Ice Age had a far-reaching impact in the Ottoman Empire. The extreme cold and drought in Anatolia led to famine and poverty. Lots of people, but also animals, including the Angora goats, died. This also resulted in the outbreak of riots and

Mahmut Pasa Bedesteni. Photo: Vekam

View on Ankara by 1799, Rijksmuseum Amsterdam

looting, the most destructive one being the Celali Rebellion (1595-1610). To protect the prosperous city and her citizens from attacking and looting rebels, massive walls were built around the city (1604 -1608). These are still visible in Ulus, on İpek Caddesi and in the Ankara Evi Parkı. The Celali Rebellion marked a turning point in the Ottoman era, with an enduring impact on the region's population and economy. It ended a wealthy period for the city of Angora.

Industrial Revolution

From 1750, machinery started to be used in Western Europe. The Industrial Revolution changed agriculture, manufacturing, mining and transportation. The advent of technology had a profound effect on the social, economic and cultural conditions of the times not only in Western Europe, but also in Anatolia and the city of Angora. The trade in *sof*, cloth, wool, leather, etc., which had brought the city so much wealth in the past, declined. The city could no longer compete with

View on Ankara by 1872, Jules Delbet
(LOC- http://loc.gov/pictures/item/20096311562/)

Western European countries, where they had started to use machinery in the textile industry. The demand for wool from the famous Angora goats declined because of England's wool production, with Angora goats bred in South Africa. With the disappearance of the trade and production, the city lost its wealth and vibrancy. To make matters worse, between 1873 and 1875 the city was hit by extremely bad weather. This led to a massive famine with over 18,000 casualties. Many citizens left the city, looking for better lives elsewhere. It was almost the final blow for the once prosperous city in central Anatolia.

The Ottoman Railway

In 1888 the Ottomans started building the *Chemins de Fer Ottomans d'Anatolie*, the Ottoman Railway in Anatolia, from İstanbul, via Eskişehir and Ankara, to Konya. When the railway arrived in 1892, it gave a slight stimulus to Ankara. It had become easier to get to the small, sleepy provincial town that was located once more on an important route through Anatolia.

However, in 1915, the city was struck again by disaster. A major fire destroyed a large part of the city to the north. In the same year, many

Armenians were forced to leave the city and much wealth disappeared with them. What was left was a half ruined, burned, largely abandoned and poor city.

Modern History

On 27 December 1919 a miracle changed the future of the city. On that day, perhaps at the lowest point in the city's history, *Mustafa Kemal Atatürk* arrived in Ankara. He decided to settle his independence movement in Ankara, because city was located on the railway and therefore easily accessible by train. To coordinate the War of Independence, he needed a good and reliable communication system. Ankara was the best spot, because it had an important telegraph and communication centre for the Ottoman railway. Furthermore the city was located in the centre of the independent piece of land in central Anatolia, the part of land that the Allies (Russia, Britain, France, Greece and Italy) had left to the Turks after World War I. Because of the lack of alterna-

Atatürk arrives in Ankara by train. Photo: Vekam

Ankara station master house, home of Mustafa Kemal Atatürk between 1920-1921.

tives, Ankara was one of the best cities in which *Mustafa Kemal Atatürk* could settle- safe in the interior of Anatolia, away from his biggest threats. On the day he arrived, *Mustafa Kemal Atatürk* took residence in the "Stationmaster's Office" in Ankara railway station. This building was allocated to him as the Supreme Military Command Headquarters. During the War of Independence, he used this station building as his house and as the place where he prepared the plans for the war. This "*Atatürk's residence*" is nowadays a small museum on the right side of Ankara Garı and can be visited. It can also be seen from the platform in the station.

On 23 April 1920, the Grand National Assembly of independent Turkey came together for the first time in Ankara. *Mustafa Kemal Atatürk* was elected as the first Speaker of the House and the Head of

Parliament building, 1923. Photo: Vekam

the Government. The Turkish Grand National Assembly passed new laws, to give a mandate for the War of Independence –a war that ended after four years on 24 July 1923. With the victory of the Turkish nationalists, the era of the Ottoman Empire came to an end, after more than six centuries.

On 29 October 1923 the republic was proclaimed and Ankara became the capital of the newly founded Republic of Turkey. The entire government machinery moved from İstanbul to Ankara. The dusty, dilapidated Ottoman province city rose from the ashes and suddenly became the political centre of Turkey and an important city for international diplomacy.

Planning the New City

This change demanded a physical adaptation of Ankara. The city had to expand. The new leaders of the young republic wanted a capital city that was a physical manifestation of the new spirit. Through new buildings and town planning, they wanted to show their modern ideas and break with the past. City planners and architects from Europe, mostly from Germany and Austria, were hired to create new modern areas and buildings in a western style. The German architect and city planner Hermann Jansen made a big city plan for the new Turkish capital in 1932. In his plan he kept the old citadel and its vicinity as an area that represented the traditional Ankara. On the south side of the

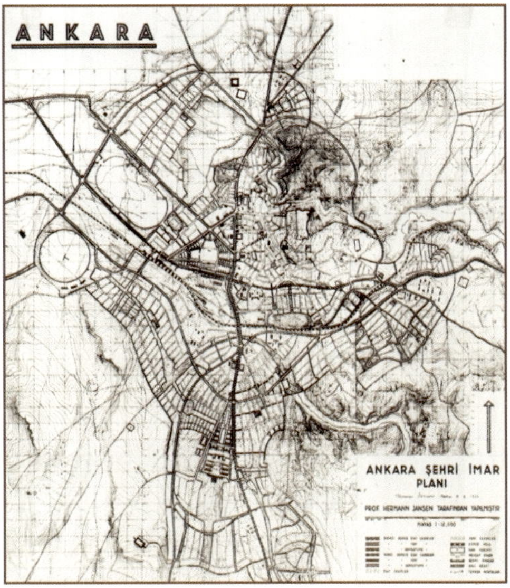

City plan by Hermann Jansen, 1932

old city he planned the new expansion of the city. This new area got the name Yenişehir (New City). The area is nowadays known as Kızılay.

He also planned the government quarter in this new part of the city –a triangular urban block on the southern end of Yenişehir, as a powerful symbol of the new Republic. This entire government quarter, including the Grand National Assembly of Turkey, was designed by the Austrian architect Clemens Holzmeister. This prominent complex is still the Turkish Parliament building.

The city planners also planned a lot of parks in Ankara. They wanted a green belt around the city and large green areas within the urban area, green corridors along valleys, public gardens and central parks along the main boulevards. Examples are Güvenpark (Park of Confidence) and Gençlik Parkı (Park of the Youth). There were expressive sculptures in these parks, which represented the prosperous and secure future of the new republic. The whole city was designed. Besides Astana (Ka-

Old first parliament building in 2012.

zakhstan), Brasilia (Brazil) and Canberra (Australia), Ankara is one of only a few artificially created capital cities in the world.

Slums in Ulus

The new leaders thought that the new capital needed to be able to accommodate 500,000 future inhabitants. In the first three decades the city grew as planned in an orderly fashion. In 1924, a year after the government moved to Ankara, the city had about 35,000 residents. In 1950 the population had already grown to 287,000. Because of unemployment and poverty in the countryside, in 1950s many people migrated from small country villages to the new capital. The result was an uncontrolled urban expansion. In 1960 the city had 646,000 and ten years later 1.2 million inhabitants. To shelter all these new people, many illegal houses were built around the city, called *gecekondu* (slum). Although many of these *slums* have been replaced, you still can see some of them, if you stand on top of Ankara castle, in the valley and on the slopes on the northeast side of the old city. The municipality is quickly tearing down all these slums and replacing them with new houses, modern built on the inside but with an authentic look on the outside.

Ankara Today

Nowadays, Ankara has over 4.5 million inhabitants and the city is still expanding. In the current Ankara you still see the mix of western modernity and old Ottoman and even Roman culture.

Ankara is a very diverse city, with modern areas with luxury shopping malls (Kentpark, Panora, etc), fashionable restaurants and nightclubs (Gazioşmanpaşa, Kavaklıdere, etc). These areas, and Ankara's wealth, are the result of rapidly increasing prosperity in Turkey in the last 10 years. Next to the modern areas, Ankara still has some old parts, with Roman ruins, Ottoman bazaars, lively small streets with fruit and vegetables. Here you will find electric gadgets, antiques and all sorts of trinkets. A place where kebap sellers are offering you their food and where you can drink hot *Türk kahvesi* (Turkish coffee) or cold *ayran* (Turkish yogurt drink), or where you can go to an old Ottoman *hamam*. A place where you can taste the lively atmosphere, like it was maybe hundreds of years ago.

Ulus,
the Old City Centre

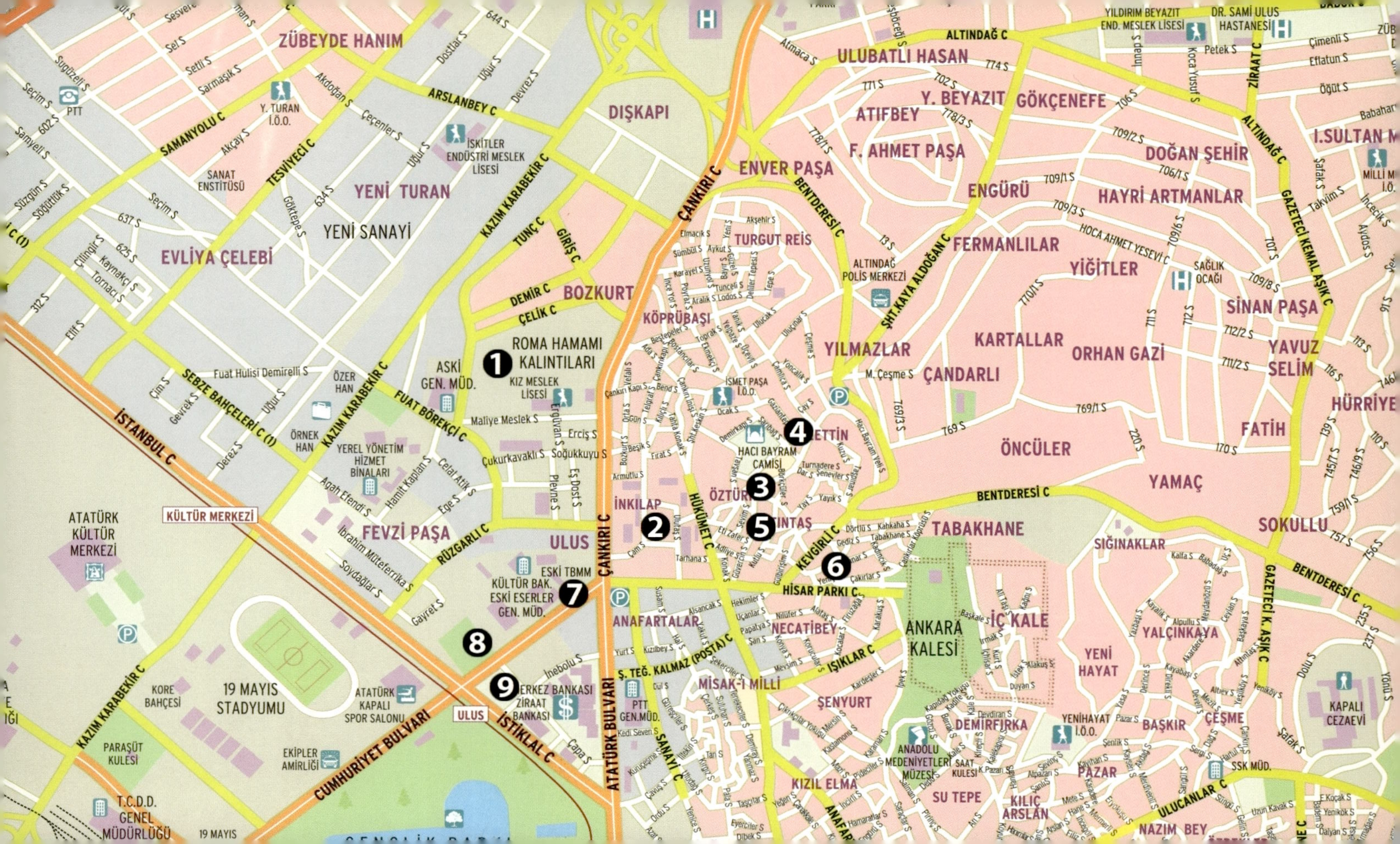

ZÜBEYDE HANIM
DIŞKAPI
ULUBATLI HASAN
ATIFBEY
Y. BEYAZIT
GÖKÇENEFE
F. AHMET PAŞA
DOĞAN ŞEHİR
I.SULTAN M
HAYRİ ARTMANLAR
ENGÜRÜ
ENVER PAŞA
YENİ TURAN
YENİ SANAYİ
EVLİYA ÇELEBİ
BOZKURT
TURGUT REİS
FERMANLILAR
YİĞİTLER
SİNAN PAŞA
KÖPRÜBAŞI
YILMAZLAR
KARTALLAR
ORHAN GAZİ
YAVUZ SELİM
ÇANDARLI
HÜRRİYE
FATİH
ÖNCÜLER
YAMAÇ
SOKULLU
TABAKHANE
SIĞINAKLAR
FEVZİ PAŞA
ULUS
İNKILAP
ÖZTÜRK
ANAFARTALAR
NECATİBEY
MİSAK-I MİLLİ
ŞENYURT
İÇ KALE
ANKARA KALESİ
YENİ HAYAT
YALÇINKAYA
BAŞKIR
ÇEŞME
DEMİRFIRKA
PAZAR
KIZIL ELMA
SU TEPE
KILIÇ ARSLAN
NAZIM BEY
KAPALI CEZAEVİ
ROMA HAMAMI KALINTILARI
ASKİ GEN. MÜD.
KIZ MESLEK LİSESİ
HACI BAYRAM CAMİSİ
ALTINDAĞ POLİS MERKEZİ
SAĞLIK OCAĞI
DR. SAMİ ULUS HASTANESİ
YILDIRIM BEYAZIT END. MESLEK LİSESİ
MİLLİ M İ.Ö.
İSMET PAŞA İ.Ö.O.
Y. TURAN İ.Ö.O.
İSKİTLER ENDÜSTRİ MESLEK LİSESİ
SANAT ENSTİTÜSÜ
PTT
ÖZER HAN
ÖRNEK HAN
YEREL YÖNETİM HİZMET BİNALARI
KÜLTÜR MERKEZİ
ATATÜRK KÜLTÜR MERKEZİ
ESKİ TBMM
KÜLTÜR BAK. ESKİ ESERLER GEN. MÜD.
MERKEZ BANKASI
ZİRAAT BANKASI
ULUS
PTT GEN.MÜD.
ATATÜRK KAPALI SPOR SALONU
19 MAYIS STADYUMU
KORE BAHÇESİ
PARAŞÜT KULESİ
EKİPLER AMİRLİĞİ
T.C.D.D. GENEL MÜDÜRLÜĞÜ
ANADOLU MEDENİYETLERİ MÜZESİ
SAAT KULESİ
YENİHAYAT İ.Ö.O.
SSK MÜD.
ALTINDAĞ C
ZİRAAT C
GAZETECİ KEMAL AŞIK C
GAZETECİ K. AŞIK C
BENTDERESİ C
ŞHT.KAYA ALDOĞAN C
ÇANKIRI C
HÜKÜMET C
KEVGİRLİ C
HİSAR PARKI C.
IŞIKLAR C
Ş. TEĞ. KALMAZ (POSTA) C
SANAYİ C
ATATÜRK BULVARI
CUMHURİYET BULVARI
İSTİKLAL C
İSTANBUL C
KAZIM KARABEKİR C
FUAT BÖREKÇİ C
RÜZGARLI C
SEBZE BAHÇELERİ C (1)
TESVİYECİ C
SAMANYOLU C
ARSLANBEY C
TUNÇ C
GİRİŞ C
DEMİR C
ÇELİK C
ULUCANLAR C
19 MAYIS

Ulus, the Old City Centre

Ulus, the old centre, is probably the most fascinating quarter of Ankara for tourists. It is the oldest part of the city and it is here where most remains from earlier civilizations are found.

The most popular places to visit in Ulus are the castle and Roman archaeological sites and the old inns and bazaars (*han*). Anadolu Medeniyetleri Müzesi (The Museum of Anatolian Civilizations) is also located in Ulus.

Ulus is a good place to buy souvenirs, including Turkish carpets and cushions, copperware, shawls and lots more. Prices are reasonable compared to İstanbul and in most cases there is room for negotiation. Although Ulus is a touristy area it's also a good place to witness traditional Turkish daily life. People who live here tend to be more conservative than in other, more modern areas.

How to get there?

Take the metro to Ulus station. Buses and dolmuşes with the sign Ulus or Altındağ also go in the right direction. If you want to go to the citadel, look for the high peak with the castle and walk in that direction. From Hisar Parkı Caddesi, you can take the stairs to go up or take Kadife Sokak, past Anadolu Medeniyetleri Müzesi It is quite a way up. If you want to take a taxi, ask them to take you to the "Kale".

Ulus also offers a variety of great restaurants, from modern restaurants located in old inns to more traditional places. There are also many hotels in this part of the city. You can easily spend half a day to a day in this quarter of the city.

The old city center Ulus can be divided into four areas, namely Altındağ, Hisar, Kale (the citadel), and Hamamönü. In this chapter these four neighborhoods are described.

Altındağ

This quarter has a lot of history. There are many Roman ruins. Ancyra used to be the capital of the Roman province Galatia. Now and then new ruins are found, like the Roman theatre, which was just found in 1982. The Ottomans also left evidence of their architectural skills, sometimes re-using Roman materials and buildings.

1 Roma Hamamı

The Roman Baths are on top of a 2,5 meter high plateau. They date back to 212-217 AD and were built in honour of Asclepius, the god of

medicine, by the Roman emperor Caracalla. The coins found in the excavations indicate that the baths were used for 500 years. Relics of Phrygian, Roman and Byzantine relics were found. Unfortunately little is left of the Roman Baths and you have to use your imagination and the information signs to imagine how it used to be. However you can clearly see the different sections such as the dressing rooms (*apoditerium*), the cold (*frigidarium*), warm (*tepidarium*) and hot rooms (*caldarium*).

How to get there?

Buses 188, 203, 252, 261, 263 in the direction Ulus or Kızılay and many more stop in the Çankırı Caddesi. For more information see www.ego.gov.tr

3 TL, Opening hours: every day 8:30 – 17:00, Çankırı Caddesi No. 43 Ulus.

2 Julianus Sütunu

The column commemorates a visit of the Roman emperor Julian to the city in 362 BC. There are no inscriptions on the col-

Near Ankara Valiliği (provinicial government headquarters) on Hükümet Meydanı, accessible from Telgraf Sokak or Hükümet Caddesi.
From Ulus Square go up Cumhuriyet Caddesi, take a left turn on to Çankırı Caddesi and then turn right (Çam Sokak) approximately 10 metres past the intersection and walk up the side street that leads towards the square (Hükümet Meydanı).

umn. It is decorated with circles and 15 metres high. The Corinthian column head is from the 6th century. Locals also refer to it as Belkıs Minaret.

How to get there?

It is a few minutes' walk from the Roman Baths.

❸ Hacı Bayram Veli Camii

Hacı Bayram-ı Veli (1352-1430) was a Turkish poet, scholar of Islam and the founder of the Bayramiye Sufi sect. His real name was *Numan* and he was born in a small village near Ankara. After completing his studies, he started teaching at a university. When he met *Somuncu Baba* on *Kurban Bayramı* (Muslim Feast of Sacrifice) his life changed. *Somuncu Baba* taught him about Sufism. As they met on the feast (*Bayram*) day his teacher called him *Bayram,* a name he kept on using during his whole life.

How to get there?

The nearest bus stop is at Çankırı Caddesi, near the Roman Bath. From there it is a 10 minutes' walk. Buses 188, 203, 252, 261, 263 in the direction Ulus or Kızılay. For more information see www.ego.gov.tr

Hacı Bayram Veli Caddesi, Sarıbağ Sokak

He built a Dervish lodge in Ankara, where many people came to learn about Sufism. This lodge stood at the place where now his tomb and the Hacı Bayram Camii are located. Nowadays the place is still frequented by followers of *Hacı Bayram-ı Veli*. It is a kind of pilgrimage site. Visitors come to his tomb and the mosque, founded in honour of the Sufi teacher.

The rectangular mosque is built between 1427 and 1428. The construction of the mosque started before *Hacı Bayram-ı Veli's* death. It is built in Seljuk style but during restorations in the 16th and 18th century other styles were introduced. For example Kütahya tiles, which can be seen on the interior mosque walls on the ground floor, are the result of a renovation in the 18th century. The mosque has two floors, the ground floor and a loft, which covers half of the prayer hall on the ground floor. The ceiling is covered with flower patterns made of wood. There is a large wooden rosette in the centre of the ceiling.

The mausoleum of *Hacı Bayram-ı Veli* dates back to 1429 and is next to the mosque. It has a square base, topped by an octagonal structure and a leaden dome. It is a typical example of mausoleum design in the 15th century.

A richly decorated door dominates the marble front façade of the tomb. The doors are not originals but reproductions. The original entrance doors can be seen at the Ankara Etnografya Müzesi (Ethnography Museum. The complex (mosque and tomb) is adjacent to the temple of Augustus.

4 Agustus Tapınağı

Next to Hacı Bayram Camii, close to and accessible from Sarıbağ Sokak.

Next to Hacı Bayram Camii you can see the remains of the temple of Augustus: a wall (12 m high and 32.5 m long) wall and a door (8.40 m high and 3.30 m wide). Originally the temple measured 36 x 55 metres.

How to get there?

As it is right next to Hacı Bayram Camii –see the section of the mosque for directions.

Although not a lot remains of this temple, it is very important because the *"Res gestae divi Augusti"* (the deeds of the Divine Augustus) is engraved on the wall, both in Latin (on the inside) and in Greek (on the outside). The original, which has not survived, was engraved upon a pair of bronze pillars and placed in front of Augustus' Mausoleum in Rome. The text is allegedly written by Augustus. It consists of a *breviarium totius imperii* (a summary of his government between 27 BC and 14 AD) in which he describes his achievements, both politically and military but also for society. The text is written shortly before his death. It can not be considered as objective history and more like as propaganda for the first emperor of the Roman Empire, whose political career was in many ways experimental.

The temple is built on the ruins of a temple consecrated to the Phrygia goddess, Men. Around 20 BC the Galatian King, Pylamenes gave order to build a temple for the goddess Rome in honour of a visit of emperor Augustus who came to visit the capital Ancyra of the Galatian province, which had just been conquered a few years before.

In the 4th or 5th century the temple was converted into a Christian church by the Byzantines. Later the Seljuks built a mosque and now one wall is even part of the 15th century Hacı Bayram Camii.

5 Güvercin Sokak – Ankara Houses

The area around Hacı Bayram Camii and Agustus Tapınağı has been subject to a tourist project of the Ankara municipality. Around Hacı Bayram Parkı new Ankara houses in a sort of Ottoman style are being rebuilt. The old houses are not being restored but houses are complete newly built. Walking down from the Wall of August to the Roman theatre you can walk through the Güvercin Sokak and Kutlu Sokak which was set up in this way in 2013. It has a lively atmosphere and some teahouses. Although mostly occupied by men in this speci-

fic area tourist are mostly welcome as well. The only authentic detail in this street is that it is used as a lamp souk. In all eastern countries specialised traders tend to stick in the same street or area next to each other. So if you are looking for a certain object you can go to that souk. If you are considering buying a lamp this would be the place in Ankara for a typical Turkish stylish lamp.

6 Roma Tiyatrosu

Located on Hisar Parkı Caddesi, next to Öğretmen Evi.

This theatre was first discovered only in 1982. Between 1983 and 1986 excavations began. It was established that the theatre dates from the 2nd century AD. The excavated statues and other artefacts are currently exhibited in the Museum of Anatolian Civilisations. On the site itself, the foundations and walls of what was once a vaulted building, orchestra, amphitheatre and stage can be seen. The total structure was 50 x 43,5 metres. It is believed to have had a capacity of 3000 to 5000 people. The eastern and western entrances of the theatre were covered with big blocks and turned later, in the late Roman and Byzantine period, into a pool.

The seats were made from the local Andesite stone. If you look to the right (standing on Hisar Parkı Caddesi) you will see some mountains and recognise the same colour stone.

Between 1986 and 2009 no excavations were carried out. After 2009 excavations started again under the guidance of the Museum of Anatolian Civilisations, as part of a city-wide plan to restore old monuments and attract more tourists. It was announced in 2011 that, after completion of the restoration, the theatre will host cultural and artistic events. At the time of writing, the work is progressing quickly and it is expected to be finished in 2014.

How to get there?

The best way to get there is to take a dolmuş in the direction of Hisar Parkı. The driver will let you out at Anafartalar Caddesi or Kevgirli Sokak. It is nearby. The nearest bus stop is at Kevgirli Sokak. Buses 303, 304, 306 and 307 in the direction of Ulus and Kızılay. For more information see www.ego.gov.tr

❼ Eski Türkiye Büyük Millet Meclisi - Kurtuluş Savaşı Müzesi

How to get there?

As it is next to the second building of the Grand National Assembly see that section for directions.

Cumhuriyet Caddesi, entrance 1 TL. Everyday, except Monday between 9:00-17:00

This Ottoman style building (First Building of the Grand National Assembly - Museum of the War of Independence) at the corner of Cumhuriyet Caddesi and Atatürk Bulvarı is an example of the First National Architect Period. It was constructed in 1915 as the headquarters of the Committee of Union and Progress, the political party that wanted to bring democracy to the Ottoman Empire. But after *Atatürk*'s arrival in Ankara on 27 December 1919, it became the headquarter of the new Assembly of Turkey. During the War of Independence all military and political decisions were taken here. It was also the place where the Turkish Republic was declared on 29 October 1923.

The building now houses the Museum of the War of Independence. There is a small exhibition about the leaders of the war showing some of their belongings. Unfortunately the explanation is only given in Turkish. However, if you ask, they will show a film in English with authentic footage of the War of Independence. In the museum you can also see the First Grand National Assembly, the meeting room as it was used between 1920 and 1924.

8 II. TBMM Binası - Cumhuriyet Müzesi

The construction of this building (Second Building of the Grand National Assembly - Republic Museum) which is about 100 metres to the left of the building of the first National Assembly, started in 1923. The first Parliament's building was only in use for 4 years but already too small. This building was initially intended to be the office of the Republican Party. But during its construction the decision was taken to house the new National Assembly here. Despite the change of plans

How to get there?

From the Ankara Metro line it is a few minutes' walk to both Parliament buildings. There is a bus stop on the Cumhuriyet Caddesi. Buses 105, 180-3, 285 in the direction of Ulus or Opera stop here. For more information see www.ego.gov.tr

Cumhuriyet Caddesi, in the direction of İstanbul Caddesi, opposite Ankara Palas. Entrance 3 TL. Every day, except Monday, between 8:45 – 17:00

the building was already opened 18 October 1924, as more space was urgently needed.

The building is typical architecture from the Republican age with broad doorposts, wooden ceilings and tiles. During the early years, the garden was also open to the public and concerts were held in the garden of the building.

Fortunately the new building lasted longer than the first Parliament's building. The National Assembly was housed here for 36 years until they moved to the new building at south of Kızılay. Before that, many important decisions about major changes and steps in the modern history of Turkey were taken in this building in Ulus.

Nowadays the building houses the Republic museum. You can see original letters, photos, speeches and quotes about new laws which were passed by the Grand National Assembly. The first paper money and coins are also on display, as well as teaching material for the new Turkish language in European script. There are audio guides (in English) of how all these things were thought over and set up to get the new Republic started.

However, most of the museum is taken up by the second National Assembly's old Plenary Hall, where the original furniture still exists. This is the place from where, between 18 October 1924 and 6 January 1961, Turkey was ruled.

9 Ankara Palas

Cumhuriyet Caddesi, across the second building of the Grand National Assembly - Republic Museum, not accessible for public. Tel: 310 24 24

Opposite the second National Assembly Building is the Ankara Palas. This place was opened in 1927 as a club where the deputies could meet, eat and drink. In the informal setting of this parliamentary club, many decisions about the country's future were prepared here. One of the frequent visitors to the parliamentary club was *Atatürk*. It was one of his favourite places in Ankara.

The building is lavishly decorated with elements of Ottoman and Seljuk design and famous Turkish artists' artwork. The complex has a large ballroom and some smaller rooms and halls. They were, and are still, in use for receptions, dinners and balls. Unfortunately, the Ankara Palas is not open for public. So, if you want to have a look inside, you need an invitation to one of these events, which regularly take place here. If you do receive an invitation, take that unique opportunity to see the palace from the inside.

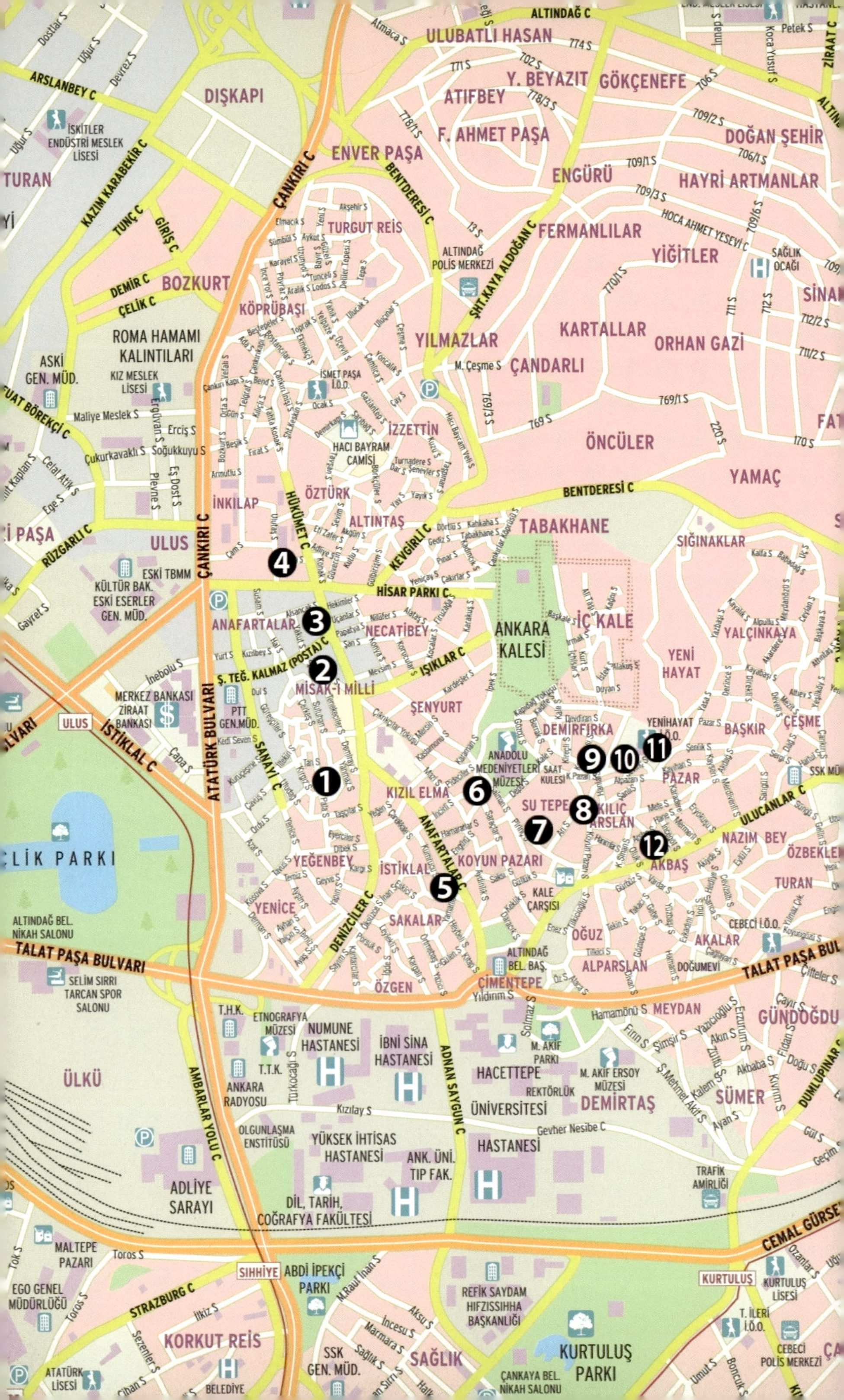
ALTINDAĞ C
ULUBATLI HASAN
ARSLANBEY C
DIŞKAPI
Y. BEYAZIT
GÖKÇENEFE
ATIFBEY
F. AHMET PAŞA
DOĞAN ŞEHİR
İŞKİTLER ENDÜSTRİ MESLEK LİSESİ
TURAN
KAZIM KARABEKİR C
ENVER PAŞA
ENGÜRÜ
HAYRİ ARTMANLAR
ÇANKIRI C
BENTDERESİ C
TUNÇ C
GİRİŞ C
TURGUT REİS
FERMANLILAR
HOCA AHMET YESEVİ C
YİĞİTLER
ALTINDAĞ POLİS MERKEZİ
SAĞLIK OCAĞI
DEMİR C
BOZKURT
ÇELİK C
KÖPRÜBAŞI
ŞHT.KAYA ALDOĞAN C
KARTALLAR
ORHAN GAZİ
ROMA HAMAMI KALINTILARI
YILMAZLAR
ÇANDARLI
ASKİ GEN. MÜD.
KIZ MESLEK LİSESİ
İSMET PAŞA İ.Ö.O.
M. Çeşme S
FUAT BÖREKÇİ C
Maliye Meslek S
Erciş S
İZZETTİN
ÖNCÜLER
Çukurkavaklı S
Soğukkuyu S
HACI BAYRAM CAMİSİ
YAMAÇ
BENTDERESİ C
ÖZTÜRK
İNKILAP
HÜKÜMET C
RÜZGARLI C
ALTINTAŞ
TABAKHANE
ULUS
KEVGİRLİ C
SIĞINAKLAR
KÜLTÜR BAK. ESKİ ESERLER GEN. MÜD.
ESKİ TBMM
HİSAR PARKI C.
ANAFARTALAR
NECATİBEY
ANKARA KALESİ
İÇ KALE
YALÇINKAYA
Ş. TEĞ. KALMAZ (POSTA) C
IŞIKLAR C
YENİ HAYAT
MİSAK-İ MİLLİ
MERKEZ BANKASI
ZİRAAT BANKASI
PTT GEN.MÜD.
ŞENYURT
ULUS
İSTİKLAL C
ATATÜRK BULVARI
SANAYİ C
DEMİRFIRKA
YENİHAYAT İ.Ö.O.
BAŞKIR
ÇEŞME
ANADOLU MEDENİYETLERİ MÜZESİ
SAAT KULESİ
PAZAR
KIZIL ELMA
SU TEPE
KILIÇ ARSLAN
ULUCANLAR C
NAZIM BEY
ÖZBEKLER
ÇELİK PARKI
YEĞENBEY
İSTİKLAL
KOYUN PAZARI
AKBAŞ
TURAN
ANAFARTALAR C
KALE ÇARŞISI
YENİCE
DENİZCİLER C
SAKALAR
ALTINDAĞ BEL. NİKAH SALONU
OĞUZ
CEBECİ İ.Ö.O.
AKALAR
ALTINDAĞ BEL. BAŞ.
ALPARSLAN
DOĞUMEVİ
TALAT PAŞA BULVARI
ÇİMENTEPE
ÖZGEN
TALAT PAŞA BUL
SELİM SIRRI TARCAN SPOR SALONU
Yıldırım S
Hamamönü S
MEYDAN
GÜNDOĞDU
T.H.K.
ETNOGRAFYA MÜZESİ
NUMUNE HASTANESİ
İBNİ SİNA HASTANESİ
M. AKİF PARKI
HACETTEPE
M. AKİF ERSOY MÜZESİ
ÜLKÜ
T.T.K.
ANKARA RADYOSU
REKTÖRLÜK
ÜNİVERSİTESİ
DEMİRTAŞ
SÜMER
AMBARLAR YOLU C
ADNAN SAYGUN C
DUMLUPINAR C
Kızılay S
Gevher Nesibe C
OLGUNLAŞMA ENSTİTÜSÜ
YÜKSEK İHTİSAS HASTANESİ
HASTANESİ
ANK. ÜNİ. TIP FAK.
ADLİYE SARAYI
TRAFİK AMİRLİĞİ
DİL, TARİH, COĞRAFYA FAKÜLTESİ
CEMAL GÜRSEL
MALTEPE PAZARI
Toros S
SIHHİYE
ABDİ İPEKÇİ PARKI
KURTULUŞ
KURTULUŞ LİSESİ
EGO GENEL MÜDÜRLÜĞÜ
STRAZBURG C
REFİK SAYDAM HIFZISSIHHA BAŞKANLIĞI
T. İLERİ İ.Ö.O.
KORKUT REİS
SAĞLIK
KURTULUŞ PARKI
CEBECİ POLİS MERKEZİ
ATATÜRK LİSESİ
BELEDİYE
SSK GEN. MÜD.
ÇANKAYA BEL. NİKAH SALONU
1
2
3
4
5
6
7
8
9
10
11
12

Hisar

How to get there?

Many dolmuşes go to Ulus. Tell the driver of an Ulus-Sıhhıye dolmuş where you want to go and he will tell or sign to you where to get out. Metro: On the Ankara Metro line get out at Ulus station. Buses: Get off at the Opera bus stop on Atatürk Bulvarı. This is across Gençlik Parkı. Buses 113, 114, 115, 132, 133, 135 and many more in the direction of Opera or Ulus. From here it is a 10 to 15 minute walk. Or, if you want to avoid the walk, take a bus to Anafartalar Caddesi: 328, 333, 336, 347, 349, 350 or one of many others that go in the direction of Ulus. For more information see www.ego.gov.tr

1 Eyne Bey Hamamı

This *hamam* dates back to 1502. It was built for *Eyne Bey,* a magistrate at the time of *Sultan Murad I*, probably at the beginning of the 15th century. The bath was damaged in a natural disaster in 1527. In 1528 it was restored but it was subsequently neglected until its complete renovation in 1992.

How to get there?

From Atatürk Bulvarı, across Gençlik Parkı, take the first street to the right: Adnan Saygun Caddesi. Eyne Bey Hamamı is on the left-hand side of the street.

Adnan Saygun Caddesi No: 11 Ulus
Tel: 309 68 65
Opening hours: 24 hours a day.
Men only. No women's section.
www.eynebeyhamami.com

It only has a men section's and is open 24 hours a day. It is quite a big *hamam*, with a swimming pool and a lot of staff for massage and scrubbing (see chapter *Practical Information >>Hamams*).

2 Sulu Han

This *han* is also called Hasan Paşa Han as it was built by *Hasan Paşa* in 1511, to serve as eating-house for the poor. It also contained a bath-house for both sexes and some small shops. In 1685 it was bought by a dervish association, who partly rebuilt and expanded it. Only the shops in the east and south façade remain from that original construction.

Şehit Teğmen Kalmaz Caddesi.

In the Ottoman days coffee and yarn were traded here. In 1929 it was partly destroyed by a fire, after which it was used as a vegetable market. The *han* was restored between 1971 and 1984 and now offers visitors a vivid impression of the old trading spirit.

In this two storey *han*, all sorts of beads and accessories for making necklaces, bracelets and other handicrafts are sold. It is also a good place to find various forms of the famous Turkish blue bead (*Nazar Boncuğu*). On the ground floor you can enjoy a cup of tea.

3 Ulus Hali

This food market is a feast for the eyes. Seasonal vegetables, fruits and fish are sold cheaply here. You can buy fresh figs (September-October) or chestnuts (later in the year). In autumn or winter you can buy *hamsi* here –little anchovies from the Black Sea.

Hal Sokak

If you walk through the food market and exit on the north side, across the street, you can go into the spice market. Its entrance is opposite the food market, slightly to the left, on a small pathway right next to the "*Pastırmacı*" sign.

At the entrance to the spice market you can see jugs of leeches. These insects were used in the old days, and are still used by (mostly) elderly people to suck out the 'bad' blood when they suffer from rheumatism or any other aches. If you are in the spice market you might want to try some Turkish spices, for example *sumak*, which is made of the sharp red berries of the sumac plant. It is said to have antioxidant properties. Whether or not that is true, it adds a tasty lemony flavour to salads or meat.

❹ Hallaç Mahmut Camii & Türbesi

Susam Sokak

The mosque was restored in the 16th century, but probably built before that time. Some sources even suggest that it was designed in 952 AD.

Next to this mosque you can see the tomb of *Hallaç Mahmut*. This religious leader was born in Ankara. Out of respect for his knowledge, people gave him the surname *Sultan Erdede*. Although he was *Hacı Bayram-ı Veli*'s teacher, whose tomb is very well visited nowadays, hardly anyone stops at *Hallaç Mahmut*'s tomb any more. As there are not many of these tombs in Ankara, and this one is not as crowded as *Hacı Bayram-ı Veli*'s tomb, it is worth paying a visit.

❺ Şengül Hamamı

Denizciler Caddesi, Acı Çeşme Sokak No: 3 Ulus
www.sengulhamami.com.
Opening hours: Daily between 6:00 – 24:00 (men's section) 6:00 – 20:00 (Friday 22:00) (women's section)

This *hamam* was probably built in the second half of the 15th century. Inside, the bath is constructed entirely from white marble and features Ottoman patterns and a beautiful dome with holes in a star pattern. Around the central massage platform there are private areas which make it a cosy *hamam*. They also offer a special coffee treatment here. You will smell like a coffee bean for hours, which

you may or may not like, but make sure you do not wear your brand new bikini if you choose this treatment as it can stain fabric. It is, however, very relaxing and leaves you with baby soft skin.

The staff is very friendly and they will fight for your attention and for the honour of doing your treatment, as they know you will tip them afterwards. Make sure you do! The prices for treatments (excluding tip) are given on the price list beside the cashier (see chapter *Practical Information >>Hamams*).

6 Samanpazarı

Çıkrıkçılar Yokuşu

This street's actual name is Çıkrıkçılar Yokuşu but everybody calls it Samanpazarı. Traditional clothes and fabrics are sold in this street, as well as all kind of accessories for weddings and the henna night for brides-to-be. On Saturdays and just before holidays this street is amazingly crowded.

HENNA NIGHT (KINA GECESİ)

Although more and more brides choose to celebrate the night before their wedding with a joint party in a hotel, the tradition of henna night is still very much alive, as you can see in Samanpazarı. The henna night is traditionally the bride's farewell party to her family. It starts early in the evening with friends and female relatives of the bride gathering at the bride's place or in a *hamam*. The bride wears a red dress and a veil over her head.

The evening usually begins with everyone sharing all the food and pastries they've brought. After dinner the singing and dancing begins. At a certain point, friends, sisters and nieces will bring in candles and make a circle around the bride while singing an emotional old song, about the bride leaving her house and parents. Then they will put henna on her hands. The henna is served on plates which you can see in Samanpazarı. It has a little bowl in the middle and is decorated with white or red tulle. The little pockets you see, often with the famous blue bead, contain henna or another small gift that the bride gives to her friends and family.

One of the bride's hands will be covered with a rose, the other with a silk pocket. Other guests may also put henna on their hands. Henna symbolizes happiness and protection. After the henna has been applied, the bride's veil comes off and everyone parties on well into the night.

❼ Salman Sokak & Zağfiran Han

If you want to buy Turkish copperware or a traditional Turkish table (*sini*), this is the street where you will find all the coppersmiths and their shops.

If you come from Çıkrıkçılar Yokuşu, halfway up Salman Sokak, you'll see an old *han* on the left-hand side: Zağfiran Han. You need to look up as it is situated above the ground level of Salman Sokak. According to the inscription the building was constructed in 1512. Zağfiran means *saffron*, which was probably traded here. At the time of writing you cannot visit this *han*, as it is being restored by the Rahmi Koç Foundation. Like Çukurhan (⓾) it will be a boutique hotel and it will become one of Ankara's new 'old jewels'.

CARAVANSERAIS

Caravanserais (*kervansaray*) were big roadside *hans*, used by caravans for rest and recuperation after a journey. They were built at points one day's journey from each other (30-40 km) along trade routes. They offered travellers security as well as an opportunity to trade and exchange information.

Most common caravanserais are built with a square or rectangular walled exterior and a single portal high and wide enough to permit large or heavily laden animals (e.g. camels) to enter. The animals stayed in the courtyard, sometimes on the side in a sheltered area. However, the courtyard was open to the sky. Around the courtyard were small chambers to accommodate travellers, merchants and servants and small shops where goods could be traded along the way. The caravanserais were usually owned by charitable institutions but the visitors nevertheless had to pay a contribution to the owners of the caravanserais, which gave them a fair income.

In Ankara, *sof* (mohair), the cloth of the Angora goats, was the most import ant commodity during the 15th and 16th centuries. The size of the caravanserais shows how much the city thrived on this commerce.

8 Pirinç Han

Pirinç Sokak

Pirinç Han is one of the most atmospheric places in Ankara. It was built in the 1730s. *Pirinç* means rice in Turkish and, as the name suggests, rice was traded here. In the 1920s the building served as a police station. In 1992 it became a *han* again. This *han* was restored in such a way that it still feels sympathetically. It has two storeys with squeaking wooden floors, confirming its age.

Today it hosts several antique and gift shops, in which you can find all kinds of stuff from old postcards to gramophone records, to unique cufflinks and hats. Knowing that the shop keepers pay a rent of 1,000 TL a month you will be surprised how they survive as the items they sell are not expensive and you will certainly find some unique souvenirs here. This is a paradise for connoisseurs and lovers of antiques and jewellery. It takes some searching but in the packed stores, you can find unique objects, for a reasonable price. In the courtyard, on the ground floor, you can sit, drink a tea or *ayran* (Turkish yogurt drink) and eat a *gözleme* (pancake filled with cheese, spinach, potatoes or etc.). In the summertime this is one of the places where they sell the famous ice creams from Atatürk Orman Çiftliği (Atatürk Forest Farm) (see chapter *Atatürk Orman Çiftliği*).

9 Koyunpazarı Sokak

In this street (and its side streets) the famous Angora goat skins and *sof* (mohair) used to be sold. You can still see people preparing and selling the wool in one of the side streets. You can read more about this famous product in the *History* chapter.

PİLAVOĞLU HAN
GÖZLEME
MANTI
KAHVE
ÇAY
TUTKU ANTİK CAFE

Other interesting souvenirs sold in this street include antiques, fabrics and handicrafts.

In this street you will find a nice café: Kirit Café. Not only do they serve various sorts of tea but, in the tradition of the *sof* trade, they also sell all kinds of modern, handmade felt articles.

⑩ Pilavoğlu Han

Koyunpazarı Sokak, across Çengelhan Rahmi Koç Museum, left from Kirit Café (towards the castle)

This *han* still has its original 17th century structure. It is probably the only *han* in Ankara that has never burnt down. The *han* served as a hotel. No trade was done in this *han*.

It was just recently opened in the summer of 2013. Luckily it has not been restored too much so you can still see the original walls made of sundried mud and the wooden porch on the second floor. Before the opening old men were playing *tavla* (backgammon) in the courtyard and although some of the workshops were still used, the *han* was slowly deteriorating. Now it is opened from Koyunpazarı Sokak, as before it was only accessible from Hanlar Sokak. It has two storeys but at the moment of writing only the ground floor can be visited. The café inside serves tea, *gözleme* and *mantı* (Turkish ravioli). Around the courtyard antiques can be bought.

⑪ Atpazarı

Atpazarı (horse market) used to be an important crossroads during Ankara's commercial heyday. Around this square some dozen city caravanserais were built very close to each other, just outside the South Gate of the citadel. All of them were built during the 15th, 16th and 17th centuries. After Sulu Han (②), Zağfiran Han (⑦) and Pirinç Han (⑧), which were described earlier you will find around this square, Çukurhan, Çengelhan, Kurşunlu Han and Mahmut Paşa Han. The latter two are currently integrated into Anadolu Medeniyetleri Müzesi (see chapter *In and Around the Citadel*).

Çengelhan Rahmi Koç Müzesi

Sutepe Mahallesi, Depo Sokak No: 1 Tel: 309 68 00 www.rmk-museum.org.tr Tues-Fri 10.00 – 17.00, Sat-Sun 10.00 – 18.00. Admission 6 TL

This *han* was originally built for Süleyman the Magnificent's favorite daughter *Mihrimah Sultan* and her husband *Rüstem Paşa*, the grand vizier, in 1522-23. It was one of the four largest *hans* and used to be the leather merchant's inn. Restoration of the *han* has been lovingly carried out by one of Turkish famous tycoons, *Rahmi Koç*. His father opened a shop in the *han* in 1917 when it was still in ruins. Although the interior is made of bricks, it looks very refined. The architecture of the building is an attraction in itself, while the museum exhibits over 1200 objects covering engineering, road transport, science, medicine, aviation and navigation. The former courtyard has a glass roof now and serves as a brasserie.

Çukurhan

Çukurhan is now one of the finest boutique hotels in Ankara, in a unique building in a unique location. The *han* was probably built in the 17th century. It was in continuous use until it caught fire in 1950. The fire destroyed the interior and the livelihood of most of the shopkeepers. After the fire the building still served as a trading place for wool and grain, although in poorer condition than before. In 1990 the last shopkeeper left and the site was abandoned. In 2007 it was put on the World Monuments Fund's Watch List of the 100 Most Endangered Sites in the World. Luckily the unstable ruin was saved by Çengelhan Inc., a company of the Rahmi Koç Foundation for Museology and Culture (*see Çengelhan above*). They now lease the *han* on a 29-year basis from the government and have turned it into a hotel with 19 individually designed rooms. Af-

How to get there?

From here you can go into the citadel (see chapter In and Around the Citadel) or walk a little bit further along the Atpazarı to the Ahi Şerafeddin (Arslanhane Camii).

Next to Çengelhan you will find Çukurhan.

ter an elaborate restoration lasting 2.5 years, during which enormous care and attention was paid to the preservation of the original building, Çukurhan was opened again in May 2010 as Divan Hotel.

⓬ Ahi Şerafeddin (Arslanhane) Camii

Can Sokak

This mosque dates back to the early 13th century and was renovated in about 1290. Many stones from the Roman and Byzantine ruins in Ankara were used in its construction. The mosque is located on a slope just outside the citadel. It is a unique and classic example of a Seljuk mosque. It has a wooden ceiling, supported by 24 wooden pillars, arranged in four rows of six units. Their stone column heads are all different, as they are reused column capitals from Roman ruins.

The mihrab, the niche in the wall, indicating the direction of Mecca, is covered with turquoise Seljuk tiles. Right next to the mihrab is the pulpit, made of walnut. Both are, in terms of style and craftsmanship, unique examples of the Seljuk tradition in Anatolia. They are thought to have been made in 1290 as well.

The official name of this mosque, Ahi Şerafeddin Camii, refers to a governor of Ankara and the founder of the mosque, *Ahi Şerafeddin* (...-1331). His tomb is situated next to the mosque. His sarcophagus, decorated with his own art techniques, is housed in the Ethnography Museum. Although the mosque is named after this governor, it is better known by its unofficial name "Arslanhane", which means lion-house, because there is an antique reused lion statue on one of the walls.

Ahi Şerafeddin's tomb lies next to a parking lot. On the other side of the parking lot, on the Atpazarı ramp, you can find another: Kesikbaş tomb. This one is open on four sides stands in the middle is a concrete sarcophagus. It dates back to the 14th century but unfortunately it is not known who is buried here.

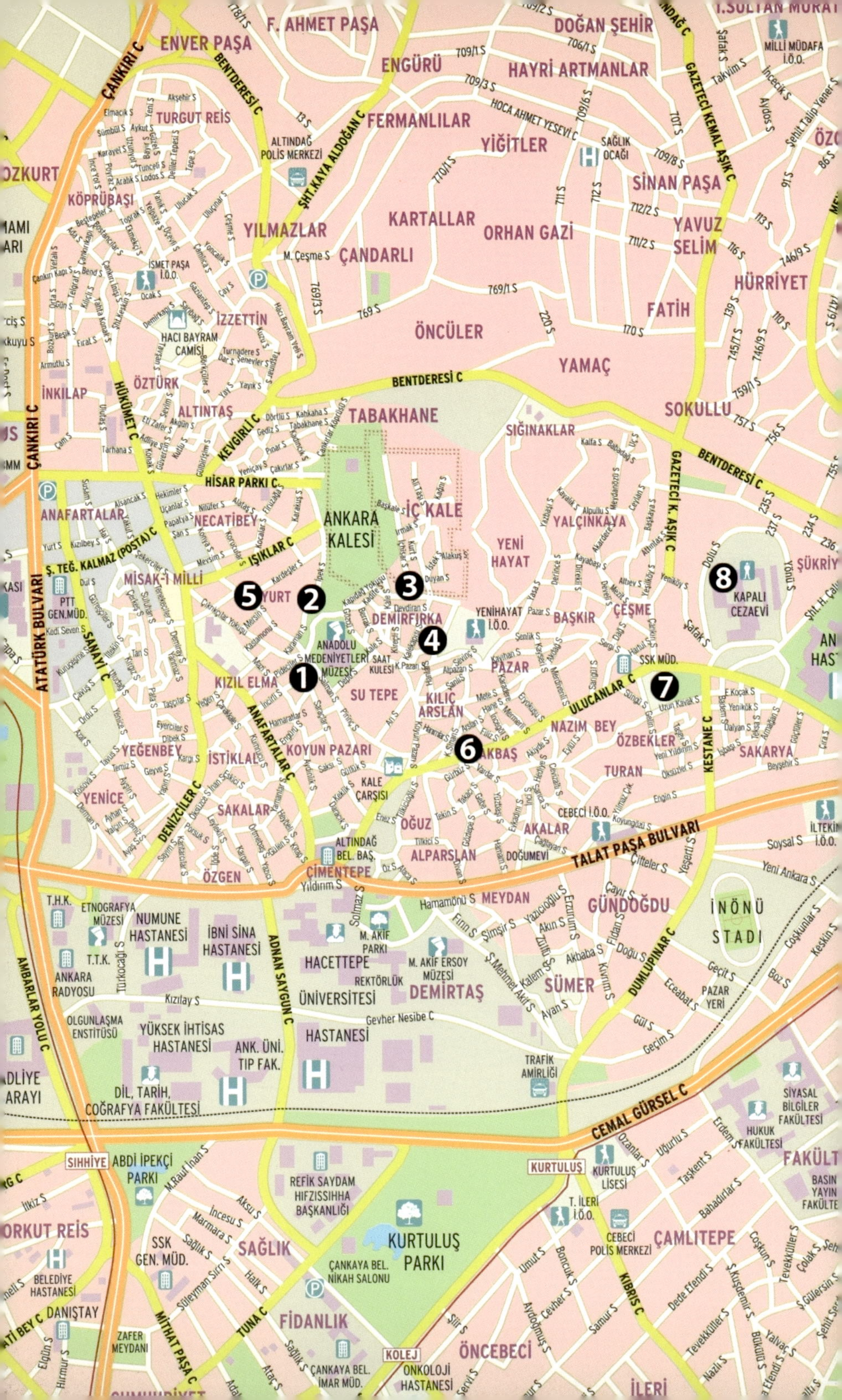
F. AHMET PAŞA
DOĞAN ŞEHİR
ENVER PAŞA
ENGÜRÜ
HAYRİ ARTMANLAR
FERMANLILAR
YİĞİTLER
TURGUT REİS
ALTINDAĞ POLİS MERKEZİ
SAĞLIK OCAĞI
SİNAN PAŞA
ÖZKURT
KÖPRÜBAŞI
KARTALLAR
ORHAN GAZİ
YAVUZ SELİM
YILMAZLAR
ÇANDARLI
HÜRRİYET
İSMET PAŞA İ.Ö.O.
İZZETTİN
FATİH
HACI BAYRAM CAMİSİ
ÖNCÜLER
YAMAÇ
ÖZTÜRK
BENTDERESİ C
İNKILAP
ALTINTAŞ
TABAKHANE
SOKULLU
SIĞINAKLAR
ÇANKIRI C
HÜKÜMET C
KEVGİRLİ C
HİSAR PARKI C
BENTDERESİ C
GAZETECİ K. AŞIK C
ANAFARTALAR
NECATİBEY
ANKARA KALESİ
İÇ KALE
YALÇINKAYA
YENİ HAYAT
Ş. TEĞ. KALMAZ (POSTA) C
IŞIKLAR C
MİSAK-I MİLLİ
YURT
DEMİRFIRKA
YENİHAYAT İ.Ö.O.
BAŞKIR
ÇEŞME
KAPALI CEZAEVİ
ŞÜKRİYE
PTT GEN.MÜD.
ANADOLU MEDENİYETLERİ MÜZESİ
SAAT KULESİ
SSK MÜD.
ATATÜRK BULVARI
PAZAR
KIZIL ELMA
SU TEPE
KILIÇ ARSLAN
ULUCANLAR C
SANAYİ C
NAZIM BEY
ÖZBEKLER
SAKARYA
YEĞENBEY
İSTİKLAL
KOYUN PAZARI
AKBAŞ
TURAN
KESTANE C
YENİCE
KALE ÇARŞISI
ANAFARTALAR C
DENİZCİLER C
SAKALAR
OĞUZ
AKALAR
CEBECİ İ.Ö.O.
İLTEKİN İ.Ö.O.
ALTINDAĞ BEL. BAŞ.
ALPARSLAN
DOĞUMEVİ
TALAT PAŞA BULVARI
ÖZGEN
CİMENTEPE
T.H.K.
ETNOGRAFYA MÜZESİ
NUMUNE HASTANESİ
İBNİ SİNA HASTANESİ
MEYDAN
GÜNDOĞDU
İNÖNÜ STADI
M. AKİF PARKI
M. AKİF ERSOY MÜZESİ
T.T.K.
ANKARA RADYOSU
HACETTEPE ÜNİVERSİTESİ
REKTÖRLÜK
DEMİRTAŞ
SÜMER
PAZAR YERİ
ADNAN SAYGUN C
DUMLUPINAR C
OLGUNLAŞMA ENSTİTÜSÜ
YÜKSEK İHTİSAS HASTANESİ
ANK. ÜNİ. TIP FAK.
HASTANESİ
Gevher Nesibe C
AMBARLAR YOLU C
ADLİYE SARAYI
DİL, TARİH, COĞRAFYA FAKÜLTESİ
TRAFİK AMİRLİĞİ
SİYASAL BİLGİLER FAKÜLTESİ
HUKUK FAKÜLTESİ
CEMAL GÜRSEL C
SIHHİYE
ABDİ İPEKÇİ PARKI
REFİK SAYDAM HIFZISSIHHA BAŞKANLIĞI
KURTULUŞ
KURTULUŞ LİSESİ
BASIN YAYIN FAKÜLTE
ORKUT REİS
SSK GEN. MÜD.
SAĞLIK
KURTULUŞ PARKI
T. İLERİ İ.Ö.O.
CEBECİ POLİS MERKEZİ
ÇAMLITEPE
BELEDİYE HASTANESİ
ÇANKAYA BEL. NİKAH SALONU
DANIŞTAY
FİDANLIK
TUNA C
KIBRIS C
ZAFER MEYDANI
MİTHAT PAŞA C
ÇANKAYA BEL. İMAR MÜD.
KOLEJ
ONKOLOJİ HASTANESİ
ÖNCEBECİ
İLERİ
1
2
3
4
5
6
7
8

In and Around the Citadel & Ulucanlar Caddesi

How to get there?

(1 to 5)
Buses 336, 363, 360, 364, 368 in the direction of Ulus. Walk for 10 minutes. For more buses and further information check www.ego.gov.tr. A lot of dolmuşes also go in this direction, although you will have to walk up the hill.

1 Anadolu Medeniyetleri Müzesi

Gözcü Sokak No: 2 Ulus
Tel: 324 31 60/61/65 www.anadolumedeniyetlerimuzesi.gov.tr
Opening hours: every day 8:30 – 17:15. Entrance fee: 30 TL, students, pensioners and children under 18 years: 15 TL

The Museum of Anatolian Civilizations is located in two *hans* dating back to the Ottoman Empire: Kurşunlu Han (from early 15th century) and Mahmut Paşa Bedesteni (built 1464-1471). The former one is currently only used as adminis-

trative building. Mahmut Paşa Bedesteni is used as an exhibition hall. It has ten domes and used to have 102 shops in which *sof* the goat hair fabric and garments made from it, were traded. The *hans* were used until 1881, when they were abandoned after a fire. Renovations started in 1938, which took 30 years altogether, but some sections opened to the public before the work had been completed.

Nowadays the museum houses relics from Ankara and surroundings, from the Palaeolithic era, through the Neolithic, Early Bronze, Assyrian trading colonies, Hittite, Phrygian, Urartian, Greek, Hellenistic, Roman, Byzantine, Seljuk and Ottoman periods. Most artefacts came from ruins in and around Ankara, from places like Gordion, Gavurkale, Polatlı, the Roman theatre and bath, etc. The exhibition is not limited to Ankara and its surroundings though. Its exhibits items that were collected from all over Anatolia. It is a unique collection with exhibits of gold, silver, glass, marble and bronze objects, as well as coins, tools, jewellery and weapons, dating back as far as the second half of the first millennium BC.

❷ Kale

The citadel or castle (Ankara Kalesi) is the most prominent landmark in Ankara, not least because it is built on a hill 978 metres high. The ou-

Open air

ter castle has seven entrances: Çankırı, İstanbul, İzmir, Namazgâh, Erzurum, Kayseri and Aynalı.

No one is exactly sure when the citadel was built. Some say it served as a garrison in the Hittite era, some say King Midas built it, others say the foundations of the citadel or castle were laid by the Galatians or the Romans. However, the (current) inner walls date back to the 7th century but its current form is from the last restoration the Byzantines made around 900. Following periods of Roman and Byzantine rule, it was captured in 1073 by the Seljuks, who made further restorations and additions. Then the crusaders conquered it, before the Seljuks won it back again in 1227.

During the Ottoman era, the castle was extensively repaired by order of *İbrahim Paşa* in 1832. In the citadel you will find the remains of all these different ages and civilizations. Old stones and columns with inscriptions of former inhabitants were reused to fortify or expand the walls. If you look closely in between the marble and red Ankara stones you will find Roman and Greek inscriptions.

The latest version of the castle consists of 42 pentagonal towers between 14 and 16 metres high. Only a few have survived until today however. The purpose of the castle was to protect the city.

The layout of the citadel differs from that of other castles, in that it has two sections: The inner castle and the outer castle. Not only the fortress remains but also the surrounding houses. The fact that there are still people living in these houses makes it a lively place.

Inner Castle

The Ottoman houses in the inner castle are the oldest in Ankara, dating back to the 17th century. They were made of wood, adobe and mud brick. The citadel is slowly being restored by the municipality. As well as the houses, this time by using more sustainable materials. The streets are also restored but with the same cobble stones.

The traditional houses were built in such a way as to maximise the space available within the walls of the castle. They had two or three storeys. The different storeys were for different seasons: In the cold season, the lower floor with thick walls and small windows kept in the

warmth. In summer the upper storeys were used, as they had thin walls and were more airy. The houses also had special gazebo rooms called *Cihannuma* for summer time. The wooden ceilings were often decorated with geometrical designs, as was common in the Ottoman period.

The highest point of the castle can be entered across the Allaaddin Camii. Pass the ladies selling handicrafts to reach this point and look over Ankara.

❸ Kınacızade Konağı

Kale Kapısı Sokak No: 28 Ankara Kalesi Ulus Tel: 324 57 14 www.kinacizadekonagi.com

Kınacızade Konağı claims to be the only remaining original mansion in the inner castle. It dates back to the 1800s. The mansion was restored in 2007. *Kıvırcık Usta*, a master in repairing and restoring antiques, is the owner of this mansion. He uses the mansion as a restaurant and wedding salon, but it is also a kind of a museum.

The mansion has private rooms that belonged to important guests. The first room is the Academician's room. It is dedicated to Prof. Dr. *Halil İnalcık*, an expert on the history of the Ottoman Empire. He worked in this room and received many national and international guests here. The first female speaker for the Turkish national broadcast company TRT, *Julide Gülizar*, also had a study here, where she read her newspaper, wrote her books and talked to youngsters, almost every day. The last room belonged to *Yurdusev Arığ*, *İsmet İnönü*'s private secretary and founder and president of the Women's Politicians Platform.

You can eat Turkish specialities in the restaurant, such as *gözleme*, (pancake filled with cheese, spinach, potatoes or etc.) If you are lucky you can sit on the small balcony and look out over the main street into the inner castle.

❹ Alaaddin Camii

Inner castle, on the left-hand side after you pass through the gate coming from And Café.

Alaaddin Camii is one of the oldest mosques in Ankara. This small and simple mosque was built in 1178 by *Muhiddin Mesut*, inside the walls of Ankara Castle. The building has evolved over the years and has been rebuilt and renovated many times. The restorations of the Ottoman sultans in particular changed the identity and character of the original property. For example, *Sultan Alaaddin Keykubat* not only renovated the mosque, but also gave it its current name.

The mosque is built, according to Seljuk tradition, in a rectangle. Stones from ruins in Ankara were reused in its construction, for example the Roman column capitals on top of the thick columns of the porch. The *minber* (pulpit) is also interesting, with its Seljuk walnut wood carvings. The doors of the mosque are reproductions of the original ones, which are displayed in the Ethnography Museum in Ankara.

❺ Zenger Paşa Konağı

Doyran Sokak No:13
Ankara Kalesi içi,
www.zengerpasa.com

Like Kınacızade Konağı, this mansion is a combined museum-restaurant. The restaurant offers a great view over the castle and the city of Ankara.

The museum shows exhibits like kitchen tools and old fire extinguishers, which must have been really important in the inner city where the wooden houses burned down several times in the past. You can often see women preparing *mantı* (Turkish ravioli), or other Turkish specialties, in the open kitchen. Entrance is free if you have something to drink or eat. When there are group visits, you may be told you cannot eat there but you can still look around.

Ulucanlar Caddesi

How to get there?

15 minute walk from the citadel.
Buses 345, 395, 392, 322, 312, 324 in the direction of Ulus and Sıhhıye. For more buses and further information see www.ego.gov.tr.

6 Ağaçayak (Ağaçoğlu) Camii

Ulucanlar Caddesi

This little mosque is worth visiting, not just because it is very old (1705-1706 AD) but because of its woodwork. Inside you can admire the timber ceiling workmanship, as well as the decorated wooden beams. The mosque is called *Ağaçayak* (meaning bottom of the tree) because of its abundant usage of timber posts and lintels. These beams are used to strengthen the main walls, which are made of mud bricks. It was restored in 2006 and although the original structure was strengthened, the timber was retained and, with it, the mosque's distinctive character.

As the mosque is located in a conservative area, women might be asked to close the curtain if there are men inside. You can step on to the platform to the left of the entrance and close the curtain. Make sure you bring a scarf, as scarves are not available for loan here.

7 Cenab-ı Ahmet Paşa Camii

Ulucanlar Caddesi, across from Ankara Ulucanlar Göz Hastanesi

This mosque is the only building in Ankara designed by the famous architect. *Mimar Sinan* (1489-1588) who was the chief architect and civil engineer for sultans *Kanuni Sultan Süleyman, Selim II,* and *Murad III.* He built more than 300 major structures, across the Ottoman Empire, including Süleymaniye Camii in İstanbul and Selimiye Camii in Edirne.

The mosque was constructed in 1566 for *Cenab-ı Ahmet Paşa*, a military governor of Ankara and vizier during the reign of *Kanuni Sultan Süleyman*. The mosque's design is typical of the Ottoman period, with its square layout and single lead dome. The *minber* (pulpit) and *mihrap* (prayer niche) are made of white marble, and the mosque itself of Ankara stone (red porphyry). It has very brightly coloured windows, which can be best admired from the inside.

According to the famous Turkish traveller *Evliya Çelebi,* this complex was used as a *Mevlana* lodge in 1640. It formed a social complex with *Cenab-ı Ahmet Paşa*'s and *Azimi*'s tombs and an Ottoman graveyard. This used to be bigger until the inner court of the mosque was re-constructed in 1929, leaving only a small part of the graveyard with the two tombs. Unfortunately the tombs cannot be visited.

You are free to go inside, except prayer times, if you take off your shoes. For women, scarves are available at the entrance.

8 Ulucanlar Cezaevi

Although the prison is not very close to any other places that are interesting to visit, it is worth seeing for those who are not too sensitive.

Ulucanlar was a prison from 1925 to 2006. The prison housed many celebrity figures throughout its history, including the late Prime Minister *Bülent Ecevit*, actor *Yılmaz Güney*, novelist *Yaşar Kemal*, the late leader of the Grand Unity Party (BBP), *Muhsin Yazıcıoğlu*, the late leader of the Nation Party (MP), *Osman Bölükbaşı*, writer and theologian *Mustafa İslamoğlu*. Information about the prisoners is only provided in Turkish, unfortunately.

Ulucanlar Caddesi. Opening hours: Monday to Sunday 10:00 – 16:00. Entrance: 5 TL, students and teachers 2 TL.

In the courtyard, Turkish folk music from the 1970s can be heard. The prison focuses on that decade, when the political situation in Turkey was polarized and chaotic. This is also what the municipality wants to show and why it has opened the prison as a museum. As President *Abdullah Gül* wrote on his Twitter account after visiting the museum: "Ulucanlar is a reminder of the fact that when there is a lack of democracy and justice, there can be nothing but cruelty."

The prison shows dormitories where inmates made music and cooked their dinner. Their private belongings, as well as the poems, notes and drawings they made are shown. Showing dormitories like these, it does not seem like such a bad place. There was even a section, called the Hilton that had a nice view over Ankara and its surrounding hills. However, there was also a dark side to the prison. In isolated dark cells the sound of interrogation and torture is broadcasted. Inside, the waxworks of inmates make the scene even more cruel and realistic. Outside, the original gallows is exhibited along with the list of 19 inmates who were executed here. One of the most famous is the Marxist-Leninist political activist *Deniz Gezmiş* –a socialist-communist student leader in the late 1960s and early 1970s.

The prison is freshly painted but the memories of what went on inside cannot be covered by the paint and restorations. It will leave an impression on you as you leave, especially as it is very recent history.

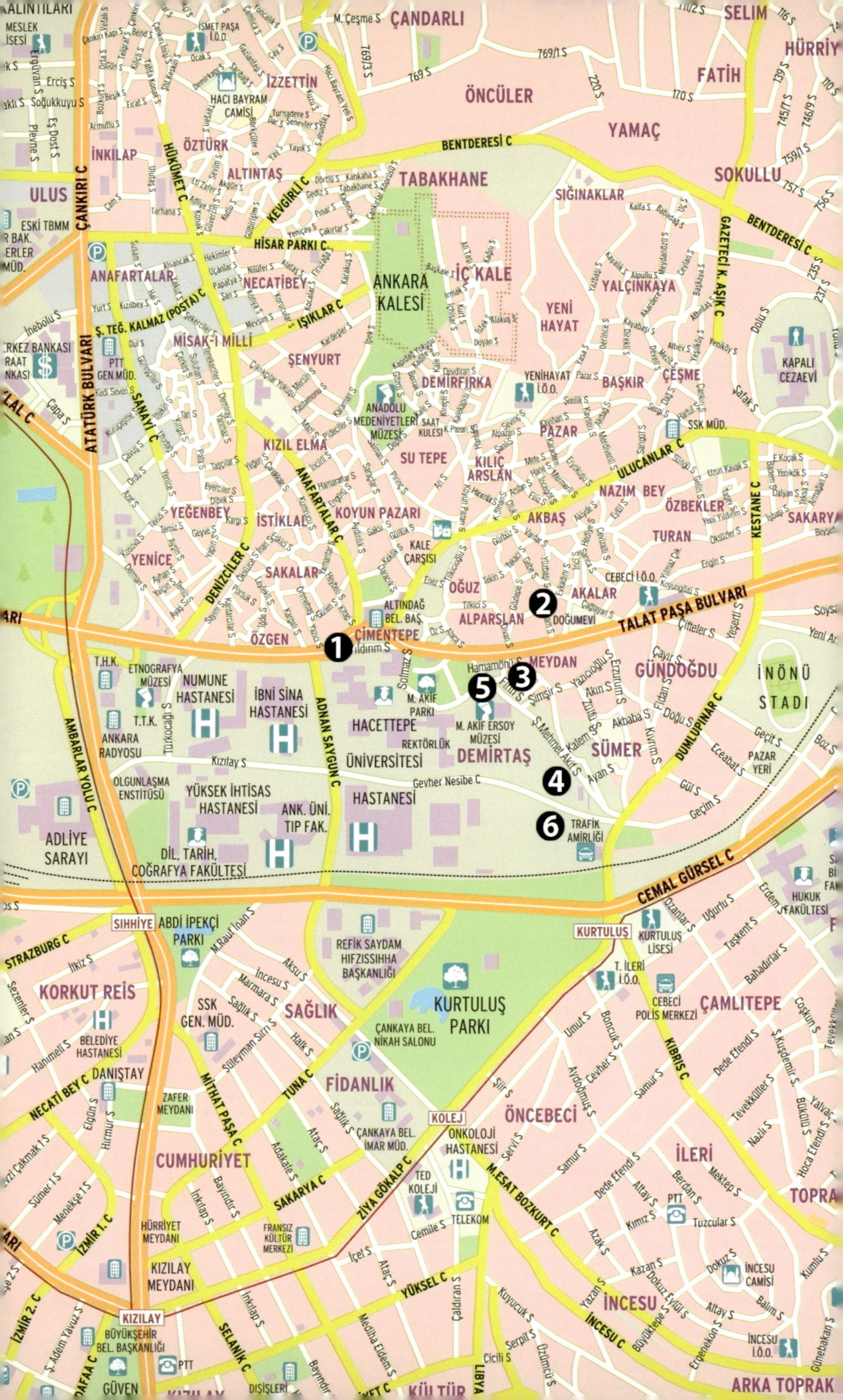
ÇANDARLI
ÖNCÜLER
YAMAÇ
SELİM
HÜRRİYET
FATİH
SOKULLU
BENTDERESİ C
İZZETTİN
HACI BAYRAM CAMİSİ
İSMET PAŞA İ.Ö.O.
MESLEK LİSESİ
ÖZTÜRK
İNKILAP
ULUS
ESKİ TBMM
ALTINTAŞ
TABAKHANE
SIĞINAKLAR
HÜKÜMET C
KEVGİRLİ C
ÇANKIRI C
HİSAR PARKI C
ANAFARTALAR
NECATİBEY
ANKARA KALESİ
İÇ KALE
YALÇINKAYA
GAZETECİ K. AŞIK C
YENİ HAYAT
IŞIKLAR C
Ş. TEĞ. KALMAZ (POSTA) C
MİSAK-I MİLLİ
PTT GEN.MÜD.
ŞENYURT
DEMİRFIRKA
YENİHAYAT İ.Ö.O.
BAŞKIR
ÇEŞME
KAPALI CEZAEVİ
ATATÜRK BULVARI
SANAYİ C
ANADOLU MEDENİYETLERİ MÜZESİ
SAAT KULESİ
PAZAR
SSK MÜD.
KIZIL ELMA
SU TEPE
KILIÇ ARSLAN
ULUCANLAR C
NAZIM BEY
ÖZBEKLER
SAKARYA
KESTANE C
YEĞENBEY
İSTİKLAL
KOYUN PAZARI
AKBAŞ
TURAN
ANAFARTALAR C
YENİCE
DENİZCİLER C
SAKALAR
KALE ÇARŞISI
OĞUZ
CEBECİ İ.Ö.O.
AKALAR
ALTINDAĞ BEL. BAŞ.
ALPARSLAN
DOĞUMEVİ
TALAT PAŞA BULVARI
ÖZGEN
ÇİMENTEPE
MEYDAN
GÜNDOĞDU
İNÖNÜ STADI
T.H.K.
ETNOGRAFYA MÜZESİ
NUMUNE HASTANESİ
İBNİ SİNA HASTANESİ
ADNAN SAYGUN C
M. AKİF PARKI
M. AKİF ERSOY MÜZESİ
T.T.K.
ANKARA RADYOSU
HACETTEPE ÜNİVERSİTESİ
REKTÖRLÜK
DEMİRTAŞ
SÜMER
DUMLUPINAR C
PAZAR YERİ
AMBARLAR YOLU C
OLGUNLAŞMA ENSTİTÜSÜ
YÜKSEK İHTİSAS HASTANESİ
ANK. ÜNİ. TIP FAK.
HASTANESİ
Gevher Nesibe C
TRAFİK AMİRLİĞİ
ADLİYE SARAYI
DİL, TARİH, COĞRAFYA FAKÜLTESİ
CEMAL GÜRSEL C
HUKUK FAKÜLTESİ
SIHHİYE
ABDİ İPEKÇİ PARKI
REFİK SAYDAM HIFZISSIHHA BAŞKANLIĞI
KURTULUŞ
KURTULUŞ LİSESİ
STRAZBURG C
KORKUT REİS
SSK GEN. MÜD.
SAĞLIK
KURTULUŞ PARKI
T. İLERİ İ.Ö.O.
CEBECİ POLİS MERKEZİ
ÇAMLITEPE
BELEDİYE HASTANESİ
DANIŞTAY
ÇANKAYA BEL. NİKAH SALONU
FİDANLIK
NECATİ BEY C
ZAFER MEYDANI
MİTHAT PAŞA C
TUNA C
ÇANKAYA BEL. İMAR MÜD.
KOLEJ
ONKOLOJİ HASTANESİ
ÖNCEBECİ
KIBRIS C
CUMHURİYET
SAKARYA C
ZİYA GÖKALP C
TED KOLEJİ
TELEKOM
M.ESAT BOZKURT C
İLERİ
PTT
TOPRAK
HÜRRİYET MEYDANI
FRANSIZ KÜLTÜR MERKEZİ
İZMİR 1. C
KIZILAY MEYDANI
YÜKSEL C
İNCESU
İNCESU CAMİSİ
KIZILAY
İZMİR 2. C
BÜYÜKŞEHİR BEL. BAŞKANLIĞI
PTT
SELANİK C
İNCESU C
İNCESU İ.Ö.O.
GÜVEN
KÜLTÜR
LİBYA
ARKA TOPRAK
1
2
3
4
5
6

Hamamönü

Hamamönü, which literally translates as *"in front of the hamam"*, is located south of the old Karacabey Hamam. The area, which dates from the 15th century, was originally known as Karacabey.

How to get there?

Take a bus or dolmuş to the Talatpaşa Bulvarı. Get off in front of the Karacabey Hamamı. Buses 312, 313, 314, 320, 339,335, 336 and many more in the direction of Sıhhiye or Ulus. If you take a bus to Gençlik Parkı, it is about 20 minute walk from there.

Under Ottoman ruler, Ankara became a wealthy city because of trade in Angora goats' wool. More and more people came to Ankara and the city expanded rapidly. The then-named Karacabey area was developed during the early 15th century, including the construction of Karacabey Camii and Karacabey Hamamı.

In the early days of the Republic, the area was populated by bureaucrats and politicians. After a few years the politicians moved to other sites in the city. The adobe houses were abandoned and Hamamönü degenerated into something of a slum, until the Altındağ municipality started work on its restoration in 2006. Today it is no longer a strictly residential area and has been transformed into a popular tourist attraction, with ateliers and galleries, restored historic Ankara houses and many restaurants and cafés attracting students and employees from the surrounding universities and hospitals.

1 Tezveren Sultan Türbesi

Intersection of Anafartalar Caddesi and Talatpaşa Bulvarı

This tomb, in the middle of the busy intersection of Anafartalar Caddesi and Talatpaşa Bulvarı, exemplifies the clash between the old city of Ankara and the new modern capital, the city architects had in mind. Before the street (connecting different university hospitals) was designed, this area was the site of various tombs.

Some say that just as the tomb was about to be destroyed the bulldozer's scoop broke and the bulldozer's operator died. Other sources say, perhaps more realistically, that the Ministry of Culture never intended to destroy the tomb. The tomb's odd location, in the middle of the intersection, is a nice image of the balance between the heritage of the old city and the construction of the new.

Despite its peculiar spot, faithful believers take the time to walk around the shrine three times clockwise and say a prayer at its feet. It is not clear whether *Tezveren Sultan* refers to a woman or a man.

❷ Karacabey Hamamı

Talatpaşa Bulvarı No: 101, Hamamönü
www.tarihikaracabeyhamami.com
Opening hours: Daily between 5:30-24:00 (men's-section) - 7:30-20:00 (women's-section)

Karacabey Hamamı, opposite the clock tower in Hamamönü, dates from 1444. It is the oldest *hamam* in Ankara, featuring beautiful domes, and was restored in 1988 and then modernised again in 2012. All of the marble in the steam baths and the 'wet areas' was renewed, but the authentic atmosphere was fortunately not affected. The *hamam* has separate men's and women's sections and offers a wide range of different treatments, which are generally all good. The male dressing area has a barber service, offering an authentic Turkish shave (see chapter *Practical Information>>Hamams*).

❸ Hamamönü

Hacettepe Mahallesi Talatpaşa Bulvarı. Enter from the square with the clock tower across the Karacabey Hamamı.

The restoration project in Hamamönü has led the area being elected a "European Destination of Excellence" in 2011. Seeing the photos from before the restoration, you can only admire the work that has been undertaken (and continues to be carried out, as the municipality continues to expand the project). In this peaceful pedestrian area you can enjoy art, music and carefully restored Anatolian houses. In some of these mansions lived Ottoman pashas and the first MPs of the Turkish Republic: Kamil Paşa Konağı, Beynamlızade Konağı and Kabakçı Konağı are among them.

As well as the historic houses, the mosques in the area have also been renovated: Hacı Musa Camii, Karacabey Camii, Sarıkadı Camii and Taceddin Camii are all worth a look.

Sanat Sokağı

This art street is home to several workshops where traditional Turkish handicrafts, like leather accessories, marbling art (*ebru*), paintings,

KONYALILAR
KIRAATHANESİ

pottery, etc. are made and sold. This is a result of a partnership between the Altındağ Municipality and the Hacettepe University. Take a look around in this street and talk to the shop owners. They will be more than happy to show you their work and if you are lucky you may even be able to have a go at something yourself in one of the workshops they organize.

Outside the main court, there is a daily handicrafts bazaar. Women from the neighbourhood sell leather items, home decorations and knit-work to the public.

In the evenings, especially at the weekends, there are music performances and an open air movie theatre held here. You can find events and fixtures posters around the area.

Restaurants and Cafés

Hamamönü has a good selection of restaurants and cafés, most of them serving Turkish cuisine. Particularly in summer time, it is nice to sit outside on one of the terraces and enjoy the quiet neighbourhood and watch the students stroll through the streets. It is also a very good place to enjoy a typical Turkish breakfast or have a Turkish coffee with *baklava* (multilayered flaky pastry with walnuts or pistachios). A restaurant of note, housed in an old mansion, is Lezzet-i Tarih, although there are plenty of options so don't hesitate to try any of the others.

④ Taceddin Camii

Mehmet Akif Ersoy Sokak

The sign at the entrance of this mosque says 1610. Some say it was originally built even earlier, during the time of *Kanuni Sultan Süleyman*. But the current mosque standing here was built by *Sultan Abdülhamit* between 1901-1902. In the western area of the mosque are the tombs of *İbrahim Taceddin* (....-1550) and his son Muttaki. *İbrahim Taceddin* was a dervish who was sent to Ankara after his study in İstanbul. He was the donor of what was then a lodge of the *Celvetiyye* sect. Their sarcophagus tombs on display here are not the originals.

Next to the mosque is a graveyard, with old Ottoman gravestones. Most of the graves belong to military personnel and their families, dating back to the end of the 19th and beginning of the 20th century. Some gravestones from Hacı Bayram Camii were also brought here when that area was changed.

❺ Mehmet Akif Ersoy Müze Evi

Mehmet Akif Ersoy Sokak, next to the Taccedin Camii in the little park. Opening hours: all days except Sunday 10:00 – 17:00. Entrance is free.

This house is famous as the national anthem, *İstiklal Marşı*, was written here by *Mehmet Akif Ersoy*.

Mehmet Akif Ersoy (1873-1936) was a poet, author, academic and member of parliament. He was a fervent patriot who contributed to the Turkish War of Independence by giving speeches in many mosques in Anatolia. One of the most important speeches he gave in Kastamonu, on 19 November 1920, in which he condemned the Treaty of Sèvres (which divided the Turkish territory among Western countries) and invited the Turkish to use their faith and guns to fight against the Western Colonialists. This speech was even published and pamphlets were distributed over the country.

Ersoy was much appreciated by *Atatürk* and was invited to come to Ankara to join the national struggle. *Tevfik Çiftdoğan*, the imam of the Taceddin Camii at the time, also admired *Ersoy* greatly and invited him to stay in this building, which was then part of the mosque.

At around that time a competition to write a new national anthem was announced, even before the new Republic was established. Initially *Ersoy* did not join the competition but when no suitable songs were entered, the Minister of Education persuaded *Ersoy* to write the anthem. It is said that *Ersoy* wrote on the walls of the lodge at night so as not to miss any inspiration that came to him during his sleep. However these writings, if they were there, are not visible anymore.

The name *Mehmet Akif Ersoy* is still very well known among Turks as the national anthem, along with his credit, is present above the blackboard in almost all classrooms. His portrait was present on the reverse of the 100 Lira banknote until 1989. As *Ersoy* was a deeply pious man he left Turkey in 1925 on a self-imposed exile to Cairo, after Turkey became a secularized state. In Egypt he taught the Turkish language at University. In 1936, just before he died, he returned to Turkey.

The museum consists of 3 rooms with wax statues: a living room, a bed room and a living room annex kitchen. The museum will only interest those with prior knowledge of the man and his stories. However, it does show the interior decor of a lodge just before the beginning of the new Republic of Turkey, which might be of separate interest.

6 Karacabey Camii

Mehmet Akif Ersoy Sokak next to the Hacettepe Hospital

This mosque was probably built in 1427, as the sign at the entrance attests. It is the only example in Ankara, built according to the Bursa type mosques, with an "Exedra" (a semi-circular niche) and a reverse-T floor plan. Its minaret has glazed bricks and tiles. The mosque was part of a complex of buildings including a tomb, fountain, bath house and two medressa's. Unfortunately not all of these buildings have survived and, as the mosque has been restored several times, its shape is no longer the original one. The little tower on one of the domes was also a later addition.

The tomb of Karacabey, son in law of *Sultan Mehmet*, who lost his life in the battle of Varna (Bulgaria) 10 November 1444, is found here.

Walk: **Modern Markets** and **Old Hans**

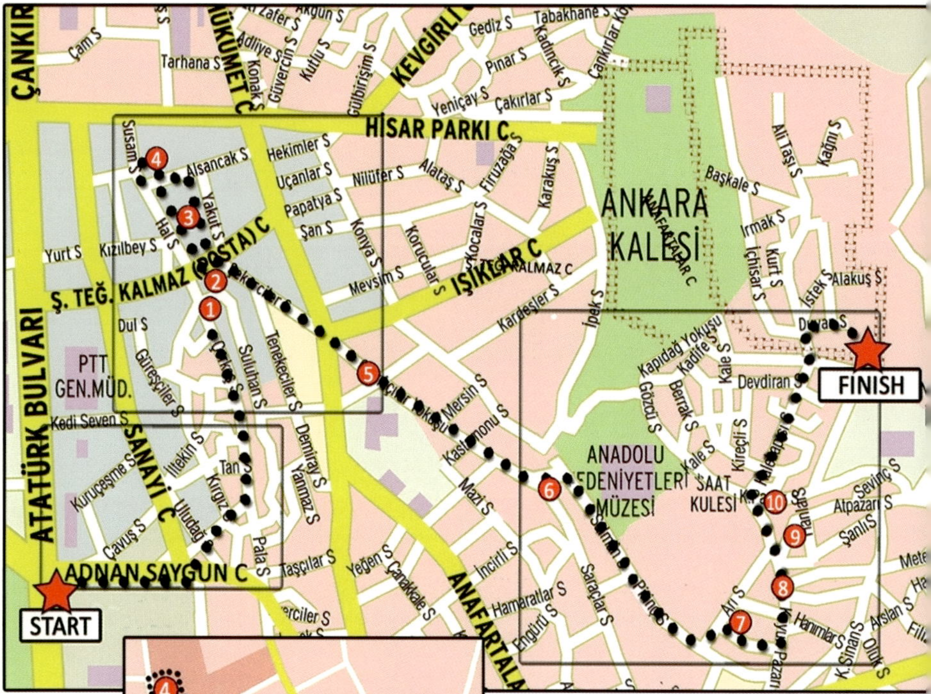

ÇANKIRI
HÜKÜMET C
Zafer S
Akgün S
Adliye S
Güvercin S
Kutlu S
Konak S
Çam S
Tarhana S
Gülbirişim S
KEVGİRLİ
Gediz S
Tabakhane S
Pınar S
Kadıncık S
Çankırılar Kö
Yeniçay S
Çakırlar S
HİSAR PARKI C
Susam S
Alsancak S
Hekimler S
Uçanlar S
Nilüfer S
Alataş S
Firuzağa S
Karakuş S
Papatya S
Yakut S
Hal S
Şan S
Konya S
Korucular S
Kocalar S
Yurt S
Kızılbey S
Ş. TEĞ. KALMAZ (POSTA) C
IŞIKLAR C
Ş. TEĞ. KALMAZ C
Mevsim S
ANKARA KALESİ
Başkale S
Ali Taşı S
Kağnı S
Irmak S
İçhisar S
Kurt S
İstek S
Alakuş S
Duvar S
Kardeşler S
İpek S
Kapıdağ Yokuşu
Kadife S
Kale S
Devdiran S
Dul S
ATATÜRK BULVARI
PTT GEN.MÜD.
Güreşçiler S
Sulu Han S
Tenekeciler S
Mersin S
Kastamonu S
Gözcü S
Berrak S
Kireçli S
FINISH
Kedi Seven S
SANAYİ C
İlterin S
Tan S
Kuruçeşme S
Kırgız S
Demirtaş S
Yanmaz S
Mazi S
ANADOLU MEDENİYETLERİ MÜZESİ
SAAT KULESİ
Sevinç S
Atpazarı S
Şanlı S
Çavuş S
Uludağ S
Pala S
Taşçılar S
Yeğen S
Çanakkale S
İncirli S
Saraçlar S
Hamamlar S
Engürü S
Arı S
Koyun Pazarı
Hanımlar S
K. Sinan S
Arslan S
Oluk S
ADNAN SAYGUN C
START
ANAFARTALAR

Ş. TEĞ. KALMAZ C
ANAFARTALAR C

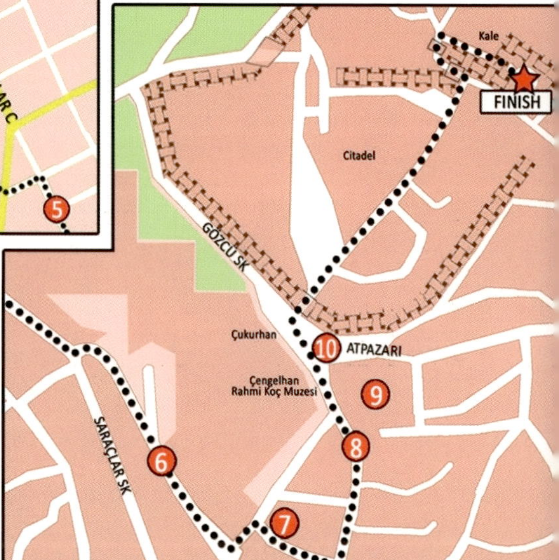

Kale
FINISH
Citadel
GÖZCÜ SK
Çukurhan
ATPAZARI
Çengelhan Rahmi Koç Muzesi
SARAÇLAR SK

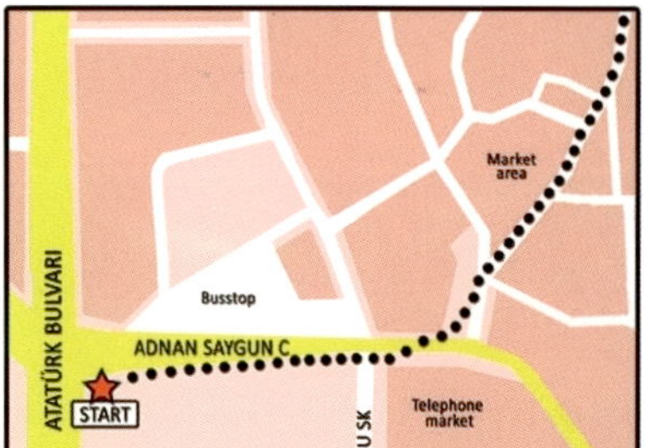

ATATÜRK BULVARI
Market area
Busstop
ADNAN SAYGUN C
START
ORDU SK
Telephone market

Walk: Modern Markets and Old Hans

This walk leads you through Samanpazarı and Hisar, up the hill to entrance of the citadel. You will be walking inside the ancient city limits –now a tiny portion of modern Ankara. Ankara was a bustling city whose residents traded with travellers on the silk route. In the old city there was a plethora of markets, bazaars and Hans (caravanserais) to service these many travellers.

The travellers, their caravans, camels and horses may be gone but the hill is still home to a vibrant and colourful market. You'll find clothing, nuts, fruits, vegetables, fresh fish, spices, copper and silverware, and the local specialty Angora wool. The products on display here paint a picture of Ankara's rich and glorious history.

More detailed information about the sights and locations found on this walk can be found in chapters *Hisar* and *In and Around the Citadel*.

The walk will take between two and three hours, depending on how many stops you make along the way. It ends at the main gate of the citadel, near the Anadolu Medeniyetleri Müzesi. This walk will give your eyes, ears and nose a treat, we hope you enjoy it.

We start at the junction of Atatürk Bulvarı and Adnan Saygun Caddesi, across from the entrance to Gençlik Parkı. Walk along Adnan Saygun Caddesi, with the car park to your right. At the first junction, about 200 m along the road, you'll diagonally cross towards a small square, with a green water fountain in the middle (Zeynep Acay Hayratı). This marks the entrance to the textile market.

Walk across this square, towards the right rear corner. Here are two covered pedestrian paths. Take the left one (Çerkeş Sokağı) which will lead you through the market. Follow this path until you see the İbadullah Camii on your right.

❶ İbadullah Camii

This mosque dates back to the late 17th or early 18th century. It is small but busy, mostly used by the vendors from the surrounding market stalls.

At the mosque, turn right into a narrow alley. This leads you to the gate of the Sulu Han.

❷ Sulu Han

This is an old marketplace, built in 1511, where vendors now sell handicrafts, beads, decorative pieces, and jewellery (see chapter *Hisar*).

Head through the doorway under the "Toilet WC" sign (trust us!). This leads into a second, smaller, courtyard. The stairs on the right will take you up to the first floor, where you find lots of lovely handicraft-shops.

Leave the Sulu Han via the main exit on the first floor. A flight of stairs leads you into a busy street, Şehit Teğmen Kalmaz Caddesi. Cross over and head slightly to the right; you're heading towards the Ulus Hali. Take the left entrance of this food market.

❸ Ulus Hali

This is the big food market; it has a large sign reading "Ankara Büyükşehir Belediyesi Tarihi Yeni Hale Hoş Geldiniz" above the entrance. Enjoy the smells and colours of the fresh fruit and vegetables, fish, bread and spices (see chapter *Hisar*).

The exit is on the other side of the rectangular market hall. From here, crossing the pedestrian area takes you to a small spice market; it's a little bit to the left along a small walkway next to the "Pastırmacı" (Pastrami seller) sign.

❹ Spice Market

Pay special attention to the jugs filled with leeches at the entrance of the market. These are still used in the traditional way to suck out "bad blood" from sufferers of rheumatism and other aches and pains.

If you want to sit for a while, perhaps have a drink or a snack, there is a nice café in the middle of the spice market with an outside terrace.

If you veered off for a tea, get back to the spices and the leeches. You'll take the first exit on the right and then, once outside, left again.

Along Susam Sokak, the street to your right, you'll see the small Hallaç Mahmut Camii (see chapter Hisar). Walk back to the covered food market and take the other route through, back towards Şehit Teğmen Kalmaz Caddesi. Cross over the street, walk a bit to the left, and take the narrow

road (Tenekeciler Sokak), opposite Kahvaltı Sarayı, heading slightly downwards.

Along Tenekeciler Sokak, vendors sell an array of pots and pans, as well as knives and other cookware.

Take the first uphill street on your left. This street ends in a flight of stairs, which you should climb, and opens out onto large junction.

Cross over the road (Anafartalar Caddesi) and turn right into Çıkrıkçılar Yokuşu, another uphill road.

5 Çıkrıkçılar Yokuşu

This street is also known as Samanpazarı. Every Saturday, and in the days before public holidays this street is buzzing with shoppers. The sellers here deal in traditional cloths and fine fabrics. Traditional dresses, such as the costumes worn by young boys to circumcision ceremonies and accessories for weddings and henna nights, is fawned over by mothers for their sons and daughters. Be wary that many of these shops are closed on Sundays.

Walk along Samanpazarı, up to its highest point. Here take a turn to the left onto the cobbled Salman Sokak, a small, steep road which immediately bends to the right.

❻ Salman Sokak

Along this street you can observe coppersmiths and braziers at work and browse their wares. Most sell traditional Turkish tables and trays (*sini*), tankards and other (mainly decorative) copper and brass items.

You will pass the Zağfiran Han on your left (see chapter Hisar). You have to look up as it is located on a higher level than the Salman Sokak. At the moment this Han is being restored.

Further along, the street widens. Walk past the trees until you see a set of stairs to your left. Climb these and, at the top, head to the right. A few metres along you'll be able to enter the Pirinç Han on your left.

❼ Pirinç Han

This small *han* is home to lots of small antique shops and galleries. On the ground floor there is a little café/restaurant with an outside terrace, serving tasty *gözleme* (Turkish pancake filled with cheese, spinach potatoes, etc.). A nice lunch! (See chapter *Hisar*.)

When leaving Pirinç Han, go to the left and follow the course of the road. At the T-junction take a left turn and head up Koyunpazarı Sokak.

8 Koyunpazarı Sokak

There are several antique and gifts shops up this steep road, as well as a few restaurants. This was the area to buy Angora goat skins and *sof* (mohair). Between 15th and 19th centuries, Ankara became very wealthy from Angora wool and Angora goat leather. You still can find wool sellers in this same neighbourhood, selling the same products they always have. At the end of the street there is a café called Kirit. They serve a lovely cup of coffee in here ("Western style") and nice Turkish food with an original modern twist. On the first floor there's a great balcony where you can sit in the shade and enjoy your Latté, overlooking the hustle and bustle below.

Just a few steps from Kirit Café up the street, at your right hand side you see Pilavoğlu Han.

9 Pilavoğlu Han

This *han* was just recently opened in the summer of 2013. It is the only *han* in Ankara with two entrances, one from Hanlar Sokak and

the other from Koyunpazarı Sokak. This 17th century *han* used to be an inn only. No trade was done here. Until the café and antique shops were opened in 2013, the *han* was used as a workshop and quiet tea garden for men to play *tavla* (backgammon).

⑩ Atpazarı

This was once, during Ankara's commercial heyday, a major commercial crossroad on the East-West trade route. About a dozen caravanserais were built around this square, just outside the South Gate of the citadel, during 15th, 16th and 17th centuries. Caravanserais were used by travellers to recover after a long journey, offering the weary travellers security as well as a chance to trade and exchange information with one-another. Sulu Han, Zağfiran Han and Pirinç Han came earlier in this walk. Here in the square you'll be able to see Çukurhan, Çengelhan (see chapter *Hisar*), Kurşunlu Han and Mahmut Paşa Han. The last two are now part of the Anadolu Medeniyetleri Müzesi (see chapter *In and Around the Citadel*).

The walk is over. You can continue by visiting the Anadolu Medeniyetleri Müzesi next to the Çukurhan, or venture into the citadel and visit the castle (see chapter *In and Around the Citadel*).

Kızılay, the New Centre

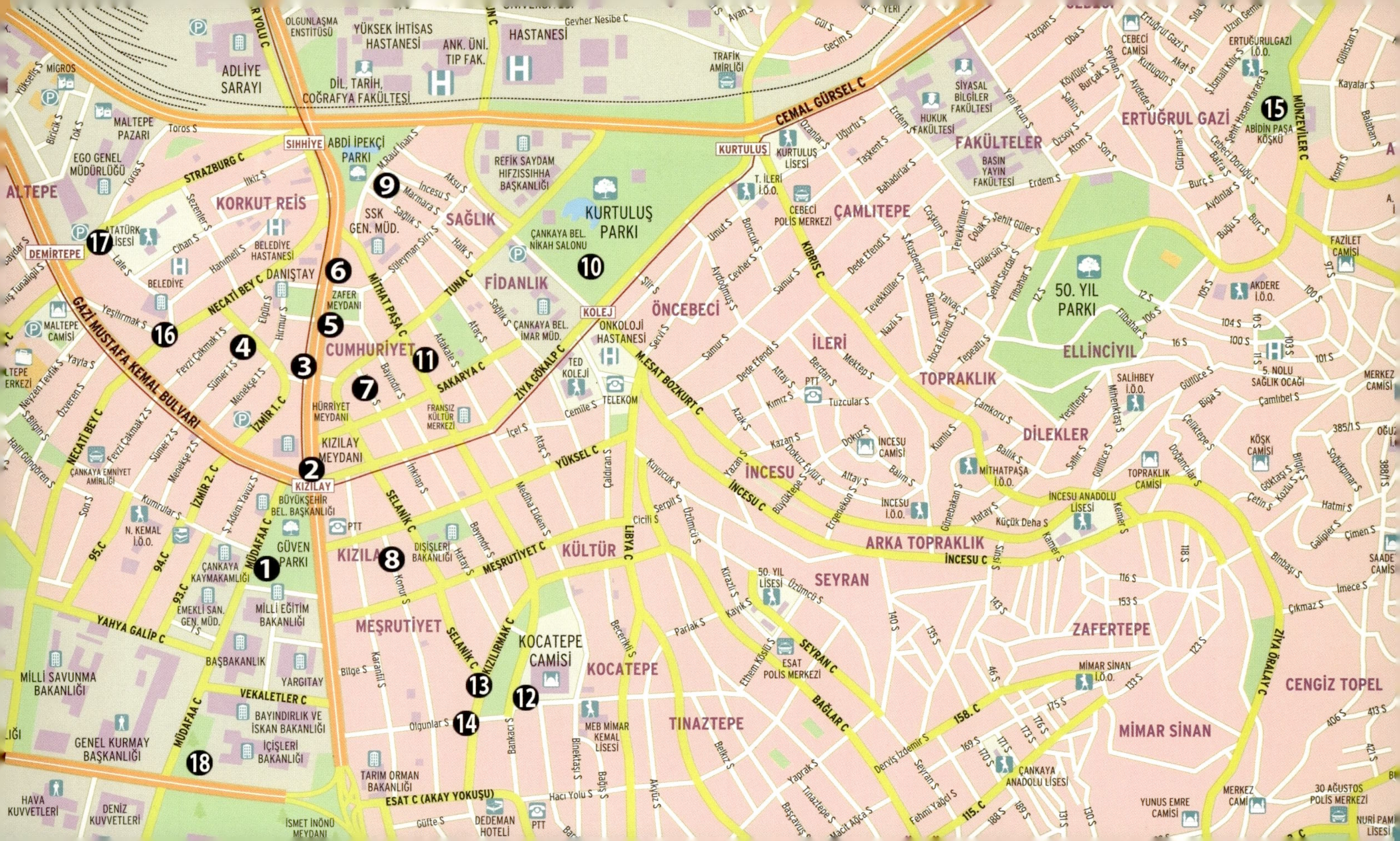

ADLİYE SARAYI
OLGUNLAŞMA ENSTİTÜSÜ
YÜKSEK İHTİSAS HASTANESİ
ANK. ÜNİ. TIP FAK.
HASTANESİ
DİL, TARİH, COĞRAFYA FAKÜLTESİ
Gevher Nesibe C
TRAFİK AMİRLİĞİ
CEMAL GÜRSEL C
SİYASAL BİLGİLER FAKÜLTESİ
HUKUK FAKÜLTESİ
FAKÜLTELER
BASIN YAYIN FAKÜLTESİ
ERTUĞRUL GAZİ
CEBECİ CAMİSİ
ERTUĞURULGAZİ İ.Ö.O.
ABİDİN PAŞA KÖŞKÜ
MÜNZEVİLER C
MİGROS
MALTEPE PAZARI
EGO GENEL MÜDÜRLÜĞÜ
ALTEPE
SIHHIYE
ABDİ İPEKÇİ PARKI
REFİK SAYDAM HIFZISSIHHA BAŞKANLIĞI
KURTULUŞ
KURTULUŞ LİSESİ
T. İLERİ İ.Ö.O.
CEBECİ POLİS MERKEZİ
ÇAMLITEPE
FAZİLET CAMİSİ
AKDERE İ.Ö.O.
50. YIL PARKI
ELLİNCİYIL
STRAZBURG C
KORKUT REİS
BELEDİYE HASTANESİ
BELEDİYE
ATATÜRK LİSESİ
DEMİRTEPE
SSK GEN. MÜD.
SAĞLIK
KURTULUŞ PARKI
ÇANKAYA BEL. NİKAH SALONU
DANIŞTAY
ZAFER MEYDANI
MİTHAT PAŞA C
TUNA C
FİDANLIK
ÇANKAYA BEL. İMAR MÜD.
KOLEJ
ONKOLOJİ HASTANESİ
ÖNCEBECİ
İLERİ
KIBRIS C
TOPRAKLIK
5. NOLU SAĞLIK OCAĞI
SALİHBEY İ.Ö.O.
MALTEPE CAMİSİ
NECATİ BEY C
CUMHURİYET
HÜRRİYET MEYDANI
SAKARYA C
ZİYA GÖKALP C
TED KOLEJİ
TELEKOM
M.ESAT BOZKURT C
İNCESU CAMİSİ
DİLEKLER
KÖŞK CAMİSİ
GAZİ MUSTAFA KEMAL BULVARI
İZMİR 1. C
KIZILAY MEYDANI
KIZILAY
FRANSIZ KÜLTÜR MERKEZİ
YÜKSEL C
İNCESU
MİTHATPAŞA İ.Ö.O.
TOPRAKLIK CAMİSİ
ÇANKAYA EMNİYET AMİRLİĞİ
İZMİR 2. C
BÜYÜKŞEHİR BEL. BAŞKANLIĞI
PTT
SELANİK C
İNCESU C
İNCESU İ.Ö.O.
İNCESU ANADOLU LİSESİ
N. KEMAL İ.Ö.O.
MÜDAFAA C
GÜVEN PARKI
ÇANKAYA KAYMAKAMLIĞI
KIZILAY
DIŞİŞLERİ BAKANLIĞI
MEŞRUTİYET C
KÜLTÜR
LİBYA C
ARKA TOPRAKLIK
50. YIL LİSESİ
SEYRAN
95.C
94.C
93.C
EMEKLİ SAN. GEN. MÜD.
MİLLİ EĞİTİM BAKANLIĞI
YAHYA GALİP C
MEŞRUTİYET
KIZILIRMAK C
KOCATEPE CAMİSİ
ESAT POLİS MERKEZİ
SEYRAN C
ZAFERTEPE
ZİYA ÖRALAY C
MİLLİ SAVUNMA BAKANLIĞI
BAŞBAKANLIK
YARGITAY
VEKALETLER C
KOCATEPE
MİMAR SİNAN İ.Ö.O.
CENGİZ TOPEL
BAYINDIRLIK VE İSKAN BAKANLIĞI
MEB MİMAR KEMAL LİSESİ
TINAZTEPE
BAĞLAR C
158. C
MİMAR SİNAN
GENEL KURMAY BAŞKANLIĞI
İÇİŞLERİ BAKANLIĞI
TARIM ORMAN BAKANLIĞI
ÇANKAYA ANADOLU LİSESİ
HAVA KUVVETLERİ
DENİZ KUVVETLERİ
İSMET İNÖNÜ MEYDANI
ESAT C (AKAY YOKUŞU)
DEDEMAN HOTELİ
115. C
YUNUS EMRE CAMİSİ
MERKEZ CAMİ
30 AĞUSTOS POLİS MERKEZİ
NURİ PAMİR LİSESİ
1
2
3
4
5
6
7
8
9
10
11
12
13
14
15
16
17
18

Kızılay, the New Centre

Kızılay can be called the true city centre. If something is going on –for example, a demonstration– the chances are it will be in Kızılay. Kızılay is also the centre for public transport, as the bus hub is located in Güvenpark.

The district dates back to the 1930s. The German architect and city planner Hermann Jansen designed *Yenişehir*, (New City), with wide boulevards and shopping streets, inspired by western cities, like Paris and Barcelona. He wanted a district where people could see, feel and experience the positive energy and vigour of the new Turkish republic.

The quarter was named after the Turkish Red Cross (*Kızılay*). Their headquarters was located at Kızılay square. It was replaced by a skyscraper, where the Kızılay shopping center (*Kızılay Alışveriş Merkezi*) is situated.

How to get there?

Kızılay and everything around Atatürk Bulvarı can be easily reached by metro (stop: Kızılay station), and with the Ankaray as well as the Metro line. As Güvenpark is the hub for most buses and many dolmuşes, you will have plenty of choice. Almost all buses and dolmuşes which go into the city, stop in Güvenpark or at Atatürk Bulvarı.

Kızılay is a lively area with lots of shops, offering a modern Turkish shopping experience and a range of prices to suit every budget. It can be quite hectic, especially at weekends. The main shopping street is Atatürk Bulvarı. But if you look closer, behind this main street, there are nice streets with restaurants and cafés to stroll around. This is also a popular nightlife area for students. But during the day it has a relaxed atmosphere, with street musicians playing Turkish music and other street artists performing their arts.

Another feature in Kızılay is *Kocatepe Camii*, the biggest mosque in Ankara. There are also parks here, as there are all over Ankara, for example Güvenpark, Kurtuluş Parkı and 50. Yıl Parkı.

❶ Güvenpark

If you come to Kızılay by bus or dolmuş, you will probably arrive at Güvenpark. The bus hub is the main feature of the park. The park itself is not big but can often be seen on Turkish television when demonstrations are held, mostly in front of the Security Monument (*Güvenlik Anıtı*). This monument was erected in 1935 and bears *Atatürk*'s advice to the Turkish people: "Turk! Be proud, work hard, and believe in yourself." There are several reliefs, representing the War of Independence, farmers farming the land, police and gendarme and human intellect. It was designed and created by the Austrian sculptors Franz Wirt, Triberer, Anton Hanak and Joseph Thorak.

In summer you will see flower, tea and sunflower seed sellers in the park.

❷ Kızılay Square

The heart of the city and of Kızılay is Kızılay Square. It is found on Atatürk Bulvarı, connecting the old part (Ulus) with the Presidential

Kızılay Square

Palace and the official government building (on the same site) in Çankaya. Kızılay Square was designed as a socio-spatial project of the newly established Turkish Republic. It was an essential node in the city development plans of 1924-1925. It was planned to be both the symbol of the new republic and the public space of the bourgeoisie. Today it has been taken over by shopping malls and the bourgeoisie have moved to other areas.

Kızılay Square has often been at the centre of Ankara's most significant moments. In the first half of the 1960s, the square was often the stage for political struggles. In 1963, after the coup, demonstrations on the square were forbidden by law in order to safeguard public safety. At that time, the square was still a pedestrian area. This changed in the 1980s when the square was turned into a traffic junction –one of the busiest in the city nowadays.

The first Turkish department store, Gima, was located on Kızılay Square, in one of the first shopping centres in Ankara, the YKM.

Selanik 2 Caddesi is a very "sweet" street with lots of restaurants offering ice creams and pastries. You will also find internet cafés with big TV screens for playing PlayStation and cafés where they play Okay –a kind of Rummikub.

9 Yenişehir Pazarı

How to get there?

It is a 6 minute walk from the Sıhhıye metro stop on the Metro line and 7 minutes from Kolej metro stop on the Ankaray (metro) line.

On the junction of Süleyman Sırrı Caddesi and Aksu Caddesi there is a big market, Çankaya Belediyesi Yenişehir Pazarı. Most days, clothes, bags and plastic kitchenware are sold here. On Wednesdays and Saturdays, you can also buy fruits and vegetables here. Thursdays are the busiest days, when it is a *Sosyete Pazarı* where (mostly fake brand) clothes are sold for cheap prices.

⑩ Kurtuluş Parkı

How to get there?

Get out at the Kolej stop or the Kurtuluş stop on the Ankaray (metro) line.

This park is one of the bigger parks and is a pleasant place to pass the time of day. It has a wedding salon and if you are lucky (mostly during the summer in weekends) you might come across a wedding party.

The park has picnic tables (but not the common BBQs!), a small playground, outdoor fitness equipment, ping pong tables, a running track, a traffic garden for kids (although closed for the moment), an ice skating rink (in winter time) and public toilets.

⑪ Mustafa Necati Kültür Evi

How to get there?

Mithatpaşa Cad. No: 35 Entrance: in general only for Members of Parliament. Sometimes accessible when an exhibition is organized.

To see if there is an exhibition see: www.tbmm.gov.tr/kultur_evi/index.htm (only in Turkish).

This lovely mansion is, unfortunately, not always accessible. If you are lucky (and the guards are friendly), there will be an exhibition taking place and they will grant you access.

Use of the garden and its cafeteria is restricted to former and present members of Parliament.

⑫ Kocatepe Camii

This huge mosque is the largest in Ankara. You can see it from a long way away. It was built by *Turgut Özal* government in the mid 1980s and was inspired by the architectural styles of Selimiye Camii in Edirne and Sultan Ahmet Camii in İstanbul. It has specific classical 16th century Ottoman style elements. The mosque has a dome of 98.5 metres and four minarets of 88 metres. The worship area is 1288 square metres.

Kocatepe Camii

The mosque is often subject to political controversy. By virtue of its size, it can easily compete with *Atatürk*'s mausoleum in Ankara's skyline. That is why some secularists see it as a symbol of the rising influence of (political) Islam in Turkey.

The inside of the mosque is very colourful with stained glass windows and eastern patterns on the wall. In the middle hangs an enormous chandelier, fitting for the size of the mosque, lighting the immense space.

How to get there?

Buses 123, 132, 133, 165, 284 direction Kızılay; 160, 174 direction Opera, 173, 188 direction Oran and many more. For more information see www.ego.gov.tr.

The mosque can be visited by everyone, except during prayer times. Women enter through the same entrance but their area is upstairs. Shawls and long skirts can be found in the cabinet on the right by the entrance.

13 Büyülü Fener Sineması

How to get there?

See Kocatepe Camii

Meşrutiyet Cad. Hatay Sok No: 18 Kızılay

This small cinema has more atmosphere than most cinemas in the big shopping malls have. It shows both commercial and cult movies, also in the original language with Turkish subtitles (*Türkçe altyazılı*).

Tickets are around 7 euros. There are concessions for students, teachers and elderly and on Tuesdays and Wednesdays during the day.

For more information and the program see *www.buyulufener.com.tr* (Turkish only)

⑭ Olgunlar Caddesi

How to get there?

Buses 114, 118, 119, 122, 123, 126 and many more in the direction of Kızılay. It is a 10 minutes' walk from Güvenpark.

In the street next to the Belgian Residence (the yellow house on Atatürk Bulvarı) there is a little market selling second-hand and new books. They mainly sell Turkish textbooks but sometimes they have English books, if you ask them.

There are some interesting books, if you look carefully, for example a children's comic book about *Atatürk*, in which different scenes from *Atatürk*'s life are depicted.

⑮ 50. Yıl Parkı

Münzeviler Caddesi

50. Yıl Parkı is slightly away from the centre of Kızılay. This park is located on a hill, which makes it an interesting exercise to go here by foot. You might consider taking a taxi. The street before the park looks shabby but do not let it scare you –the park is worthwhile visiting because of its lo-

How to get there?

The buses do not stop nearby. As it is quite a walk up you might consider taking a taxi. For all sporty people the buses who stop at 750 metres from the park are 220, 221, 297-3 direction Mamak-Batıkent, 321, 324 329, 330, 332, 342 and many more in the direction of Kızılay. For more buses and current information see www.ego.gov.tr.

cation. From the hill you have a view of Ankara in different directions. You can walk through the park or drive around by car. The entrance fee for cars is 4 TL.

The park has a small playground for children and pavilions from which you can enjoy the view.

The best view is probably from the Rivana café, where they serve nice sandwiches. If you have never tried it before try a sandwich with hellim cheese, which is grilled, to give it a crispy texture.

16 Maltepe Camii

Maltepe Camii is squeezed in between traffic jammed streets. Coming from Gazi Mustafa Kemal Bulvarı, there is a terrace in front, with a fake

How to get there?

The metro stop Demirtepe on the Ankaray line is just next to the mosque.

stone wall and waterfall. It could be a pleasant spot, if the park and stairs around had not been used as a public toilet.

Maltepe Camii itself is a majestic building. It was designed by architect *Recai Akçay* and built between 1954 and 1959. To finance the construction of the mosque a foundation was set up in 1950, in which the public could participate. This foundation (although under a different name) is still responsible for the mosque. The total cost for building was (5.000.000 old Turkish liras) and current expenses are all met by public donations to this foundation.

The mosque is built in classical Ottoman style, with a dome and two minarets. The outside is white stone. Inside the walls are covered with the tiles from Kütahya (some 300 km west from Ankara and famous for its porcelain). It has stained glass windows and a big chandelier in the middle.

This mosque does not welcome guests as openly as Kocatepe Camii, but like other mosques, it can be visited outside prayer times.

Women can enter through the entrance on the right-hand side of the minaret, around the corner. As there are no shawls and skirts available, make sure you bring your own.

17 75. Yıl Cumhuriyet Eğitim Müzesi

How to get there?

The metro stop Demirtepe on the Ankaray line is on the other side of Strazburg Caddesi.

Strazburg Cad. Lale Sok. No: 6.
Tel: 231 28 99
Weekdays 9.30 – 17.00. Entrance is free.

This small museum is interesting for those who went to school in Turkey, displaying old educational equipment and documents. There are more than 400 exhibits, including telescopes, jars of fluid-preserved specimens, pinned insects and butterflies and land maps. Although the museum was only opened in 1998, it looks dusty and it is clear that little effort is put in to maintaining the museum or attracting the public.

⑱ Türkiye Büyük Millet Meclisi (TBMM)

The current building of Türkiye Büyük Millet Meclisi (TBMM), Turkey's Grand National Assembly, was designed by the Austrian architect Clemens Holzmeister. He wanted to encapsulate the power and eternity of the Turkish Republic in his design. It is a powerful, solid and almost symmetrical building. Construction started in 1939. Because of World War II, the new parliament building was not opened and used until January 1961.

The main entrances to the Parliament Building are at the front, on the left and right under the bridges. The Honorary entrance is in the middle of the front facade. 5 bronze doors lead into the Marble Hall. From here the official guests can walk, via galleries with columns and two indoor gardens, straight to the centre of the Parliament Building and the heart of Turkish democracy, the Plenary Hall.

How to get there?

Between Atatürk Bulvarı and Dikmen Caddesi. Access only for groups, official requests have to be submitted in advance to the Guidance and Advertising Bureau of the TBMM. Tel: 420 68 87 www.tbmm.gov.tr

In the Plenary Hall, there are 578 orange chairs, allocated to the Members of Parliament. The seats are arranged in an amphitheatre layout. They face a lectern for speakers, the seats allocated to the ministers and in the middle the seat of the parliamentary chairman. An important statement of *Atatürk* is engraved on the white marble wall in the background:

"Egemenlik kayıtsız şartsız milletindir."

"Sovereignty belongs unconditionally and without any reservation to the nation."

The first-floor galleries are allocated to the President of Turkey, military and civilian bureaucrats on the left-hand side and on the right-hand side to the representatives of diplomatic missions in Turkey.

The balconies at the back of the Plenary Hall are for the press and former members of the Parliament on the first floor and for the public on the second floor.

Behind the Parliament Building is a second building, where the offices of the 550 deputies of the Parliament, their secretaries and support staff and administrative and service units are situated.

There are guided tours for groups. But you need to make an appointment in advance with the Guidance and Advertising desk of the TBMM. You need to write an official visit request stating the reason for your interest and giving background information about the group. Requests can always be refused. Tours are not made for individuals.

Tours take place outside the meeting times of the parliament, which are on Tuesdays, Wednesdays and Thursdays and very occasionally on other days. So requests for guided tours on Mondays or Fridays are more likely to be granted. Submit your request well in advance.

At the moment it is not possible to visit the meetings of the parliament without an invitation from one of the MPs. Turks can contact

the representative of their region with an official request to visit a debate. TRT, the state broadcaster, however, broadcasts most of the debates in the Plenary Hall live on TRT3 (generally from Tuesday-Thursday, between 3 PM-7 PM). Seeing these debates can be interesting, as they can be heated sometimes; and not only in terms of what is said. In the heat of the moment, "occasionally" MPs even tackle each other physically.

According to the Guidance and Advertising Bureau you can visit the gardens of the Parliament. To enter the Parliament area, you go, with a valid ID-card, to the Dikmen gate of the TBMM complex and tell the guides the reason for your visit. Do not try to enter through the main entrance (from İsmet İnönü Bulvarı) because as soon as you enter the stairs the security will ask you to leave.

On the website you can see a virtual tour of the inside of the building.

Around the **Train Station & Hipodrum Caddesi**

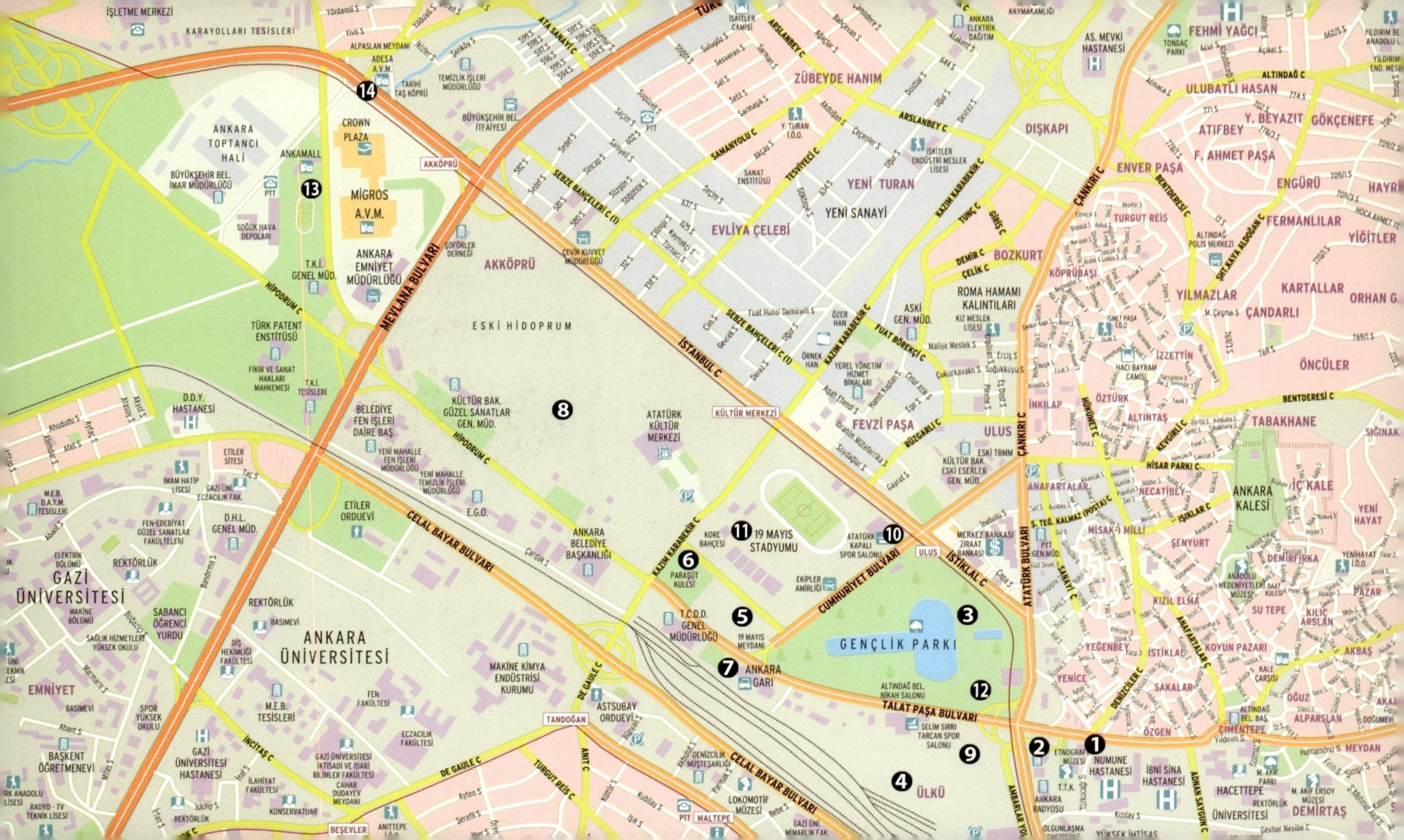
İŞLETME MERKEZİ
KARAYOLLARI TESİSLERİ
ANKARA TOPTANCI HALİ
BÜYÜKŞEHİR BEL. İMAR MÜDÜRLÜĞÜ
ANKAMALL
CROWN PLAZA
MİGROS A.V.M.
SOĞUK HAVA DEPOLARI
T.K.İ. GENEL MÜD.
ANKARA EMNİYET MÜDÜRLÜĞÜ
ADESA A.V.M.
ALPASLAN MEYDANI
TARİHİ TAŞ KÖPRÜ
TEMİZLİK İŞLERİ MÜDÜRLÜĞÜ
BÜYÜKŞEHİR BEL. İTFAİYESİ
AKKÖPRÜ
ŞOFÖRLER DERNEĞİ
ÇEVİK KUVVET MÜDÜRLÜĞÜ
MEVLANA BULVARI
HİPODRUM C
TÜRK PATENT ENSTİTÜSÜ
FİKİR VE SANAT HAKLARI MAHKEMESİ
T.K.İ. TESİSLERİ
D.D.Y. HASTANESİ
ESKİ HİDOPRUM
BELEDİYE FEN İŞLERİ DAİRE BAŞ.
KÜLTÜR BAK. GÜZEL SANATLAR GEN. MÜD.
YENİ MAHALLE FEN İŞLERİ MÜDÜRLÜĞÜ
YENİ MAHALLE TEMİZLİK İŞLERİ MÜDÜRLÜĞÜ
E.G.O.
ETİLER ORDUEVİ
ETİLER SİTESİ
İMAM HATİP LİSESİ
GAZİ ÜNİ. ECZACILIK FAK.
M.E.B. D.A.Y.M. TESİSLERİ
FEN-EDEBİYAT GÜZEL SANATLAR FAKÜLTELERİ
D.H.L. GENEL MÜD.
ELEKTRİK BÖLÜMÜ
REKTÖRLÜK
GAZİ ÜNİVERSİTESİ
MAKİNE BÖLÜMÜ
SABANCI ÖĞRENCİ YURDU
SAĞLIK HİZMETLERİ YÜKSEK OKULU
EMNİYET
BAŞKENT ÖĞRETMENEVİ
RADYO - TV TEKNİK LİSESİ
ANKARA ÜNİVERSİTESİ
DİŞ HEKİMLİĞİ FAKÜLTESİ
M.E.B. TESİSLERİ
SPOR YÜKSEK OKULU
GAZİ ÜNİVERSİTESİ HASTANESİ
İLAHİYAT FAKÜLTESİ
KONSERVATUAR
GAZİ ÜNİVERSİTESİ İKTİSADİ VE İDARİ BİLİMLER FAKÜLTESİ
CAHAR DUDAYEV MEYDANI
ECZACILIK FAKÜLTESİ
FEN FAKÜLTESİ
MAKİNE KİMYA ENDÜSTRİSİ KURUMU
ANITTEPE İ.Ö.O.
BEŞEVLER
TANDOĞAN
ASTSUBAY ORDUEVİ
DE GAULLE C
TURGUT REİS C
ANIT C
CELAL BAYAR BULVARI
DENİZCİLİK MÜŞTEŞARLIĞI
LOKOMOTİF MÜZESİ
MALTEPE
GAZİ ÜNİ. MİMARLIK FAK.
ANKARA BELEDİYE BAŞKANLIĞI
ATATÜRK KÜLTÜR MERKEZİ
KÜLTÜR MERKEZİ
KAZIM KARABEKİR C
KORE BAHÇESİ
PARAŞÜT KULESİ
19 MAYIS STADYUMU
T.C.D.D. GENEL MÜDÜRLÜĞÜ
19 MAYIS MEYDANI
ANKARA GARI
ATATÜRK KAPALI SPOR SALONU
EKİPLER AMİRLİĞİ
CUMHURİYET BULVARI
GENÇLİK PARKI
ALTINDAĞ BEL. NİKAH SALONU
TALAT PAŞA BULVARI
SELİM SIRRI TARCAN SPOR SALONU
ÜLKÜ
ULUS
İSTİKLAL C
MERKEZ BANKASI
ZİRAAT BANKASI
ATATÜRK BULVARI
ETNOGRAFYA MÜZESİ
T.T.K.
ANKARA RADYOSU
NUMUNE HASTANESİ
İBNİ SİNA HASTANESİ
HACETTEPE ÜNİVERSİTESİ
M. AKİF ERSOY MÜZESİ
DEMİRTAŞ
ADNAN SAYGUN C
AMBARLAR YOLU
İSTANBUL C
SEBZE BAHÇELERİ C (1)
EVLİYA ÇELEBİ
YENİ SANAYİ
YENİ TURAN
ZÜBEYDE HANIM
ARSLANBEY C
SAMANYOLU C
TESVİYECİ C
SANAT ENSTİTÜSÜ
Y. TURAN İ.Ö.O.
İŞKİTLER ENDÜSTRİ MESLEK LİSESİ
İŞKİTLER CAMİSİ
ATA SANAYİ C
ANKARA ELEKTRİK DAĞITIM
DIŞKAPI
AS. MEVKİ HASTANESİ
TONGAÇ PARKI
FEHMİ YAĞCI
ULUBATLI HASAN
ALTINDAĞ C
ATIFBEY
Y. BEYAZIT
GÖKÇENEFE
F. AHMET PAŞA
ENVER PAŞA
ENGÜRÜ
HAYRİ
ÇANKIRI C
BENTDERESİ C
TURGUT REİS
KÖPRÜBAŞI
BOZKURT
TUNÇ C
GİRİŞ C
DEMİR C
ÇELİK C
ROMA HAMAMI KALINTILARI
KIZ MESLEK LİSESİ
ASKİ GEN. MÜD.
ÖZER HAN
ÖRNEK HAN
YEREL YÖNETİM HİZMET BİNALARI
FUAT BÖREKÇİ C
FEVZİ PAŞA
RÜZGARLI C
ESKİ TBMM
KÜLTÜR BAK. ESKİ ESERLER GEN. MÜD.
ALTINDAĞ POLİS MERKEZİ
ŞHT. KAYA ALDOĞAN C
FERMANLILAR
YİĞİTLER
YILMAZLAR
KARTALLAR
ORHAN G.
ÇANDARLI
ÖNCÜLER
İZZETTİN
HACI BAYRAM CAMİİ
ÖZTÜRK
ALTINTAŞ
İNKILAP
HÜKÜMET C
TABAKHANE
SIĞINAK
HİSAR PARKI C
ANAFARTALAR
NECATİBEY
ANKARA KALESİ
İÇ KALE
YENİ HAYAT
S. TEĞ. KALMAZ (POSTA) C
MİSAK-I MİLLİ
IŞIKLAR C
ŞENYURT
PTT GEN. MÜD.
SANAYİ C
ANADOLU MEDENİYETLERİ MÜZESİ
SAAT KULESİ
DEMİRFIRKA
YENİHAYAT İ.Ö.O.
PAZAR
KIZIL ELMA
SU TEPE
KILIÇ ARSLAN
ANAFARTALAR C
YEĞENBEY
İSTİKLAL
KOYUN PAZARI
AKBAŞ
KALE ÇARŞISI
YENİCE
DENİZCİLER C
SAKALAR
OĞUZ
ALPARSLAN
AKALAR
DOĞUMEVİ
ALTINDAĞ BEL. BAŞ.
ÇİMENTEPE
ÖZGEN
MEYDAN
M. AKİF PARKI
1
2
3
4
5
6
7
8
9
10
11
12
13
14

Around the Train Station & Hipodrum Caddesi

1 and 2 Ankara Devlet Resim ve Heykel Müzesi & Etnografya Müzesi

These two museums are right next to each other at the top of the hill on Talatpaşa Bulvarı.

History

Ankara Devlet Resim ve Heykel Müzesi, together with its neighbour the Etnografya Müzesi, are lovely examples of early Turkish Republic architecture. Both buildings were built at *Atatürk*'s request and both are the work of architect *Arif Hikmet Koyunoğlu* as a result of his winning the competition for their design in 1926. The complex was completed in 1930.

> **How to get there?**
>
> *Take a bus to Opera Köprüsü towards the train station (Gar) (464, 410, 352, 255, 397, 398-3 and many more) or walk from Sıhhiye Metro station (Ankara Metro line). For more information see www.ego.gov.tr*

Namazgâh Hill, on which the buildings stand, was a sacred place for the residents of Ankara. Prayers were held here on important Islamic holidays, as was the service after the Greeks' defeat during the War of Independence in 1923. After *Atatürk*'s death it became a sacred place once more, as *Atatürk*'s sarcophagus was located here temporarily.

Personally involved in the construction and decoration of the buildings, *Atatürk* wanted Turkey's new capital to have a distinguished centre for cultural events. In 1932, the buildings were opened as a 'community centre'. *Atatürk* often used it for ceremonies and meetings. Concerts, theatre productions, ballet and opera performances were all held here. A well-equipped library was also established within the centre. Many important political and cultural events of the Turkish Republic's history took place here –for example, the first opera to be written in Turkish was performed on this centre's stage. For his first visit to Turkey, the Shah of Persia was received here in 1934.

After the closure of the community centre, in 1952, the buildings went through several periods of different usage by various institutions until they were finally opened as museums in 1980. The concert hall here continues to perform its original purpose.

❶ Ankara Devlet Resim ve Heykel Müzesi

On display within this State Art and Sculpture Museum is a collection of Turkish avant-garde paintings from 1850 until the present day. The collection is presented thematically and by art movement. The gallery is a little "busy" but contains some very interesting modern paintings. Besides giving you an historical overview of Turkish art, it also gives you a historical perspective of Turkish art movements' take on political and social issues. Small details in many of the paintings can be seen

to express the artist's opinions or statements on the then-current situations.

Talatpaşa Bulvarı, Türkocağı Sokak. Every day, except Monday 9.00 – 12.00 and 13.00 – 17.00. Entrance is free.

At the top of the main stairs you will find a painting that *Atatürk* received from Lenin as a present, which may be of interest.

❷ Etnografya Müzesi

Atatürk's sarcophagus was housed here from the 21st of November 1938 until his current resting place, Anıtkabir, was finished in 1953. In the hallway, the past location of his tomb is saved as a memory.

Talatpaşa Bulvarı, Türkocağı Sokak. Every day, except Monday, 09.00 – 16.50 Entrance fee is 5 TL.

In the museum's other rooms there are exhibits portraying common professions of olden-times Ankara and Anatolia, mostly from the Ottoman period. Trades such as barbers, braziers, calligraphers, dervishes and so on, are shown in reproduced locations and with the requisite tools and items. Traditional events such as a henna night, weddings, circumcision gatherings and such have also been staged to observe, and traditional handicrafts like woodcarving, embroidery, carpets and manuscripts are on display. All the written information on and around the exhibits is displayed in both Turkish and English.

3 Gençlik Parkı

How to get there?

On the Ankara Metro line get off at Ulus. Also lots of buses and dolmuşes go to Gençlik Parkı. Look on the signs of the buses or ask the driver to give you a sign.

Gençlik Parkı is in the centre of Ankara at one of the lowest points in the city. Various small rivers from the mountains meet here in an area which used to be covered with marshland. After the marshes were drained the area became a large public park and it was opened on 19 May 1943, National Youth Day.

At the heart of the park is an artificial lake surrounded by a permanent fairground, an open air theatre and many food and drink kiosks with picnic benches. The park also hosts the Ankara Municipality Con-

vention Hall, a youth centre and a cultural centre. A science museum is under construction at time of writing. On summer nights the park is crowded with people coming to see the events, such as live music concerts and laser, light, fountain shows performed in the pond.

4 CerModern

Not far from the main train station, an old disused train depot houses modern art centre, CerModern. This museum was opened in April 2010 and is home to a diverse variety of art projects. There are many distinct spaces, including a large main exhibition hall, a photography gallery, artist studios and a sculpture park. The museum has four exhibitions a year in the main hall, attracting top world-class exhibitors. The museum also has a nice restaurant and a museum shop, of course.

How to get there?

Buses 204, 418, 420, 415, 464, 410 480, 481 towards Kızılay or Ulus. Get off at Talatpaşa Bulvarı on the south side of Gençlik Parkı (next to the fairground). Altınsoy Caddesi is on the other side of the Talatpaşa Bulvarı than the Gençlik Parkı. For more information see www.ego.gov.tr

Altınsoy Caddesi No: 3 Altındağ www.cermodern.org Tel: 310 00 00 Entrance fee depends on the exhibition.
Exhibition Halls and Café Tuesday - Sunday: 10:00-18:00 Closed on Mondays
Library Monday - Friday: 10:00-18:00 Closed on weekends

In the summer, CerModern organizes an open air cinema with international (usually 'cult') films in English or with English subtitles. They also organize art activities for children, in a scheme called CerÇocuk (see chapter *Ankara for Kids*).

5 Türk Hava Kurumu Müzesi

How to get there?

Buses 124, 157-3, 202-3, 203, 204, 254, 255, 270, 350 and many more towards Kızılay, Ulus or Gar stop outside the Hipodrom Caddesi. It is opposite the station so ask for "Gar" if you want help. For more information see www.ego.gov.tr.

Hipodrom Caddesi No: 2 Altındağ. Entrance free. Opening hours: daily, except Monday. 1 November - 31 March between 09:00 to 18:00 / 1 April - 30 October between 10:00 to 19:00

This museum was opened in 2002, with the intention of increasing interest in aeronautics. The museum reveals the history of Turkish aviation and its aviation pioneers, with historical documents, photographs and miniature models of aeroplanes. Most information within the museum is available in English. Outside there are some small planes and helicopters on display. The museum also has a small cafeteria and a (very) small playground for children.

Although many people might be interested in the subject of this museum, the museum itself is not an absolute must see. The exhibition and the plane models are dusty and uncared for, and the museum as a whole feels somewhat dated.

A part of the museum is the parachute tower (*Paraşüt Kulesi*). This 41 meter high concrete structure was built in 1937 for practicing parachute jumps. A similar construction in Russia served as inspiration. For years the tower dominated the skyline of Ankara until high-rise buildings began to arrive. In 2000 the tower was restored and, on summer days, parachute jumping is available.

6 Kore Şehitleri Anıtı

When North Korea invaded South Korea in 1950, Turkey joined the UN alliance to fight against the communist invaders. Committing nearly 5,500 troops, Turkey was one of the major participants. Most of the enlisted men came from the small towns and villages of Eastern Turkey.

How to get there?

Buses 124, 157-3, 202-3, 203, 204, 254, 255, 270, 350 and many more towards Kızılay, Ulus or Gar stop outside the Hipodrom Caddesi. It is opposite the station so ask for "Gar" if you want help. For more information see www.ego.gov.tr.

Hipodrom Caddesi, next to Türk Hava Kurumu Müzesi, Altındağ. Open air.

Korean Martyrs' Monument

Turkish troops remained in Korea until 1954. During the war 741 Turkish soldiers died (about 15% of its troops) and 2,147 were wounded. In addition, 234 Turkish soldiers were taken as prisoners of war and 175 were unaccounted for. The troops were honoured with a monument in Seoul for their sacrifices. Internationally, joining the Western alliance against the Soviets paid off for Turkey as they were accepted into the North Atlantic Treaty Organization (NATO) in 1952.

This monument in Ankara, called "The Garden of Korea" *(Kore Bahçesi)* is a gift from the Korean government for Turkey's help during the conflict. As the soldiers had to be buried as soon as possible after their death, according to Islam, the sarcophagus in the monument is a representation of the fallen soldiers' graves. The real graves are in the UN cemetery in Pusan, South Korea.

7 Railway Museums

Hipodrom Caddesi, next to the TCDD train station, Altındağ. Monday till Friday from 9:00 till 12:00 and 13:00 to 17:00. Entrance is free.

How to get there?

Buses 124, 157-3, 202-3, 203, 204, 218,254, 255, 270 , 350 and many more towards Kızılay, Ulus or Gar stop. Ask the driver or look at the signs for the word station (Gar). For more information see ww.ego.gov.tr.

The railway museum in Ankara has 3 different buildings around Ankara Gar, the main train station, hence "Museums". These are: Milli Mücadele Atatürk Konutu, Demiryolları Müzesi ve Sanat Galerisi and TCDD Açık Hava Müzesi.

Oddly, during opening hours the doors might sometimes be closed. Do not hesitate to knock on the doors, windows or the gate, even several times. Someone will come to let you in. This might give you some idea of the number of visitors usually attending.

Milli Mücadele Atatürk Konutu

This small museum is accessible from platform 1. Go into the station and as you enter the platform turn right. You will see an old house, formerly station master's house. Nowadays it's the Railway Museum and the *Atatürk*'s residence.

On the ground floor, historical items from the Ottoman railway companies and TCDD, the current Turkish railway company, are on display. They show old (glass) photographs, train tickets from the Ottoman era, restaurant wagon silverware, models of old wagons, locomotives and station buildings, furniture from the sultan´s personal train and Ottoman-era telephone and telegraph machines. Ankara was an important telegraph centre for the Ottoman railway. This was one of the reasons why *Atatürk* chose the city as his base.

When *Atatürk* arrived on 27 December 1919, he chose to live in the stationmaster's residence. He used it as his home and as an office, from where he coordinated the War of Independence. Many important strategic decisions were made in this house, next to the communication centre of the railway companies.

On the first floor you can still see *Atatürk*'s fully furnished temporary accommodation, with a study room, bedrooms, a bathroom and a meeting room. *Atatürk* lived here until spring 1921, when he moved into a nice vineyard house outside the city in Ordu Köşkü in Çankaya (see chapter *South of the City Centre Çankaya*).

Further along platform 1, behind the museum building, you will find *Atatürk*'s private train car in which he travelled the country from 1935 until his death in 1938. The car had all mod cons: a bathroom, a bedroom, an office, a kitchen and the latest (for the time) communications equipment. Unfortunately, the train can only be looked at from the outside.

The location is a historically interesting place but the museum itself is slightly dated and tired. The presentation and decoration could do with a refresh.

Demiryolları Müzesi ve Sanat Galerisi

Hipodrom Caddesi, next to the TCDD train station, Altındağ. Tel: 309 05 15/40 94. Monday till Friday from 9:00 till 12:00 and 13:00 to 17:00. Entrance is free.

Part 2 of the Railway Museum(s) can be found next door to the main building. Don't enter the main station doors but rather head to the building on the left (looking from the front).

This building, built in 1924, had been destined to become a hotel but these plans never came to fruition. Contrary to what its name suggests, the museum is not an art gallery. Through some interesting drawings the museum explains railway techniques and steam engines. They have old train and railway items, like an old station clock, photos, training models, train interiors and, yes, some paintings.

TCDD Açık Hava Müzesi

Celal Bayar Bulvarı, Altındağ. Entrance is free. Weekdays 9:00-12:00 and 13:00-17:00. Gate may be closed, ask for attention of the guard.

Part 3 of the Railway Museum(s), at the rear of the station complex: the TCCD Open Air Museum. You can get there through the station, by taking the underground passageway from platform 1. After taking the staircase to the left, the museum is around 300 metres along the road (Açık Hava Buharlı Bulvarı).

This museum has ten big steam locomotives on display, which were previously used by Turkish Railways, and other railway material such as crane-trains (which were used for loading coal). The trains are arranged in the open air, connected by footpaths, constructed as a "railway marshalling yard" between the locomotives in the grass. There are no working trains on display, unfortunately.

8 Atatürk Kültür Merkezi

This futuristic building, looking a bit like a spaceship which just landed holds frequent fairs or exhibitions. Often these fairs are devoted to other cities or areas in Turkey, to stimulate tourism and highlight local produce. Generally you will find lots of local crafts to look at and purchase, and regional foods to try. The events are very much pitched at local people, so don't expect a lot of English or other language assistance, but that doesn't mean it's not interesting to have a look around. Atatürk Kültür Merkezi is not open to visitors outside of exhibition times.

How to get there?

On the Ankara Metro line get off at Atatürk Kültür Merkezi .

Hipodrom Cadessi Ulus
Tel: 384 50 50 www.akm.org.tr

9 Concert Hall (to be)

At the time of writing there is a huge balloon like structure surrounded by cranes and workmen, along from the station and near the junction with Atatürk Bulvarı. A new concert hall is being built, apparently using some experimental construction techniques. It will be interesting to see how this (large) complex comes together and what events it will offer.

10 Ankara 19 Mayıs Stadı

Entrance Cumhuriyet Caddesi. Ticket sales İstanbul Caddesi.

Ankara 19 Mayıs Stadium is one of Ankara's big sport stadiums. The name of the stadium refers to 19 May 1919, the date when *Mustafa Kemal Atatürk* started the War of Independence, and the city's annual May 19th celebrations take place here.

It is the home ground to three different football teams of Ankara: Ankaragücü, Gençlerbirliği and Hacettepe. This building was construc-

How to get there?

On the Ankara Metro line get off at Ulus. Buses 124, 157, 203, 204, 218, 222, 254, 255, 266, 270 etc. towards Kızılay, Opera or Ulus. Get off at Cumhuriyet Caddesi. See also www.ego.gov.tr

ted in 1935 and is starting to show its age. There are plans for a new stadium, which will be built on top of the current location. It will be totally covered with have a capacity of 20,600 people, and be ready in 2016.

Turks generally take football very seriously. If you go to a match and drink tea and eat sunflower seeds with the local fans you will realise this. The atmosphere is generally very good. The standard of the football may vary. The big İstanbul teams do visit here. For the fixtures list and tickets, check www.biletix.com.

Tickets can also be bought at İstanbul Caddesi gate and are very reasonably priced depending on the seats.

⓫ Ankara Arena

Ankara Arena next to Ankara 19 Mayıs Stadı was built for the 2010 FIBA basketball World Championships. It opened in April 2010 and has a capacity of 10,400. Although mostly used for basketball, it is sometimes used for pop concerts and other large indoor events.

Events and tickets at www.mybilet.com/place/1018/ankara-arena-spor-salonu

Gar Meydanı, Ulus Tel: 309 91 91

⓬ Opera Sahnesi

The Opera House is located at the edge of Gençlik Parkı on Ankara Bulvarı. It is home to the Turkish State Opera, the Turkish Ballet and the Turkish State Theatre. The building was designed as an exhibition centre in 1933 and converted into a theatre in 1948. The building is architecturally interesting, sharing characteristics of both Turkish and German architecture from the first half of the 20th century. The stage is no longer of adequate size for major theatre productions, but there are plans for a new opera, ballet and theatre house to be constructed nearby, with more stages and seating capacity. For the program and tickets, check *www.dobgm.gov.tr*

How to get there?

Many buses (113, 114, 115, 133, 145 etc.) and dolmuşes drive past Opera Sahnesi, along the Atatürk Bulvarı. There is a large collection of bus stops just outside. For more information see www.ego.gov.tr

⑬ Ankamall

Ankamall is the second largest shopping mall in Turkey, covering an area of 176,000 square metres. It hosts international and national retailers as well as a food court and an entertainment centre, including a movie theatre (with IMAX). It was opened in 1999. It is one of very few malls easily accessible by public transport, so if you need to experience an Ankara shopping mall this might be the one.

How to get there?

At the Ankara Metro line get off at Akköprü stop. Look around, you can't miss it! As it is not really in walking distance of the train station, you better take the metro.

Akköprü Mevki, Konya Devlet Yolu
No: 2 Yenimahalle Merkez
www.ankamall.com.tr

⑭ Akköprü

Fatih Sultan Mehmet Bulvarı

Just to the northwest of the Ankamall shopping centre lies Ankara's oldest

bridge. This historical construction lies unnoticed close to the busy highway. It is preserved amazingly well and therefore a walk from the shopping mall is well worthwhile. Take the bridge over the highway and pass the petrol station. After a few metres you'll find this old beauty on the left-hand side.

The bridge was built by the Seljuk *Sultan Alaaddin Keykubat* in 1222 over the confluence of the Çubuk river, the İncesu Creek and the Hatip river. It was an important passage on the old trade route from Baghdad to the West. This was the place where farewells were bid to the soldiers and pilgrims leaving for Western Anatolia.

The bridge is built from basalt stone and re-used materials (among which are many stones not originally from the Ankara area). An inscription right of the middle vault bears *Keykubat*'s name and the year.

West of the City Centre

ATATÜRK ORMAN ÇİFTLİĞİ
TARIM ARAZİSİ
HAYVANAT BAHÇESİ
ŞARAP FABRİKASI
TİGEM TESİSLERİ
TİGEM CAMİSİ
ÇİFTLİK POLİS MERKEZİ
TÜRKİYE ZİRAİ DONATIM KURUMU
BİRA FABRİKASI
A.O.Ç. BAHÇE FİDANI SATIŞ YERİ
A.O.Ç. SÜT ÜRÜNLERİ FAB.
PTT
ÇİFTLİK C
POLATLI C
ŞENOL C
SİLAHTAR C
GAZİ
ANKARA FİZİK REHABİLİTASYON MERKEZİ
DEVLET MEZARLIĞI
ATATÜRK EVİ
ATA KÖŞKÜ
MARMARA OTELİ
MARMARA HAVUZU
ORMAN GENEL MÜDÜRLÜĞÜ
PLANLAMA DAİRE BAŞKANLIĞI
ORMAN GENEL MÜDÜRLÜĞÜ TESİSLERİ
ORMAN GENEL MÜD. TESİSLERİ
SÖĞÜTÖZÜ C
ALPASLAN TÜRKEŞ C
GAZİ ORDUEVİ
GAZİ ÜNİVERSİTESİ
REKTÖRLÜK
SABANCI ÖĞRENCİ YURDU
EMNİYET
BAŞKENT ÖĞRETMENEVİ
ATATÜRK ANADOLU LİSESİ
RADYO - TV TEKNİK LİSESİ
JOKEY KULÜBÜ TESİSLERİ
ATLI SPOR TESİSLERİ
ASKİ
FATİH ÜNİVERSİTESİ HASTANESİ
D.D.Y. HASTANESİ
ETİLER SİTESİ
İMAM HATİP LİSESİ
D.H.L. GENEL MÜD.
ANKARA ÜNİVERSİTESİ
GAZİ ÜNİVERSİTESİ HASTANESİ
M.E.B. TESİSLERİ
FEN FAKÜLTESİ
ECZACILIK FAKÜLTESİ
MAKİNE KİMYA ENDÜSTRİSİ KURUMU
ASTSUBAY ORDUEVİ
TANDOĞAN
DE GAULLE C
ETİLER ORDUEVİ
CELAL BAYAR BULVARI
MEVLANA BULVARI
E.G.O.
ANKARA BELEDİYE BAŞKANLIĞI
KÜLTÜR BAK. GÜZEL SANATLAR GEN. MÜD.
ATATÜRK KÜLTÜR MERKEZİ
ESKİ HİDOPRUM
AKKÖPRÜ
T.K.İ. GENEL MÜD.
ANKARA EMNİYET MÜDÜRLÜĞÜ
TÜRK PATENT ENSTİTÜSÜ
HİPODRUM C
BEŞEVLER
BAHÇELİEVLER
MEBUSEVLERİ
ANITKABİR
ANITTEPE
GENÇLİK C
TURGUT REİS C
ANIT C
ÖNDER C
MAREŞAL FEVZİ ÇAKMAK C
TAŞKENT C (1)
MUAMMER AKSOY C (2)
AZERBEYCAN C
KAZAKİSTAN C (4)
5 C (CENGİZ HAN)
54 C
GABDULLA TUKAY C
DOÇ. BAHRİYE ÜÇOK C
İNCİTAŞ C
BAŞKENT ÜNİ. HASTANESİ
1
2
3
4
5

West of the City Centre

How to get there?

Ankaray train stops at Tandoğan station. It is a 10 minutes' walk to the entrance of Anıtkabir. Buses: 168, 212, 267, 272, 294, 484 direction Beşevler and many more. For actual information see www.ego.gov.tr

In the 1930s, the city planner Herman Jansen devised on the west side of city centre a residential area –an area with houses and gardens, where the civil servants of the young republic could live with their families. For instance the quarter Bahçelievler (houses with gardens). But it's no longer that quiet residential area between the orchards as it was planned. It's a lively part of town, with universities, many restaurants, shops and an area where many students live.

In this part of the city you can find the national library, the state cemetery, the zoo and one of the biggest attractions of Ankara, Anıtkabir. This is the mausoleum of the founder of modern Turkey, *Mustafa Kemal Atatürk*.

Anıtkabir

Anıt Caddesi. Entrance is free. Opening hours: winter 09.00 – 16.00, summer 09.00 -17.00. Closed on Mondays.

Anıtkabir, literally "memorial tomb", is one of the most interesting places to visit in Ankara. This impressive mausoleum is the final resting place of *Mustafa Kemal Atatürk,* the founder and the first President of the Turkish Republic, as well as *İsmet İnönü,* the first Prime Minister and second President.

After *Atatürk*'s death (at 9:05 on 10 November 1938, at Dolmabahçe Palace in İstanbul) his body was brought to Ankara and placed in a sarcophagus in the main hall of the Ethnography Museum (see chapter *Around the Train Station*). The museum was to be merely a temporary resting place. The final destination could be nothing less

than a grand tomb. In 1941, a competition was arranged for the design of *Atatürk*'s Mausoleum. From the 49 entries, the design submitted by Turkish architects *Ahmet Emin Onat* and *Orhan Arda* was chosen. They had designed an impressive symmetrical building. Architecture connoisseurs refer to it as a textbook example of the "Second National Architecture Movement", a period of Turkish architecture between 1940 and 1950. On 10 November 1953, fifteen years after *Atatürk*'s death, his body was brought to Anıtkabir, his final resting place.

1.	Peace Park		TOWERS
2.	Lion Road	T1.	Independent Tower
3.	Ceremonial Ground	T2.	Freedom Tower
4.	Flag Pole and Flag	T3.	Soldier's Tower
5.	Stairs	T4.	Victory Tower
6.	Relief; Battle of Sakarya Relief	T5.	Peace Tower
7.	Relief; Battle of Commander in Chief	T6.	23 April Tower
8.	Hall of Honour	T7.	Misak-i Milli Tower
9.	Atatürk and War of Museum Independence	T8.	Revolution Tower
10.	Tomb of İsmet İnönü	T9.	Republic Tower
11.	Toilets	T10.	Tower Defense West

Anıtkabir Nowadays

Mustafa Kemal Atatürk still plays an important role in the life of many Turks. For them he is still a role model. His statues can be found all over Turkey, as can his portraits. At schools his heroic life story is told to young children. Unofficially, every Turk should visit *Atatürk*'s Mausoleum Anıtkabir, at least once. So, every day, thousands of people from all over the country make the trip to Anıtkabir to pledge their allegiance and devotion to *Atatürk*.

On national holidays and especially on the 10th of November, the day of *Atatürk*'s passing, several hundreds of thousands of visitors visit the Mausoleum. There are frequent official visits and laying of wreaths whenever foreign delegates visit Ankara. Despite all these visitors, the ambiance is always peaceful. There is an unwritten code of quiet respect that all visitors are expected to abide by.

The design is full of symbols and references to Turkish values. Different stones and marble taken from different regions of Turkey refer to the unity of the Turkish people. In the design you will also find elements of the various cultures that have lived in the country. For example, the sculptures and reliefs in the walls are inspired by the Hittite civilisation. In the eaves you can see Seljuk saw tooth ornamentations. On the ceilings of the towers and the Hall of Honour, you might recognize Ottoman carpet motives.

Anıtkabir consists of four parts: the Peace Park (before entering the complex), the Road of Lions (2), the Ceremonial Square (3) and the Hall of Honour (8).

Peace Park (1)

The whole Anıtkabir complex covers an area of 750,000 square metres. Most of the area is taken up by green space, called the Peace Park. This park surrounds the Mausoleum. You will find nearly 50,000 trees, which were donated by around 25 different countries including Afghanistan, China, Egypt, France, Germany, Greece, Israel, India, Iraq, Spain, the United Kingdom and the United States. A walk through the park is an interesting botanic experience, taking you past trees, flowers and shrubs from over 100 worldly varieties. From the main entrance the road walks you through the park on your way to the Mausoleum. You may also leave the main road and take one of the many walking routes.

The park's name comes from one of *Atatürk*'s most well-known quotes: "Peace at home, peace in the world".

The Road of Lions (2)

The official entrance to the Mausoleum is via the Road of Lions. This is a 262 metre long pedestrian path, lined on each side by 12 lion stat-

ues meant to represent Anatolia, to symbolise the nation's power and serenity. They lie peacefully next to the road but show their teeth as a sign of constant vigilance. These statues are very much in the style of Hittite sculptures.

On both sides of the Lion Road are high juniper trees. This takes away the view of the surrounding area, focusing visitors on the view ahead of a giant Turkish flag flying on a 33 metre flagpole. While walking along the path, visitors have time to contemplate the meaning of visiting Anıtkabir. The marble paving stones are separated by a 5 centimetre wide gap, intended to compel them to focus on their path and behave respectfully on their way to the Mausoleum.

The Ceremonial Square (3)

At the end of the Road of Lions you reach the Ceremonial Square. This square has an area of 10,868.25 m^2 (129 m x 84.25 m) and a capacity of 15,000 people. It is paved with 373 different geometrical Ottoman carpet patterns made of red, white and black limestone.

The Ceremonial Square is surrounded by the Mausoleum building with its eight towers. Including the two towers at the entrance of the

Road of Lions, the complex has a total of ten. Each tower is dedicated to an important value of the Republic, such as independence, freedom, reforms, victory, or the nation's soldiers. Inside each tower the dedicated subject is portrayed in reliefs and supplemented with engraved statements made by *Atatürk*.

Assuming entry via the Road of Lions, on your left side you will see the Hall of Honour.

Hall of Honour (8)

42 steps bring you up to the main part of the Mausoleum. On the right and left side of the stairs are large reliefs visualising two important battles in the War of Independence. The right side depicts the Battle of Sakarya (1921) (6). In this battle the Greeks were halted in their advance towards Ankara. The left relief depicts the Battle of Commander-in-Chief (1922) (7), in which the Greeks were finally defeated at Izmir.

Hall of Honour is a rectangular building, 72 m x 52 m, surrounded by 14.4 m tall columns. Through a grand copper gate you enter the Hall which is decorated with marble from all over Turkey. The 17 m high ceiling is decorated with a mosaic in the design of an Ottoman carpet. Beside the 12 bronze torches, the hall is almost empty. Pride of place is given to a massive 40 tonne red marble sarcophagus. This is *Atatürk*'s symbolic tomb, his real tomb is 7 m below.

Atatürk and War of Independence Museum (9)

Via Misak-i Milli Tower, to the left of the flagpole and the right of the Hall of Honour, you can reach the Atatürk and War of Independence Museum. This consists of three parts. The first area displays some of *Atatürk*'s belongings; his pens, guns, swords, clothing and many other personal effects. The second section deals with the War of Independence. Here the major battles of the war are shown in a very visual way. The third area is about what *Atatürk* achieved during his presidency. This section covers many topics, such as education, transport, women's rights, foreign affairs, etc. It is an exhibition of the changes *Atatürk* was able to implement.

The Tomb

Half way through the third area of the museum, you pass the sealed entrance to *Atatürk*'s real tomb. This tomb is seven metres below the marble sarcophagus in the Hall of Honour. It is never open to the public, but the interior can be seen on a video display. The tomb is an octagon in Seljuk and Ottoman style, decorated with red, white and black marbles. In the middle is a smaller sarcophagus. This is the true location of *Mustafa Kemal Atatürk*'s remains. The sarcophagus is surrounded by vases filled with soil from every province in Turkey. It was *Atatürk*'s wish always to be able to see a Turkish flag, even after his death. For this reason in each corner of the octagon stands a Turkish flag, apart from the corner housing the large copper door. On this large door there is a detailed relief of *Atatürk*'s face looking toward the Ankara castle, via a window in the outer wall, where the eighth flag flies. Thus, as he wished, he is forever looking upon a flying Turkish flag.

The Tomb of İsmet İnönü (10)

Opposite the Hall of Honour, between the Tower of Peace and the Tower of Victory, is another symbolic sarcophagus, this time in honour of *İsmet İnönü*. The real tomb of this first Prime Minister and second President of the Republic of Turkey is beneath this symbolic sarcophagus.

Atatürk Orman Çiftliği (AOÇ)

Close to the Ankara Zoo is an area that *Atatürk* had intended to become a farm. Around this farm is a lush forest area with picnic places, a park *(Gazi Orman Çiftliği Parkı)* and several restaurants. In 1992 this area was declared a protected natural and historical site.

Atatürk gave the order to build a forest farm by saying:

"Eyes which do not see the green are deprived of colour pleasure. Let us establish a forest here so the blind can see the green."

This shows how important he felt it was to create natural places where the people of the new capital could walk around, breath in healthy air both in summer and winter.

❷ Atatürk Orman Çiftliği Müze ve Sergi Salonu

The Atatürk Forest Farm Museum and Exhibition Room offers information about the farm, its history and the War of Independence (mostly photos). Close to the entrance there is a collection of photos of *Atatürk* on the farm on display. From its foundation on 5 May 1925 un-

▶ Photo: Vekam

til January 1937 he managed the farm himself. After research a team of experts warned *Atatürk* that the area was quite barren and did not have the suitable characteristics for agriculture. *Atatürk* replied with *"If we cannot improve such a place, who would come and improve it?"* and went ahead anyway. He even financed the acquisition of the farm personally (for a lot more than it was worth, according to these experts).

How to get there?

Gazi Mahallesi train station is in walking distance from the farm. Many EGO buses go to AOÇ. 164 direction Beytepe, 212 direction Yenimahalle - Beşevler, 220 and 221 direction Mamak-Batıkent, 294 direction Batıkent, 385 and 385-2 Cebeci - Lalegül. For more buses and the latest information see www.ego.gov.tr

Alparslan Türkeş Caddesi No: 68 (Çiftlik Caddesi) Gazi. Entrance is free. Opening hours: every day 8:00 – 18:00

Atatürk planned this farm to be a model of modern farming. In those days more than half of the national income came from agriculture. 70% of the working population was occupied with farming and, although agriculture was so important, modern techniques were severely lacking. In his quest to modernise the country, *Atatürk* used this farm to test modern production methods and agricultural machinery.

The farm started with a milk processing facility but later also produced beer and wine. After the Atatürk Forest Farm expanded into a full-size facility, it filled a significant gap in providing some of Ankara's needs. Products like wine, ice, milk, butter, yogurt, fruit juices, honey, vinegar and grape molasses *(pekmez)* are still produced on the farm and can be bought at Atatürk Orman Çiftliği Satış Mağazası and other shops in this area. In Ankara you will see AOÇ brand ice creams sold in the summer-time, made from both cow and goat milk. We recommend you try one –the goat milk variety is somewhat heavy but the cow milk version is delicious!

❸ Atatürk Evi

Entrance is free. Opening hours: every day 8:00 - 12:00 and 13:00 – 18:00
Crosspoint Söğütözü Caddesi and Alparslan Türkeş Caddesi., Beştepeler Mahallesi, Gazi/Ankara

This house is a full replica of the house where *Atatürk* was born in 1881 in *Selanik* (now *Thessaloniki*) which at the time was part of the Ottoman Empire. The actual house,

How to get there?

Some 20 minutes' walk from the Atatürk Farm Museum (through a nice area).
Gazi Mahallesi train station is half an hour walk from the house.
EGO buses: 164 direction Beytepe and 391 Cebeci, bus stop Silahtar Caddesi, walk for 6 minutes along Çiftlik Caddesi towards Alparslan Türkeş Caddesi.
For the latest information see www.ego.gov.tr

in modern-day Greece, is owned by the Turkish Consulate who has turned it into a museum.

It is a three storey house. Most of the rooms (the bedrooms, the kitchen and the guest room) can be visited. Some of *Atatürk*'s belongings are displayed on the 2nd floor. The size, proportions and most of the interior furnishing match the original in Thessaloniki.

On 10 November 1981 this replica house was opened to mark *Atatürk*'s hundredth birthday. This location was chosen as *Atatürk* was very fond of this area.

For a 360° "virtual tour" of the house see *www.aoc.gov.tr/Ataturk-Evi/index.html*

4 Devlet Mezarlığı

This national and military cemetery is home to the graves of Turkish Presidents, as well as close companions-in-arms (commanders only) of *Atatürk* during the War of Independence. It is atop a hill and offers nice views over Ankara and Anıtkabir.

As *Atatürk* had given the order to build a recreation area in this area, with a "Blacksea Pool", this remained intact after the cemetery was built. It is a nice place to sit and have a drink.

In 1982 the Ministry of National Defence organised a contest for the cemetery's design. The architect *Özgür Ecevit* and the agronomist *Ekrem Gürenli* won the contest and their design was constructed. In the middle of the cemetery a huge octagon monument, like a spi-

der, draws the attention. It is called *Simge* (symbol) and represents a Turkish community tent in which all people are united and which gives shelter against the sun and precipitation. Under *Simge* is *Anısal Duvar* (Memorial Wall) into which the names of the buried are carved. For every new president of Turkey a stone is added. This shows the continuity of the republic.

Alparslan Türkeş Caddesi, Gazi/ Ankara Entrance is free. If you come by car, they will ask for your car papers (as a kind of deposit). Opening hours: Summer: 09:30-17:00. Winter: 09:30-16:30 Closed on Monday and Tuesday. Saturday: 10:00-17:00.

Sculptures

Around the monument, along the *Cumhuriyet Tarihi Yolu* you will see marble sculptures representing milestones in the War of Independence and the development of the Turkish Republic. These were carved by a team of Turkish sculptors led by the renowned artist *Rahmi Aksungur*. It is the first large sculpture arrangement in Turkey.

One of the first statues symbolises *Atatürk*'s landing in Samsun on the 19th of May 1919. Other sculptures represent the congresses in Erzurum and Sivas and the establishment of the new parliament in Ankara.

In the war section, five columns stand in the water with inscriptions from the *Atatürk*'s *Büyük Söylev* (Grand Speech). Another sculpture stands for the Peace Treaty of Lausanne and completes this section.

On both sides of the road in this area you can see reliefs. These represent the foundation of the regular armed forces, the first and second *İnönü* Battles, *Battle of the Sakarya* and the *Battle of Dumlupınar.* The last artwork is a single abstract sculpture which symbolizes the abolition of the office of caliphate by the Republic. An important step and change after the Ottoman Empire.

Museum

Inside the museum you will find documents, photos and belongings of the Presidents and high-ranked officers of the War of Independence. Although all of the artefacts might not appeal to foreign tourist some do attract particular attention such as the congratulatory messages thrown from French airplanes on 29 October 1923, the day the Turkish Republic was declared.

The museum is such that, when looking through the window in the east façade, you can see Anıtkabir, representing the bond between *Atatürk* and his comrades in the war and the presidents who symbolise the continuity of the Turkish Republic.

How to get there?

Around 10 minutes' walk from the Atatürk House.
Some 40 minutes' walk from the Gazi Mahallesi train station.
EGO buses: 308 direction Örnek Beştepe and 391 Cebeci stop almost in front of the cemetery.
For the latest information see www.ego.gov.tr

❺ AOÇ Hayvanat Bahçesi

Diagonally opposite the Atatürk Farm Museum is the Ankara Zoo. If you are used to Western zoo's you will probably be shocked by this one. In the current zoo animals live in small areas and very close to each other. So close that, in March 2011, a tiger was able to kill a lion by squeezing its front paw through a gap in the fence and cutting the lion's jugular vein, causing it to bleed to death.

Some of the animals mentioned on the sign at the entrance, such as the elephant, are no longer around but nobody has thought to change the sign. Cats, birds, monkeys, llamas, snakes, an aquarium and lots of different dogs can be found.

A new zoo is planned next-door to the current one, which will provide more space and a more natural environment for the animals. This new zoo will also measure up to the European regulations for animal welfare and contribute to the European Endangered Species Program.

How to get there?

Gazi Mahallesi train station is in walking distance from the zoo.
Also a lot of EGO buses go here, for instance 164 direction Beytepe, 212 direction Yenimahalle- Beşevler, 220 and 221 direction Mamak-Batıkent, 294 direction Batıkent, 385 and 385-2 Cebeci-Lalegül. For more buses and the latest information see www.ego.gov.tr

Alparslan Türkeş Caddesi (Çiftlik Caddesi), Gazi. Entrance is free. Parking: 5 TL
Opening hours: Summer weekdays: 08:30-18:00, weekends 08:30 – 19:00 Winter: every day 08:30-17:00

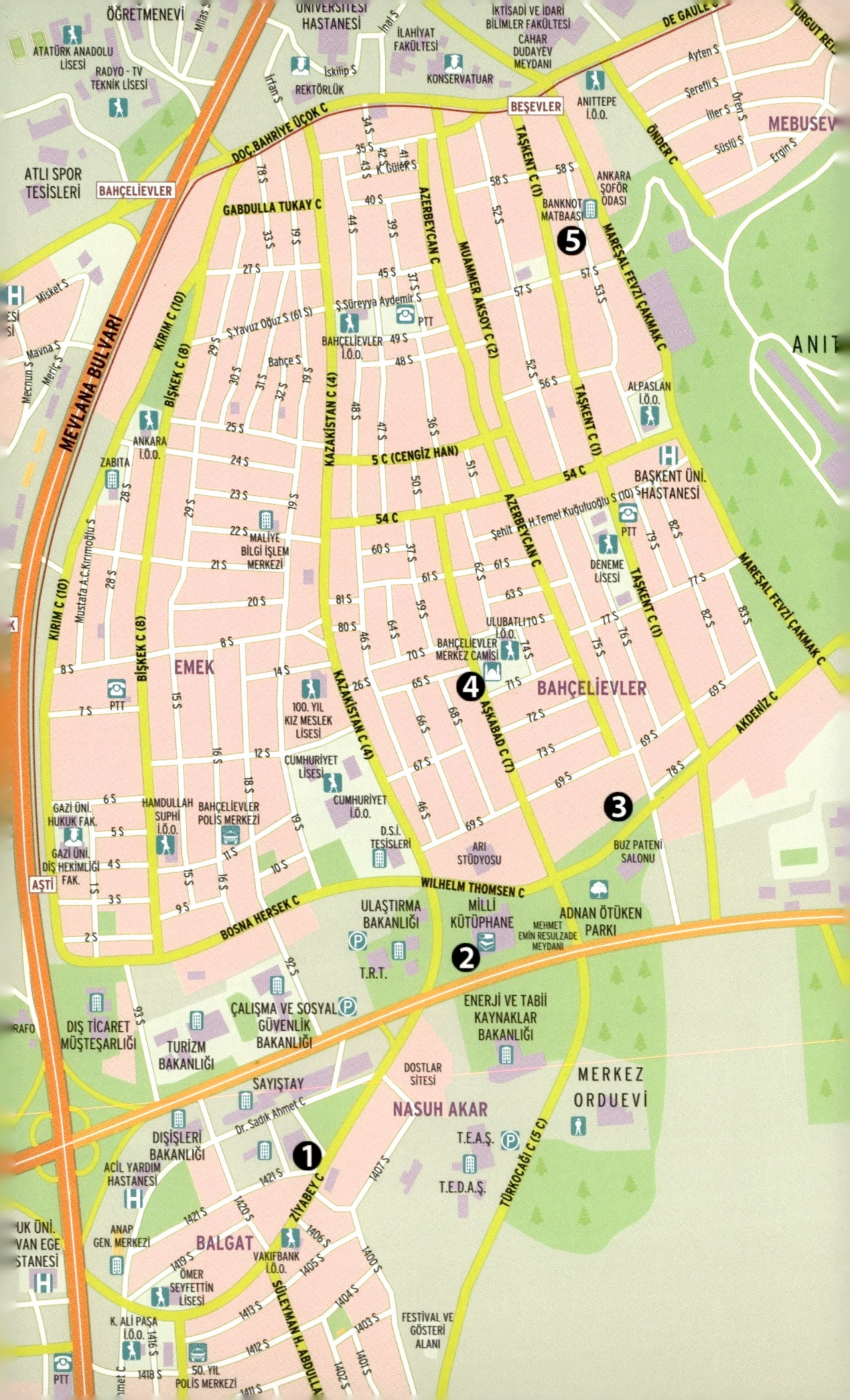

ÖĞRETMENEVİ
ÜNİVERSİTESİ HASTANESİ
İKTİSADİ VE İDARİ BİLİMLER FAKÜLTESİ
DE GAULLE C
TURGUT REİS
ATATÜRK ANADOLU LİSESİ
RADYO - TV TEKNİK LİSESİ
İLAHİYAT FAKÜLTESİ
CAHAR DUDAYEV MEYDANI
İskilip S
İrfan S
REKTÖRLÜK
KONSERVATUAR
Ayten S
Şerefli S
İller S
Ören S
Süslü S
Ergin S
MEBUSEV
BEŞEVLER
ANITTEPE İ.Ö.O.
ÖNDER C
DOÇ. BAHRİYE ÜÇOK C
ATLI SPOR TESİSLERİ
BAHÇELİEVLER
GABDULLA TUKAY C
TAŞKENT C (1)
ANKARA ŞOFÖR ODASI
BANKNOT MATBAASI
MAREŞAL FEVZİ ÇAKMAK C
AZERBEYCAN C
MUAMMER AKSOY C (2)
KAZAKİSTAN C (4)
Misket S
Mavna S
Meriç S
Mecnun S
MEVLANA BULVARI
KIRIM C (10)
BİŞKEK C (8)
Ş.Yavuz Oğuz S (61 S)
Ş.Süreyya Aydemir S
PTT
BAHÇELİEVLER İ.Ö.O.
Bahçe S
ALPASLAN İ.Ö.O.
ANIT
ANKARA İ.Ö.O.
ZABITA
5 C (CENGİZ HAN)
54 C
BAŞKENT ÜNİ. HASTANESİ
Şehit H.Temel Kuğuluoğlu S (10)
MALİYE BİLGİ İŞLEM MERKEZİ
DENEME LİSESİ
Mustafa A.C.Kırımoğlu S
ULUBATLI İ.Ö.O.
BAHÇELİEVLER MERKEZ CAMİSİ
EMEK
AŞKABAD C (7)
BAHÇELİEVLER
100. YIL KIZ MESLEK LİSESİ
CUMHURİYET LİSESİ
CUMHURİYET İ.Ö.O.
AKDENİZ C
GAZİ ÜNİ. HUKUK FAK.
HAMDULLAH SUPHİ İ.Ö.O.
BAHÇELİEVLER POLİS MERKEZİ
GAZİ ÜNİ. DİŞ HEKİMLİĞİ FAK.
AŞTİ
D.S.İ. TESİSLERİ
ARI STÜDYOSU
BUZ PATENİ SALONU
WILHELM THOMSEN C
BOSNA HERSEK C
ULAŞTIRMA BAKANLIĞI
MİLLİ KÜTÜPHANE
MEHMET EMİN RESULZADE MEYDANI
ADNAN ÖTÜKEN PARKI
T.R.T.
DIŞ TİCARET MÜSTEŞARLIĞI
ÇALIŞMA VE SOSYAL GÜVENLİK BAKANLIĞI
ENERJİ VE TABİİ KAYNAKLAR BAKANLIĞI
TURİZM BAKANLIĞI
SAYIŞTAY
DOSTLAR SİTESİ
MERKEZ ORDUEVİ
NASUH AKAR
Dr. Sadık Ahmet C
DIŞİŞLERİ BAKANLIĞI
T.E.A.Ş.
T.E.D.A.Ş.
ACİL YARDIM HASTANESİ
ZİYABEY C
TÜRKOCAĞI C (5 C)
ANAP GEN. MERKEZİ
BALGAT
VAKIFBANK İ.Ö.O.
ÖMER SEYFETTİN LİSESİ
SÜLEYMAN H. ABDULLA
FESTİVAL VE GÖSTERİ ALANI
K. ALİ PAŞA İ.Ö.O.
50. YIL POLİS MERKEZİ
1
2
3
4
5

Bahçelievler & Beşevler

Bahçelievler was developed as a housing cooperative, like many other areas of Ankara, by Hermann Jansen between 1936 and 1938. He planned for row houses on the north side and semi-detached houses in the south of the area. Two-storey homes with gardens, a school and a marketplace were planned at the centre.

In 1945 Bahçelievler was redesignated for residence of state-officials. In later years they moved away. With the increasing population in the 1950s the area began to change, as people transformed or rebuilt their houses into multi-storey apartments, and increased floor area by extending into the spacious gardens. Today you can see very few of the original houses, which are generally attractive but unfortunately neglected. Fortunately for the area most buildings particularly around 7. Cadde (7th street) are under 4 storeys. This is in contrast to many of the other areas in Ankara, where towering apartment blocks have become the norm.

The majority of Bahçelievler residents are elderly people, although you will find a large number of students walking around. The National Library *(Milli Kütüphane)* can be found to the south of the area, and Gazi University and Ankara University are up in the north. Around the universities there are several student dormitories, some for girls only (such as the *On Mayıs / 11 May* building on Bahriye Üçok Caddesi).

On a more negative note, the area's name is also firmly connected with a massacre which took place here on the 8th of October 1978, when 7 unarmed students, members of the Turkish Workers Party, were killed by ultra-nationalists. Luckily the atmosphere has changed in the years since and Bahçelievler is now a nice area for shopping, mainly for clothes and shoes, or eating and drinking in the many restaurants and cafés.

How to get to there?

Take a dolmuş in the direction of Bahçelievler or Beşevler.
For 4 and 5: the metro stops at Beşevler or Bahçelievler stations.
Buses: 168 direction Beşevler-Bahçelievler, 305 Örnek-Emek-Bahçeli, 464 Subayevleri-Emek-Bahçelievler. For the latest information see www.ego.gov.tr

❶ Mustafa Ayaz Müzesi

Mustafa Ayaz was born in 1938 in the village of Kabataş, in the province of Trabzon. From 1966 to 1987 he taught art at the Faculty of Fine Arts of the University of Hacettepe in Ankara. In the same year he acquired the title of professor and was appointed to the Faculty of Fine Arts of Bilkent University. He resigned in 1988 and since then he has continued working in his own atelier and has held dozens of exhibitions in Turkey and abroad. He is a prolific and acclaimed modern artist.

Ziyabey Caddesi No: 25 Balgat Tel: 285 89 98
www.mustafaayaz.com
Opening hours: every day except Monday 12.00 – 18.00. Entrance: 10 TL, students and teachers 3 TL

The museum established through his own means and endeavours. The goals of the Mustafa Ayaz Foundation, which runs the museum, are to foster a love of art in society, educate society through art and contribute to the promotion of contemporary Turkish art. Besides the works of *Mustafa Ayaz*, which are exhibited on the top floor, other contemporary artists hold exhibitions in this museum on a regular basis. The museum, with a total usable space of 5000 m^2, is big compared to other museums in Ankara. Aside from exhibitions, workshops, drawing, sculpture and ceramic courses and preparation courses for the Faculties of Fine Arts are offered here.

How to get there?

As the museum is actually in Balgat, the other side of Bahçelievler, the metro station of Beşevler or Bahçelievler are quite a walk. EGO buses 143, 153, 263 and 301 in the direction of Güvenpark-Balgat stop at Ziyabey Caddesi. For the latest information see www.ego.gov.tr

❷ Milli Kütüphane

The national library is a huge and modern "centre of knowledge" with more than 8000 books and papers dating back 100 years. It is one of six libraries in Turkey which receive copies of all literature published in the country. Unfortunately the library is not open to all visitors. Only library members can visit. Foreign researchers can access with a temporary card.

Wilhelm Thomsen Caddesi
Bahçelievler
www.mkutup.gov.tr
Opening hours: Weekdays 9:00 – 22:00 Weekends 09:30 – 21:30

❸ Gençlik ve Spor İl Müdürlüğü Buz Pateni Sarayı (Belpa)

A big indoor skating palace, where they also provide skating courses.

Akdeniz Caddesi No: 57 Bahçelievler Tel: 222 02 42
Weekdays from 9:30 – 19:00. Saturdays 12:15 -19:30. Sundays 12:15 -16:00
Entrance fee: 9 TL on weekdays, 10 TL in the weekend.

❹ 7. Cadde (Aşkaabat Caddesi)

Although it seems as if Ankara gains a new shopping mall every month, Bahçelievler's main "high street" is still very popular. Unfortunately more and more chain stores, the same as found in the big malls, are starting to penetrate this street, but several small unique shops survive.

The primary wares of most shops here are clothing, shoes, gifts, trinkets and perfume. There are lots of cafés and bars along the street too. Clothes in the shops here are more modern and fashionable than those found in Kızılay. Unfortunately parking facilities are severely limited, but the area can be easily reached by dolmuş and metro.

Because of the trees, low buildings and lively student population, 7. Cadde is a nice place to take a stroll or stop for a drink in the afternoons. There are plenty of nice café's to choose from. One of them is "7on Heaven". From the terrace you can look out onto the swarming pedestrians and cars in the street.

Do not forget to wander into the side streets. You can find some nice shops there as well, such as the second hand clothes shop "Obje", 61. Sokak No.13. Second-hand shops, particularly clothing, are rarely seen in Turkey (outside İstanbul) as Turkish people generally prefer not to buy anything used.

A "must have" while on 7th street is an ice cream from "Sim". It sells the typically chewy Turkish ice cream *(Maraş dondurması),* and this is one of the best places to try it.

❺ Azerbaycan Caddesi & Prof. Muammer Aksoy Caddesi

If you continue north from 7th street (towards the Beşevler metro station) you can walk through 3. Cadde, also called Azerbaycan Caddesi. This street is a little quieter than 7th street and has more trees and original houses. It also offers very nice café's, restaurants and coffee houses. The next street along, Prof. Muammer Aksoy Caddesi (2. Cadde), is also an interesting place for a stroll.

An interesting phenomenon in these streets, shared with many other areas including the back streets of Kızılay, are the internet café's. These almost always have big-screen TVs outside with comfortable seating where you can play "Pro Evolution Soccer" (and nothing else!) on PlayStation consoles.

South of the City Centre

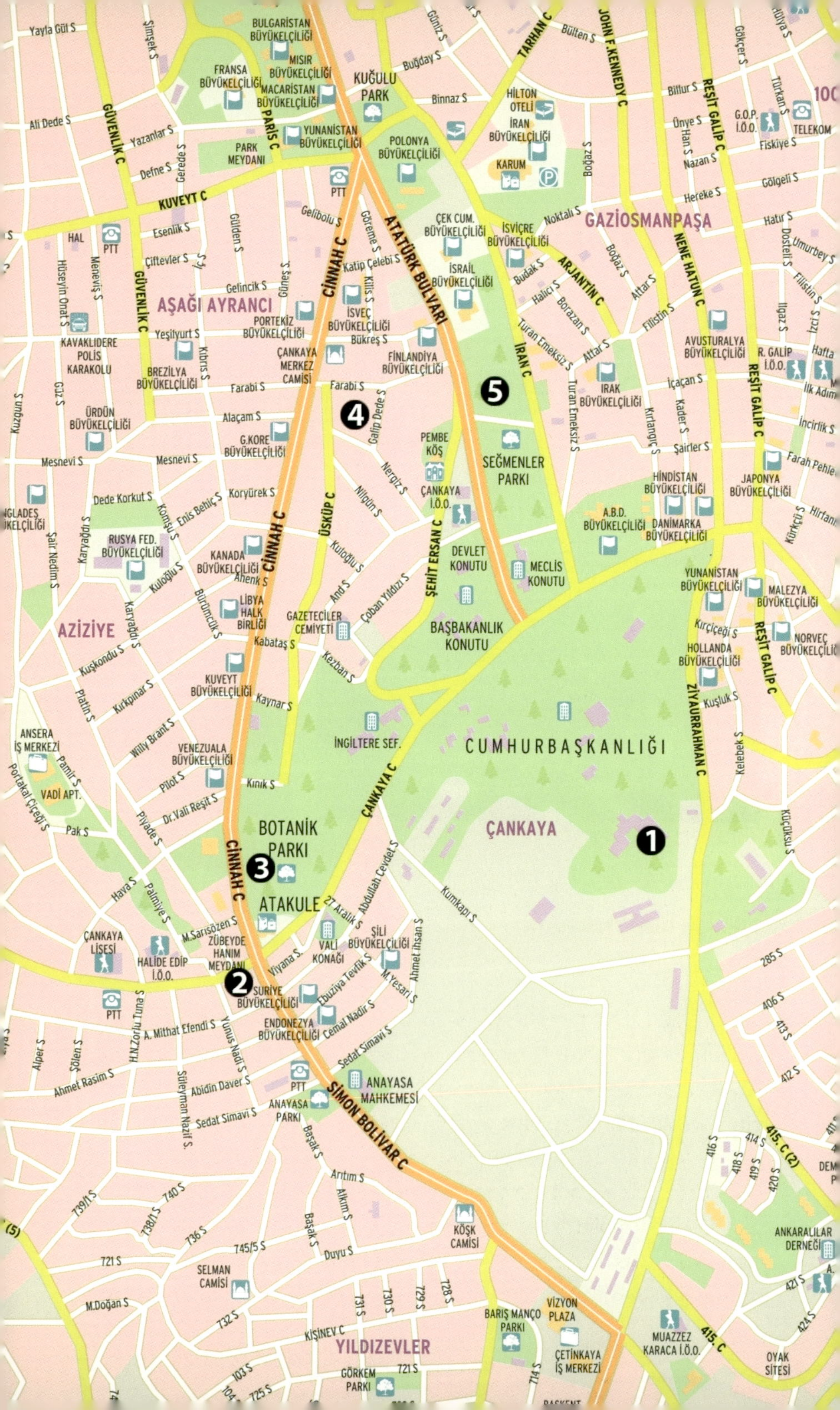

BULGARİSTAN BÜYÜKELÇİLİĞİ
FRANSA BÜYÜKELÇİLİĞİ
MISIR BÜYÜKELÇİLİĞİ
MACARİSTAN BÜYÜKELÇİLİĞİ
KUĞULU PARK
YUNANİSTAN BÜYÜKELÇİLİĞİ
POLONYA BÜYÜKELÇİLİĞİ
HİLTON OTELİ
İRAN BÜYÜKELÇİLİĞİ
KARUM
PARK MEYDANI
PTT
HAL
ÇEK CUM. BÜYÜKELÇİLİĞİ
İSVİÇRE BÜYÜKELÇİLİĞİ
GAZİOSMANPAŞA
İSRAİL BÜYÜKELÇİLİĞİ
AŞAĞI AYRANCI
PORTEKİZ BÜYÜKELÇİLİĞİ
İSVEÇ BÜYÜKELÇİLİĞİ
KAVAKLIDERE POLİS KARAKOLU
ÇANKAYA MERKEZ CAMİSİ
FİNLANDİYA BÜYÜKELÇİLİĞİ
BREZİLYA BÜYÜKELÇİLİĞİ
AVUSTURALYA BÜYÜKELÇİLİĞİ
R. GALİP İ.Ö.O.
IRAK BÜYÜKELÇİLİĞİ
ÜRDÜN BÜYÜKELÇİLİĞİ
G.KORE BÜYÜKELÇİLİĞİ
PEMBE KÖŞ
SEĞMENLER PARKI
ÇANKAYA İ.Ö.O.
HİNDİSTAN BÜYÜKELÇİLİĞİ
JAPONYA BÜYÜKELÇİLİĞİ
A.B.D. BÜYÜKELÇİLİĞİ
DANİMARKA BÜYÜKELÇİLİĞİ
RUSYA FED. BÜYÜKELÇİLİĞİ
KANADA BÜYÜKELÇİLİĞİ
DEVLET KONUTU
MECLİS KONUTU
YUNANİSTAN BÜYÜKELÇİLİĞİ
MALEZYA BÜYÜKELÇİLİĞİ
AZİZİYE
LİBYA HALK BİRLİĞİ
GAZETECİLER CEMİYETİ
BAŞBAKANLIK KONUTU
NORVEÇ BÜYÜKELÇİLİĞİ
HOLLANDA BÜYÜKELÇİLİĞİ
KUVEYT BÜYÜKELÇİLİĞİ
İNGİLTERE SEF.
CUMHURBAŞKANLIĞI
ANSERA İŞ MERKEZİ
VENEZUALA BÜYÜKELÇİLİĞİ
VADİ APT.
BOTANİK PARKI
ÇANKAYA
ATAKULE
ÇANKAYA LİSESİ
HALİDE EDİP İ.Ö.O.
ZÜBEYDE HANIM MEYDANI
VALİ KONAĞI
ŞİLİ BÜYÜKELÇİLİĞİ
SURİYE BÜYÜKELÇİLİĞİ
ENDONEZYA BÜYÜKELÇİLİĞİ
ANAYASA MAHKEMESİ
ANAYASA PARKI
KÖŞK CAMİSİ
SELMAN CAMİSİ
ANKARALILAR DERNEĞİ
BARIŞ MANÇO PARKI
VİZYON PLAZA
ÇETİNKAYA İŞ MERKEZİ
MUAZZEZ KARACA İ.Ö.O.
OYAK SİTESİ
YILDIZEVLER
GÖRKEM PARKI
G.O.P. İ.Ö.O.
TELEKOM
KUVEYT C
GÜVENLİK C
PARİS C
CİNNAH C
ATATÜRK BULVARI
TAHRAN C
JOHN F.KENNEDY C
REŞİT GALİP C
NENE HATUN C
ARJANTİN C
İRAN C
ÜSKÜP C
ŞEHİT ERSAN C
ÇANKAYA C
ZİYAURRAHMAN C
SİMON BOLİVAR C
415. C

South of the City Centre

The city of Ankara is located in a mountain basin. South of Kızılay, the new centre, the southern slope of the valley starts to climb again. For a long time, this Çankaya hillside was covered with vineyards, orchards and gardens interspersed with some big villas. Like everything else in Ankara, this changed when the capital started to expand. *Atatürk* took residence in one of the big residences on the hillside. The area became part of the big city plan for the new capital. The embassy district was planned at the foot of the hill. Large embassy compounds were built, along with roads and new houses.

Nowadays, the southern hillside is a fashionable area, with an interesting mix of residential areas, business and cultural centres, restaurants and bars, shops and big parks. You can still see imposing embassy buildings, the presidential palace and *Atatürk*'s *Çankaya Köşkü* (Çankaya Villa) here.

In this chapter we describe some of the neighbourhoods on the south side of the city –Çankaya, Gaziosmanpaşa, Kavaklıdere, Ayrancı and Dikmen– and highlight the most interesting sights in these neighbourhoods.

Çankaya

The area on top of the hill is called Çankaya. Not to be confused with the large borough of Çankaya municipality, which is named after this small area. Traditionally, this neighbourhood was the place where the city's wealthiest inhabitants lived. Even at the time of the Roman Empire, the richest inhabitants of Ancyra built their summer houses and villas here. The neighbourhood still houses the city's wealthiest inhabitants –many politicians, high-ranking government officials and foreign diplomats live here. A gated area, where the official residence of the President of the Turkish Republic is situated, occupies a large part of the neighbourhood. The houses of the Prime Minister and the most important ministers are also situated in Çankaya. Spread over the neighbourhood, and also in the adjacent neighbourhoods, are many foreign embassies. On top of the Çankaya hill, next to the presidential complex, is Atakule– prominent and remarkable, 125 m high, communications and observation tower, in the heart of the neighbourhood.

1 Çankaya Ordu Köşkü

Ziaur Rahman Caddesi, Entrance C Presidential Palace. Tel: 470 24 85 muzekosk@tccb.gov.tr. Entrance: free. Opening hours: Saturday and Sunday 13:00-15:00 and by appointment.

On top of the Çankaya hill is the Presidential site. This gated area stretches over 438 acres and is guarded by the Presidential Guard. This is the site where *Atatürk* used to live. He moved into the orchard house in the summer of 1921 and lived there until June 1932. Previ-

Çankaya Ordu Köşkü. Photo: Vekam

How to get there?

Buses 113, 115, 388, 413 in the direction of Opera, Ulus and Çankaya stop at the Ziaur Rahman Caddesi, as do many dolmuşes. For more information see www.ego.gov.tr

ously the land had belonged to the wealthy Armenian jeweller and merchant, Ohannes Kasabian.

The house had a big library, various bedrooms and bathrooms, a dining room, an ambassadors' reception room, a central hall with a billiard table (frequently used by *Atatürk*) and a central heating system. Since 1950 *Atatürk*'s Residence is a museum, which can still be visited. The villa is carefully preserved as a tribute to *Atatürk*'s memory, with its original fittings and furniture.

As Atatürk Köşkü is located on the current Presidential Compound, the museum has limited opening hours. According to official information, the museum is open on Saturday and Sunday, from 13:00-15:00, or by appointment. However, it's best to call in advance, to check if the museum is open, as it may be closed for security reasons.

2 Atakule

Atakule, a 125 metres high tower which is one of the landmarks of Ankara, is situated at the top of the Botanic Parkı.

How to get there?

Dolmuşes in the direction of Hoşdere and Cinnah Caddesi pass. Ask the dolmuş driver for the Atakule. Ego buses: 113, 115-3, 135, 176, 185, 188 and 413. For more buses and information see www.ego.gov.tr

Corner Cinnah Caddesi and Çankaya Caddesi Opening hours: every day 9:30 – 22:00 (although sometimes closed due to renovation). Entrance: 10 TL

It was built by the architect *Ragıp Buluç* between 1987 and 1989. It was built to commemorate the 66th anniversary of Ankara as the Turkish capital and to give Ankara a landmark that would be visible from everywhere and could offer a panoramic view of the city.

"*Ata*" means "ancestor" in Turkish, but usually refers to *Mustafa Kemal Atatürk*, and "*kule*" means "tower". The tower used to have a revolving restaurant at the top, which made a full 360 degree rotation in one hour. From the top you will have a great view of the city but bear in mind that the Presidential Residence may not be photographed.

Atakule was the first shopping mall in Ankara. For a few years it was the only shopping mall in Ankara. Also this old shopping mall has been closed for renovation at the time of writing.

If the tower cannot be visited, walk through the Botanic Garden to the top of Simon Bolivar Caddesi –you can also get a good view of the city from there.

3 Botanik Parkı

How to get there?

As the Botanik Parkı is just behind the Atakule, ask the dolmuş or bus driver to get out at the Atakule. See instructions above. Walk from there.

Between Cinnah Caddesi and Çankaya Caddesi. Entrance from Cinnah Caddesi.

The park is situated behind Atakule, in a valley bordered by Cinnah and Çankaya Caddesi. Although it is a pleasant park, it is not what you would expect from a botanic garden. There are no signs explaining what trees are planted. During the summer there are not many flowers. In the centre of the park there is a pond (which is now almost empty) and a dilapidated greenhouse, which used to be a nice pavilion. The best thing about the Botanik Parkı is that it smells lovely. The air here is much fresher than on Cinnah or Çankaya Caddesi, where you are walking through traffic exhaust fumes.

The Bell of Peace, located in the park, is rung each year on the anniversary of the first atomic bomb, 6 August, and in recent years, also on International Peace Day, 21 September.

4 Pembe Köşk

Walking down from Botanik Parkı, parallel to Atatürk Bulvarı and Seğmenler Parkı, you will pass the residence of the first Prime Minister and second President of Turkey, *İsmet İnönü*. It is a large Ottoman orchard villa. *İnönü* lived here from 1925 to 1973. The house was also used for important meetings, concerts, gallery openings, pool and chess tournaments and the city's first ball, on 22 February 1927.

Şehit Ersan Caddesi, open on national holidays only.

The building now houses a collection of *İnönü*'s personal belongings and diplomatic photographs. It belongs to the İnönü Foundation and is only open to the public on national holidays.

5 Seğmenler Parkı

This park is named after *Seğmenler*, traditional folk dancers and horsemen who came to dance at weddings but also served as militia. When *Mustafa Kemal Atatürk* arrived in Ankara on 27 December 1919, they gave him a wholehearted welcome, ready and willing to lay down their lives for the national independence struggle.

In the park you can see statues made by sculptor *Burhan Aklar*. The park is a pleasant shortcut if you are walking from Gaziosmanpaşa to Çankaya.

Between İran Caddesi and Atatürk Bulvarı

The park was designed by *Selami Sözer* and built in the memory of the 100th birthday of *Atatürk*, in 1983. It is 67,000 square metres in area and houses an amphitheatre, ponds (not for swimming) and a children's playground.

Seğmen. Photo: Vekam

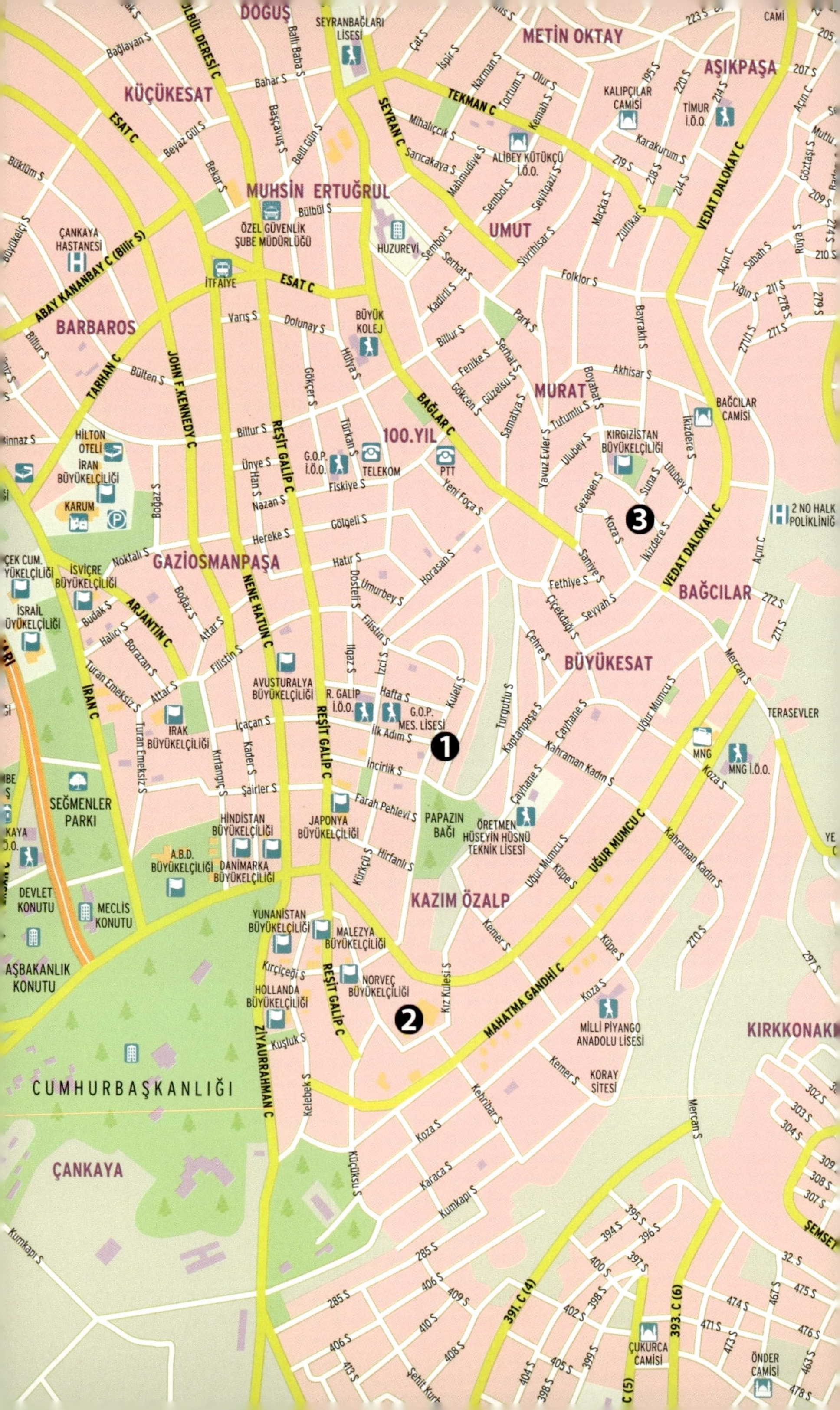

DOĞUŞ
SEYRANBAĞLARI LİSESİ
METİN OKTAY
AŞIKPAŞA
KÜÇÜKESAT
ESAT C
TEKMAN C
SEYRAN C
KALIPÇILAR CAMİSİ
TİMUR İ.Ö.O.
ALİBEY KÜTÜKÇÜ İ.Ö.O.
VEDAT DALOKAY C
MUHSİN ERTUĞRUL
ÖZEL GÜVENLİK ŞUBE MÜDÜRLÜĞÜ
HUZUREVİ
UMUT
ÇANKAYA HASTANESİ
ABAY KANANBAY C (Billir S)
İTFAİYE
BARBAROS
BÜYÜK KOLEJ
TARHAN C
JOHN F. KENNEDY C
REŞİT GALİP C
BAĞLAR C
MURAT
BAĞCILAR CAMİSİ
HİLTON OTELİ
İRAN BÜYÜKELÇİLİĞİ
KARUM
100. YIL
G.O.P. İ.Ö.O.
TELEKOM
PTT
KIRGIZİSTAN BÜYÜKELÇİLİĞİ
2 NO HALK POLİKLİNİĞİ
3
GAZİOSMANPAŞA
NENE HATUN C
ÇEK CUM. BÜYÜKELÇİLİĞİ
İSVİÇRE BÜYÜKELÇİLİĞİ
İSRAİL BÜYÜKELÇİLİĞİ
ARJANTİN C
BAĞCILAR
BÜYÜKESAT
AVUSTURALYA BÜYÜKELÇİLİĞİ
R. GALİP İ.Ö.O.
G.O.P. MES. LİSESİ
1
İRAN C
IRAK BÜYÜKELÇİLİĞİ
TERASEVLER
MNG
MNG İ.Ö.O.
SEĞMENLER PARKI
HİNDİSTAN BÜYÜKELÇİLİĞİ
JAPONYA BÜYÜKELÇİLİĞİ
PAPAZIN BAĞI
ÖĞRETMEN HÜSEYİN HÜSNÜ TEKNİK LİSESİ
UĞUR MUMCU C
A.B.D. BÜYÜKELÇİLİĞİ
DANİMARKA BÜYÜKELÇİLİĞİ
DEVLET KONUTU
MECLİS KONUTU
KAZIM ÖZALP
YUNANİSTAN BÜYÜKELÇİLİĞİ
MALEZYA BÜYÜKELÇİLİĞİ
NORVEÇ BÜYÜKELÇİLİĞİ
HOLLANDA BÜYÜKELÇİLİĞİ
2
MAHATMA GANDHİ C
MİLLİ PİYANGO ANADOLU LİSESİ
KIRKKONAKLAR
BAŞBAKANLIK KONUTU
KORAY SİTESİ
CUMHURBAŞKANLIĞI
ZİYAURRAHMAN C
ÇANKAYA
391. C (4)
393. C (6)
ÇUKURCA CAMİSİ
ÖNDER CAMİSİ
ŞEMSET

Gaziosmanpaşa

Gaziosmanpaşa is probably one of the most stylish and luxurious neighbourhoods in Ankara. The area is, like Çankaya, part of the Diplomatic Quarter of Ankara. Several embassies and consulates are located in Gaziosmanpaşa. For a long time, this neighbourhood has been home to the city's elite. Not only politicians, doctors, lawyers and successful business people live here, Gaziosmanpaşa (or GOP as the district is popularly called) is also a popular quarter for diplomats and other foreigners working for international organizations or foreign companies. For a long time the area was a retreat for people living in the city. There were tea gardens on the slopes of the hill, dotted between the vineyards and orchards. People from the city came here for relaxation (see (❶) *Papazın Bağı*).

Gaziosmanpaşa is nowadays a mainly upper class residential area. Big houses and apartment blocks are situated along quiet tree-lined streets, surrounded by small parks. Because land in the area is so expensive, and new residential areas are being built outside the city, more and more offices have been built here in recent years. However the district still has its distinctive character. Gaziosmanpaşa is also a popular area to stay for those who are visiting Ankara for a few days. The neighbourhood has a lot of hotels, from simple boutique to upper class business hotels.

The quarter houses bars and cafes, trendy clubs, international restaurants and luxury clothes shops selling international brands. These are mainly located on Arjantin Caddesi, Filistin Sokak and Turgutlu Sokak and in the side streets of these busy streets, which are arranged in a grid patterns.

❶ Papazın Bağı

Gaziosmanpaşa was once an area of vineyards and orchards, with houses and farms dotted between the grapevines and fruit trees. When Ankara started growing faster and faster in the fifties, and more and

How to get there?

Bus 112 and 114 stop at the Kuleli Sokak, almost in front of the garden. For more information see www.ego.gov.tr

Kuleli Sokak No: 61 Gaziosmanpaşa

more people moved into the city, Gaziosmanpaşa became an area, just outside the city, where people went to escape from the hustle and bustle. It's difficult to imagine today, but among the orchards and vineyards, there were old gardens with ponds, where coolness and tranquillity could be found.

One of these gardens still exists, although you have to know where it is to find it. It is Papazın Bağı, an old vineyard and orchard, which was part of the former summer residence of the priest of Ankara. The garden has been open to visitors since 1963 and is a 14,000 square metres green area, with ponds, fountains and waterfalls, surrounded by small terraces. Here you can eat *köfte* (meatball), *mantı* (Turkish ravioli) or *gözleme* (Turkish pancake filled with cheese, spinach, potatoes, etc.) and drink tea or *ayran* (yogurt drink) in the shade of century-old plane trees. In the winter you can sit inside one of the cottages. It's the hidden old green paradise in the middle of Ankara.

❷ Grand Hyatt Ankara with Crane on the Top

Uğur Mumcu Caddesi, Gaziosmanpaşa

On top of the hill of Çankaya, on the busy Uğur Mumcu Caddesi, is a remarkable high building. It was meant to become the Grand Hyatt Hotel in Ankara. But this never happened. The building has been empty and disused for years. The reason for this drama is clearly visible on the top of the high construction: a huge crane which can be seen from everywhere in Ankara.

The Grand Hyatt was a prestigious project for Ankara, because the city had a lack of five star hotel rooms. It was planned to be a 35-storey building, with 263 rooms, a conference centre, restaurants, a shopping mall and a sports club.

The construction, which started in 1991, went smoothly at first, but soon there was a series of setbacks. The biggest problem came, after 14 years of building, when most of the work was done and only some minor details had to be finished. That problem was the crane on the roof of the hotel. It is almost impossible to remove it and would cost a lot of money. It could be done bit by bit, using two other cranes, for example, but this would take two months and all the roads around the hotel would have to be closed during that time.

Another option was to move the crane with a giant

Russian helicopter but the costs for the removal of the crane were unquantified. Nobody wanted to pay these skyrocketing costs. So, after 14 years of building work, costing a total of 105 million dollars, the project ground to a halt and a legal battle began between the owner of the hotel and the construction company to determine whose fault it was, and who should pay.

Meanwhile, the crane has been on the roof for nearly 20 years. Not only residents, but also politicians, are concerned about the crane. It cannot stay on the roof forever, because it will rust. A small part falling down could cause major damage and even casualties. Also the empty high-rise building, dominating the city skyline, is now is home to vermin and damages the image of the capital city. In the coming years a solution for the crane must be found. But the question is: who is going to pay for it?

3 Gallery Nev

How to get there?

Bus 160, 317, 318 and 319 in the direction of Ulus and Opera stop at Vedat Dalokay Caddesi which is two streets away. For more information see www.ego.gov.tr

Gallery Nev holds exhibitions of international and Turkish artists' work every month. It exhibits all sorts of art: from

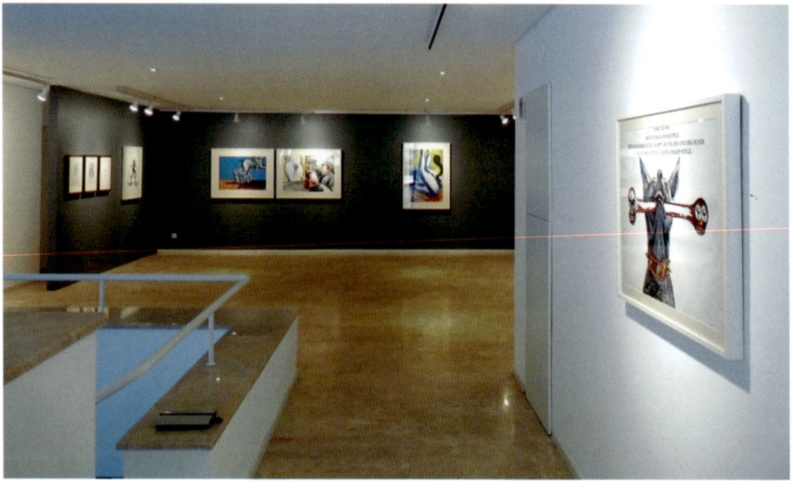

Gezegen Sokak No: 5 Gaziosmanpaşa
Tel: 437 93 90 www.galerinev.com/en
Opening hours: 11:00 – 19:00 except Sunday.

drawings and paintings to photography, but always related to Turkey. The gallery was opened in 1984 by architects *Ali Artun* and *Haldun Dostoğlu*. If you happen to be in the neighbourhood it's worth calling in to see the latest exhibition. The staff will be happy to provide you with (English) information.

❹ Restaurants and Nightlife

How to get there?

Bus 112, 114, and 161 in the direction of Kızılay, Gaziosmanpaşa, Ulus or Çankaya stop at the junction of Filistin Sokak and Arjantin Caddesi. For more information see www.ego.gov.tr

Gaziosmanpaşa is a popular area in which to go out. There are lots of restaurants, offering a wide range of international cuisines. You will not find only kebab restaurants, but also Asian or hamburger restaurants and eateries serving French and Italian cuisines. Most restaurants are located on and in the side streets of Filistin Sokak and Arjantin Caddesi. The neighbourhood also has lots of bars and some clubs. As so often in nightlife districts, the bars, clubs and restaurants change regularly. A popular eatery may suddenly close its doors and after a few weeks you will find a new restaurant in the same place.

In chapter *Restaurants* you will find a selection of restaurants in Gaziosmanpaşa.

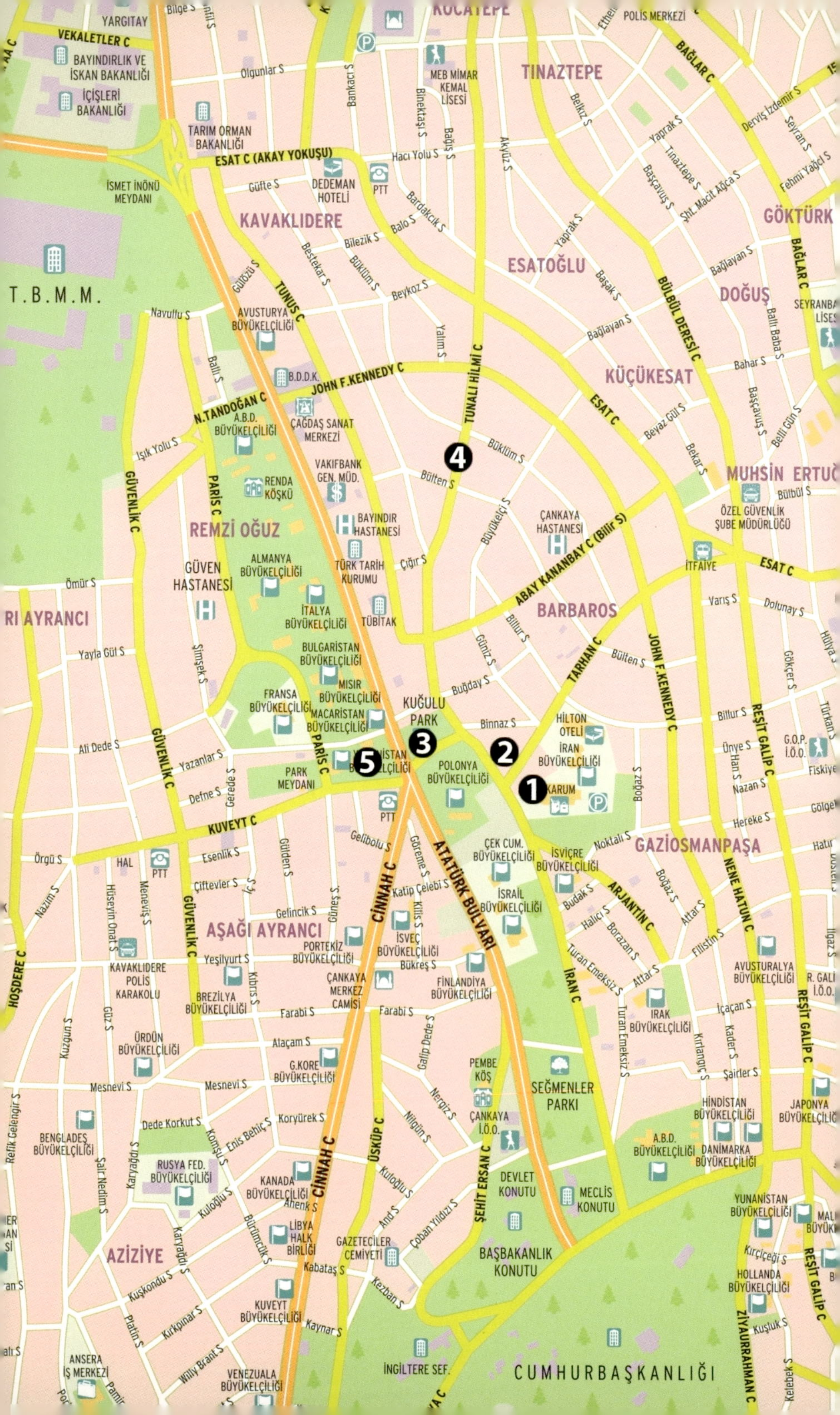
KOCATEPE
TINAZTEPE
KAVAKLIDERE
ESATOĞLU
GÖKTÜRK
DOĞUŞ
KÜÇÜKESAT
MUHSİN ERTUĞ
REMZİ OĞUZ
BARBAROS
GAZİOSMANPAŞA
AŞAĞI AYRANCI
AZİZİYE
T.B.M.M.
CUMHURBAŞKANLIĞI
YARGITAY
VEKALETLER C
BAYINDIRLIK VE İSKAN BAKANLIĞI
İÇİŞLERİ BAKANLIĞI
TARIM ORMAN BAKANLIĞI
ESAT C (AKAY YOKUŞU)
İSMET İNÖNÜ MEYDANI
DEDEMAN HOTELİ
PTT
MEB MİMAR KEMAL LİSESİ
POLİS MERKEZİ
BAĞLAR C
TUNUS C
AVUSTURYA BÜYÜKELÇİLİĞİ
B.D.D.K.
JOHN F.KENNEDY C
N.TANDOĞAN C
A.B.D. BÜYÜKELÇİLİĞİ
ÇAĞDAŞ SANAT MERKEZİ
VAKIFBANK GEN. MÜD.
RENDA KÖŞKÜ
BAYINDIR HASTANESİ
TÜRK TARİH KURUMU
TÜBİTAK
ALMANYA BÜYÜKELÇİLİĞİ
İTALYA BÜYÜKELÇİLİĞİ
BULGARİSTAN BÜYÜKELÇİLİĞİ
MISIR BÜYÜKELÇİLİĞİ
FRANSA BÜYÜKELÇİLİĞİ
MACARİSTAN BÜYÜKELÇİLİĞİ
GÜVEN HASTANESİ
GÜVENLİK C
PARİS C
TUNALI HİLMİ C
ESAT C
BÜLBÜL DERESİ C
ÇANKAYA HASTANESİ
ABAY KANANBAY C (Bilir S)
İTFAİYE
ÖZEL GÜVENLİK ŞUBE MÜDÜRLÜĞÜ
TARHAN C
JOHN F.KENNEDY C
KUĞULU PARK
HİLTON OTELİ
İRAN BÜYÜKELÇİLİĞİ
POLONYA BÜYÜKELÇİLİĞİ
KARUM
PARK MEYDANI
KUVEYT C
HAL
ÇEK CUM. BÜYÜKELÇİLİĞİ
İSVİÇRE BÜYÜKELÇİLİĞİ
İSRAİL BÜYÜKELÇİLİĞİ
ARJANTİN C
CİNNAH C
ATATÜRK BULVARI
PORTEKİZ BÜYÜKELÇİLİĞİ
İSVEÇ BÜYÜKELÇİLİĞİ
ÇANKAYA MERKEZ CAMİSİ
FİNLANDİYA BÜYÜKELÇİLİĞİ
KAVAKLIDERE POLİS KARAKOLU
BREZİLYA BÜYÜKELÇİLİĞİ
ÜRDÜN BÜYÜKELÇİLİĞİ
G.KORE BÜYÜKELÇİLİĞİ
İRAK BÜYÜKELÇİLİĞİ
AVUSTURALYA BÜYÜKELÇİLİĞİ
NENE HATUN C
REŞİT GALİP C
PEMBE KÖŞ
ÇANKAYA İ.Ö.O.
SEĞMENLER PARKI
HİNDİSTAN BÜYÜKELÇİLİĞİ
JAPONYA BÜYÜKELÇİLİĞİ
A.B.D. BÜYÜKELÇİLİĞİ
DANİMARKA BÜYÜKELÇİLİĞİ
BENGLADEŞ BÜYÜKELÇİLİĞİ
RUSYA FED. BÜYÜKELÇİLİĞİ
KANADA BÜYÜKELÇİLİĞİ
LİBYA HALK BİRLİĞİ
GAZETECİLER CEMİYETİ
ÜSKÜP C
ŞEHİT ERSAN C
DEVLET KONUTU
MECLİS KONUTU
BAŞBAKANLIK KONUTU
YUNANİSTAN BÜYÜKELÇİLİĞİ
HOLLANDA BÜYÜKELÇİLİĞİ
ZİYAURRAHMAN C
KUVEYT BÜYÜKELÇİLİĞİ
İNGİLTERE SEF.
ANSERA İŞ MERKEZİ
VENEZUALA BÜYÜKELÇİLİĞİ
HOŞDERE C
İRAN C
G.O.P. İ.Ö.O.
SEYRANBAĞLARI LİSESİ
1
2
3
4
5

Kavaklıdere

This quiet area is located at the foot of the Çankaya hill. The name Kavaklıdere means "stream with poplars". For a long time, there was a small stream here that flowed from the mountains, through these hills, into the valley. Nowadays this stream is still running, but underground. In the neighbourhood you can still see some poplars. The water made the land in this area very fertile. Until the 70's there were large vineyards on these slopes of the Çankaya hill. The fields belonged to the Kavaklıdere Winery. Nowadays you will find residential areas in Kavaklıdere, just like in Gaziosmanpaşa (apartment blocks, built in the 60s and 70s.) This neighbourhood is most famous for its busy shopping street, Tunalı Hilmi Caddesi (4).

Some big international hotel chains have also chosen to establish their luxury hotels in this stylish neighbourhood. In Kavaklıdere you will find bookshops, clothes shops, outlets, cafés, bars, restaurants and patisseries, theatres and cinemas. Next to the Sheraton Hotel is a luxury shopping mall Karum (2) one of the first shopping malls in Ankara. The central meeting point in Kavaklıdere is Kuğulu Park (3) (park with swans although most of the birds in the pond are geese and ducks).

How to get there?

Buses 112, 113, 114, 115, 135, 317 in the direction of Ulus stop at Kuğulu Park, the centre of Kavaklıdere. For more information and buses see www.ego.gov.tr

HISTORY OF THE KAVAKLIDERE VINEYARD

The name Kavaklıdere is well known throughout Turkey and beyond. This is not because the area is so well known, but because it is the name of a large Turkish winery, which has its origins in the hills of this area.

After 1923, when Ankara became the capital of the Republic of Turkey, many people moved to the city. As did the young couple *Sevda* and *Cenap*. *Cenap And* had studied economics in Germany and he got a job at the newly founded İş Bankası, the first commercial bank in Turkey.

The young couple were fascinated in viticulture. For as long as anyone could remember, there had been vineyards on the Çankaya hillside. Although many of these vineyards had been neglected during and after the war, *Sevda* and *Cenap* saw the potential of the hills. They bought some of the neglected vineyards in the Kavaklıdere area, with the intention of starting a winery in the future.

They started producing wine in 1929 with the help of experts, including *Balaj Usta,* a foreman at the Ziraat Bankası in Ankara, who had been living in Hungary, where he had learned winemaking techniques using local grapes. He became a good friend of *Sevda* and *Cenap* and helped them make their dream of producing wine from the Kavaklıdere vineyards become a reality. The first years were hard because of wrong grapes and failures in the production process. However, they persevered and improved the quality of their wine. More experts from Europe were called in to help, wine equipment and materials were imported from Europe and, with these new facilities and the *Kalecik Karası,* a local grape variety, the wine improved.

In 1932 they showcased their product at an exhibition for local products in Gençlik Parkı in Ankara. Their stand was even visited by *Atatürk*, who came to see and taste the products from all over Turkey in person. When he tasted *Kalecik* wine of the Kavaklıdere Winery, he praised the new family business for their efforts. *"This is the genuine wine of Kavaklıdere"* he said. *Atatürk*'s words spread and the next day a large and enthusiastic group of people came to the wineries pavilion, asking for the famous wine.

The family company was growing and growing. Offices, wineries and houses for the family were built on the Kavaklıdere vineyards. Kavaklıdere produced wine here for many years and became one of the largest wine producers in Turkey.

At the same time Ankara kept growing and growing. The vineyards became surrounded by buildings. Despite the growing demand for the Kavaklıdere wine, options for expanding the vineyards within the Kavaklıdere area became very limited. The price of land in the neighbourhood, which has increased significantly since the sixties, was also a factor. In the seventies the management of the winery decided to sell the vineyards and to move the winery outside the city. They bought a property in Akyurt, across from Esenboğa Airport, where a vineyard of more than 20 hectares was planted. They also constructed a very modern production bottling and storage facility, with a 40 thousand hectolitres capacity. In 1987 they started producing wine in the new winery, and the annual production capacity and sales increased. Nowadays Kavaklıdere is still the most productive wine producer in Turkey, producing over 15 million bottles of wine a year.

Mr. *Başman*, one of the current owners of the Kavaklıdere winery, with in the background a photo of the founder and his brother-in-law *Cenap And*.

Although the winery is no longer located on the hills of Kavaklıdere, the old name is honoured and used. The Kavaklıdere wine can be purchased in almost every Turkish supermarket, liquor store and restaurant. In the area where the vineyards were situated for decades, you still see some of the winery's old buildings. Some hidden between the high apartment blocks and offices, for example on Arjantin Caddesi and on the corner of Attar Sokak and Borazan Sokak. *And* family's house is on the Atatürk Bulvarı, just next to Kuğulu Park.

The highest building in Kavaklıdere is perhaps the main reminder of the old vineyard; at the site of the old winery, the Sheraton Hotel is constructed in the shape of a wine bottle.

1 Sheraton Hotel

How to get there?

Buses 112, 114, 115 and 161 stop at İran Caddesi, close to Karum. You can walk to Sheraton Hotel from here. You can also walk from Kuğulu Park as a lot of buses stop here. For more information see www.ego.gov.tr

Noktalı Sokak, Kavaklıdere

The Sheraton Hotel is housed in one of the most prominent buildings of Kavaklıdere; it is a round white tower, which rises high above the surrounding buildings. It is an orientation point from many parts of Ankara.

The hotel building, completed in 1991, was designed by the German architecture firm Architekten von Gerkan, Marg und Partner. With a total of 29 floors above ground and a height of 143 m, the hotel has 311 rooms, several bars and restaurants, meeting rooms and a convention centre. The five-star hotel has hosted many world leaders, ministers, royal guests and artists. Famous guests have included Queen Elizabeth, Barack Obama and Hillary Clinton.

Until 2009 the tower was the tallest skyscraper in Ankara. The shape of the tower is inspired by a wine bottle, due to its location on the area of the former Kavaklıdere winery (see the section *History of the Kavaklıdere Vineyard*).

❷ Karum

Next to the Sheraton Hotel is Karum shopping mall and business centre. It was one of the first shopping malls in Ankara. Like the Sheraton tower, Karum was designed by the German architecture firm Architekten von Gerkan, Marg und Partner. The building consists of a covered atrium, surrounded by shop and office floors. The construction, which began in 1986, lasted five years. Karum opened its doors in October 1991. Now, two decades after the opening, your first impression will probably be that this shopping mall has had its best years. The interior looks a bit outdated and the shops

How to get there?

Buses 112, 114, 115 and 161 stop at İran Caddesi, close to Karum. You can also walk from Kuğulu Park as a lot of buses stop here. For more information see www.ego.gov.tr

İran Caddesi, Kavaklıdere

are small, which is why you do not find the same chains as you do in other malls in Ankara. Karum hosts mainly small (luxury) boutiques, jewellers, opticians and phone shops on the ground, first and second floor. There are offices on the top floor.

There are also some restaurants and coffee bars in the basement. If you like shopping or feel a sense of nostalgia for the luxury of the early nineties, Karum is worth a visit.

3 Kuğulu Park

Kuğulu Park is a small but lively park, centrally located at the start of the busy Tunalı Hilmi shopping street. Kuğulu Park means "park with swans". The park takes its name from the swans that used to live here before their habitat was affected by all the busy roads around the park. The pictures of swans in the tunnel connecting Atatürk Bulvarı to Cin-

nah Caddesi, just next to the park, are a reminder. Luckily there are still a small number of swans in the pond.

The park has a small playground for young children and a restaurant/tea house with a terrace overlooking the park. In the middle is a pond with fountains, surrounded by benches.

Although very small, Kuğulu Park is a real meeting point. It is a place where families go with their kids, to feed the ducks and swans. A park where people cool off under the trees on hot summer days. Where people drink tea while talking about local and national issues of varying importance. And where chestnut vendors prepare and sell their hot delicacies on cold winter days.

In the autumn and winter of 2012, the park was completely renovated. The pond was refurbished and the pathways reconstructed. It is a little oasis of peace and nature in the middle of the busy city.

4 Tunalı Hilmi Caddesi

Tunalı Hilmi Caddesi, popularly known as "Tunalı", is a lively shopping street with a large variety of shops. It is a mixed street, where shops of famous Turkish fashion chains, shopping arcades, opticians, bookstores, hotels, shoe stores, pastry shops and shops with trinkets, alternate. There are many cafes and restaurants between, and above, these shops.

The street is named after the Member of Parliament and Young Turk, *Tunalı Hilmi Bey* (1871-1928). There is a statue of *Tunalı Hilmi Bey* in Kuğulu Park (see the photo of Kuğulu Park in the previous page).

From Kuğulu Park, the street runs for about a mile in a northern direction. Most shops are located in the first part of the street. The street is one-way for cars and therefore it can be packed with cars and buses, especially during rush hour.

In Ankara, this street and the surrounding area is a famous meeting place, with an important part to play in the city's social life. There are also many bars and restaurants in the side streets of Tunalı, such as Bestekar Sokak, Bülten Sokak, Büklüm Sokak, Tunus Caddesi and John F. Kennedy Caddesi. These venues are especially popular among young people and students. For more information about bars and restaurants in this area, see chapter *Restaurants*.

5 Siyah Beyaz Art Gallery & Bar

This gallery is well known in the art scene. There is a new exhibition here every month. Not only paintings but also hats and other objects d'art are exhibited.

The entrance is through an apartment building. Do not be discouraged by a closed door. Just knock and (during opening hours)

they will happily let you in. *Serra Sade*, the director, can give you information in English about the exhibitions and activities. Besides being a gallery Siyah Beyaz is also a bar which opens from 18:00 to late and has live music on Wednesday evenings until midnight and Friday and Saturday evenings until 4:00 in the morning.

Kavaklıdere Sokak No: 3/1-2 Tel: 428 26 41 www.galerisiyahbeyaz.com Opening hours: 11:00 – 19:00 except Monday

The gallery, founded by *Faruk Sade*, was paid a tribute by film director *Ahmet Boyacıoğlu*; in 2010, he made a film about this bar with the same title "Siyah Beyaz" (Black and White). In his own words, it's a film "about loneliness, growing old, friendship, solidarity, and that special bond you feel for Ankara." If you feel you have a bond with Ankara, it might be interesting to watch.

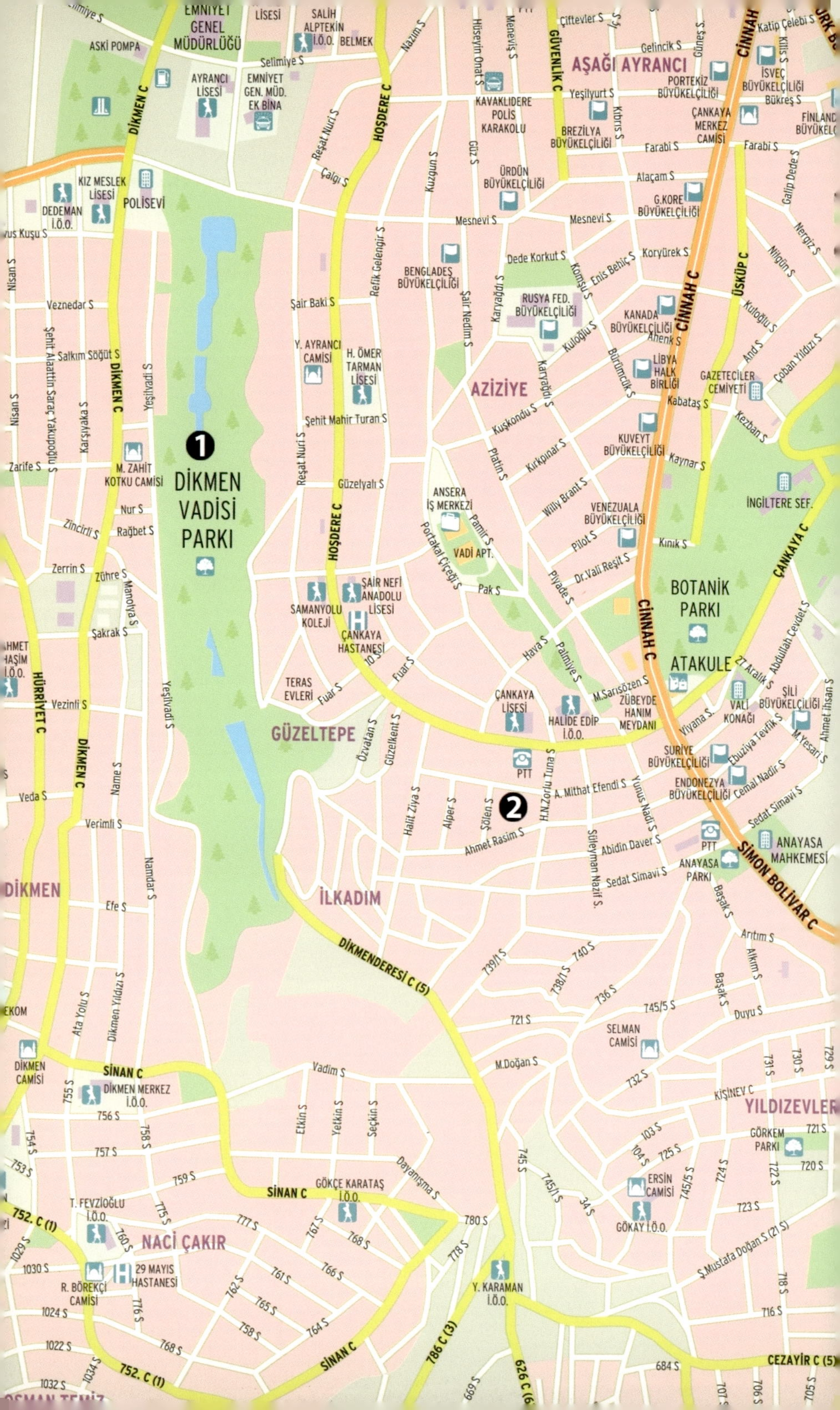
EMNİYET GENEL MÜDÜRLÜĞÜ
LİSESİ
SALİH ALPTEKİN İ.Ö.O.
BELMEK
ASKİ POMPA
AYRANCI LİSESİ
EMNİYET GEN. MÜD. EK BİNA
Selimiye S
DİKMEN C
HOŞDERE C
Nazım S
Hüseyin Onat S
Menevis S
GÜVENLİK C
Çiftevler S
AŞAĞI AYRANCI
Gelincik S
Güneş S
CİNNAH
Katip Çelebi S
Kilis S
İSVEÇ BÜYÜKELÇİLİĞİ
Bükreş S
PORTEKİZ BÜYÜKELÇİLİĞİ
Yeşilyurt S
KAVAKLIDERE POLİS KARAKOLU
ÇANKAYA MERKEZ CAMİSİ
BREZİLYA BÜYÜKELÇİLİĞİ
Kıbrıs S
Farabi S
Reşat Nuri S
Çalgı S
Kuzgun S
Güz S
ÜRDÜN BÜYÜKELÇİLİĞİ
Alaçam S
Galip Dede S
KIZ MESLEK LİSESİ
POLİSEVİ
DEDEMAN İ.Ö.O.
Mesnevi S
G.KORE BÜYÜKELÇİLİĞİ
Nisan S
Refik Belendir S
BENGLADEŞ BÜYÜKELÇİLİĞİ
Dede Korkut S
Koryürek S
Enis Behiç S
Nergiz S
Nilgün S
Veznedar S
Şair Baki S
Şair Nedim S
Karyağdı S
RUSYA FED. BÜYÜKELÇİLİĞİ
Komşu S
CİNNAH C
ÜSKÜP C
KANADA BÜYÜKELÇİLİĞİ
Ahenk S
Kuloğlu S
Şehit Alaattin Saraç Yakupoğlu S
Salkım Söğüt S
Y. AYRANCI CAMİSİ
H. ÖMER TARMAN LİSESİ
AZİZİYE
LİBYA HALK BİRLİĞİ
Bürümcük S
GAZETECİLER CEMİYETİ
And S
Çoban Yıldızı S
Karşıyaka S
Yeşilvadi S
Kuşkondu S
Kabataş S
Kezban S
Şehit Mahir Turan S
1
DİKMEN VADİSİ PARKI
Zarife S
M. ZAHİT KOTKU CAMİSİ
Platin S
Kırkpınar S
KUVEYT BÜYÜKELÇİLİĞİ
Kaynar S
Güzelyalı S
ANSERA İŞ MERKEZİ
Pamir S
Willy Brant S
VENEZUALA BÜYÜKELÇİLİĞİ
İNGİLTERE SEF.
Nur S
Zincirli S
Rağbet S
Portakal Çiçeği S
VADİ APT.
Pilot S
Kınık S
Zerrin S
Zühre S
Manolya S
ŞAİR NEFİ ANADOLU LİSESİ
SAMANYOLU KOLEJİ
Pak S
Dr.Vali Reşit S
Piyade S
BOTANİK PARKI
ÇANKAYA C
Şakrak S
ÇANKAYA HASTANESİ
10 S
Hava S
Palmiye S
CİNNAH C
ATAKULE
27 Aralık S
Abdullah Cevdet S
AHMET HAŞİM İ.Ö.O.
HÜRRİYET C
TERAS EVLERİ
Fuar S
ÇANKAYA LİSESİ
HALİDE EDİP İ.Ö.O.
M.Sarısözen S
ZÜBEYDE HANIM MEYDANI
VALİ KONAĞI
ŞİLİ BÜYÜKELÇİLİĞİ
Ahmet İhsan S
Vezinli S
GÜZELTEPE
Özvatan S
Güzelkent S
Viyana S
Ebuziya Tevfik S
M.Yesari S
DİKMEN C
Name S
PTT
H.N.Zorlu Tuna S
SURİYE BÜYÜKELÇİLİĞİ
Veda S
Halit Ziya S
Alper S
Şölen S
2
A. Mithat Efendi S
Yunus Nadi S
ENDONEZYA BÜYÜKELÇİLİĞİ
Cemal Nadir S
Verimli S
Ahmet Rasim S
Süleyman Nazif S
Abidin Daver S
PTT
Sedat Simavi S
ANAYASA MAHKEMESİ
Namdar S
DİKMEN
İLKADIM
Sedat Simavi S
ANAYASA PARKI
SİMON BOLİVAR C
Efe S
Başak S
Arıtım S
DİKMENDERESİ C (5)
739/1 S
740 S
738/1 S
Alkım S
736 S
Başak S
745/5 S
Duyu S
EKOM
Ata Yolu S
Dikmen Yıldızı S
721 S
SELMAN CAMİSİ
DİKMEN CAMİSİ
SİNAN C
Vadim S
M.Doğan S
731 S
730 S
729 S
732 S
755 S
DİKMEN MERKEZ İ.Ö.O.
756 S
KİŞİNEV C
YILDIZEVLER
754 S
758 S
Etkin S
Yetkin S
Seçkin S
103 S
GÖRKEM PARKI
721 S
757 S
745 S
104 S
725 S
724 S
722 S
720 S
753 S
759 S
Dayanışma S
ERSİN CAMİSİ
745/5 S
SİNAN C
GÖKÇE KARATAŞ İ.Ö.O.
745/1 S
34 S
T. FEVZİOĞLU İ.Ö.O.
775 S
GÖKAY İ.Ö.O.
723 S
752. C (1)
777 S
767 S
780 S
760 S
NACİ ÇAKIR
768 S
778 S
Ş.Mustafa Doğan S (21 S)
1029 S
1030 S
29 MAYIS HASTANESİ
761 S
766 S
762 S
718 S
R. BÖREKÇİ CAMİSİ
Y. KARAMAN İ.Ö.O.
765 S
1024 S
776 S
764 S
716 S
758 S
786 C (3)
1022 S
768 S
SİNAN C
CEZAYİR C (5)
1034 S
752. C (1)
626 C (6
684 S
1032 S
669 S
707 S
706 S
705 S

Ayrancı & Dikmen

This is mostly a residential quarter, inhabited by families, young professionals and older couples, and is a bit further out of the city centre, but it has some places worth visiting –notably Dikmen Valley, a huge landscaped park.

❶ Dikmen Vadisi

Dikmen Vadisi (Dikmen Valley) is the biggest park in the centre of Ankara and one of the best places in the city to go for a walk. The park is divided into different sections and it takes at least an hour to complete a circuit of the park. It also has ponds and fake waterfalls. For children there are plenty of play grounds.

How to get there?

Take the buses 117, 145, 173, 183, 186 or 187 in the direction of Ulus. For more information see www.ego.gov.tr. A lot of dolmuşes go to Hoşdere Caddesi. Get out on that street near the Dikmen Valley. Ask the driver for Dikmen Vadisi.

Between Dikmen Caddesi and Hoşdere Caddesi

There is an excellent view of Dikmen Valley from the Recep Usta restaurant (see chapter *Restaurants*).

❷ Şefik Bursalı Müzesi

> *Ahmet Mithat Efendi Sokak No: 36/3. Opening hours: every day except Sunday from 9.00 – 12.00 and 13.00 to 17.00. Entrance: is free.*

If you liked the style of art displayed in the Ankara Devlet Resim ve Heykel Müzesi (see chapter *Around the Train Station*), you might like to go to this museum. It is very small but the paintings give a good overview of Turkey during the artist's life. *Şefik Bursalı* was born in Bursa in 1903. He studied in İstanbul and later on in Europe. From 1936 onwards, he lived in this house in Ankara. Throughout his whole life he travelled a lot around Turkey. Most of the paintings in this museum are from his hometown Bursa.

North of the City Centre, **Keçiören**

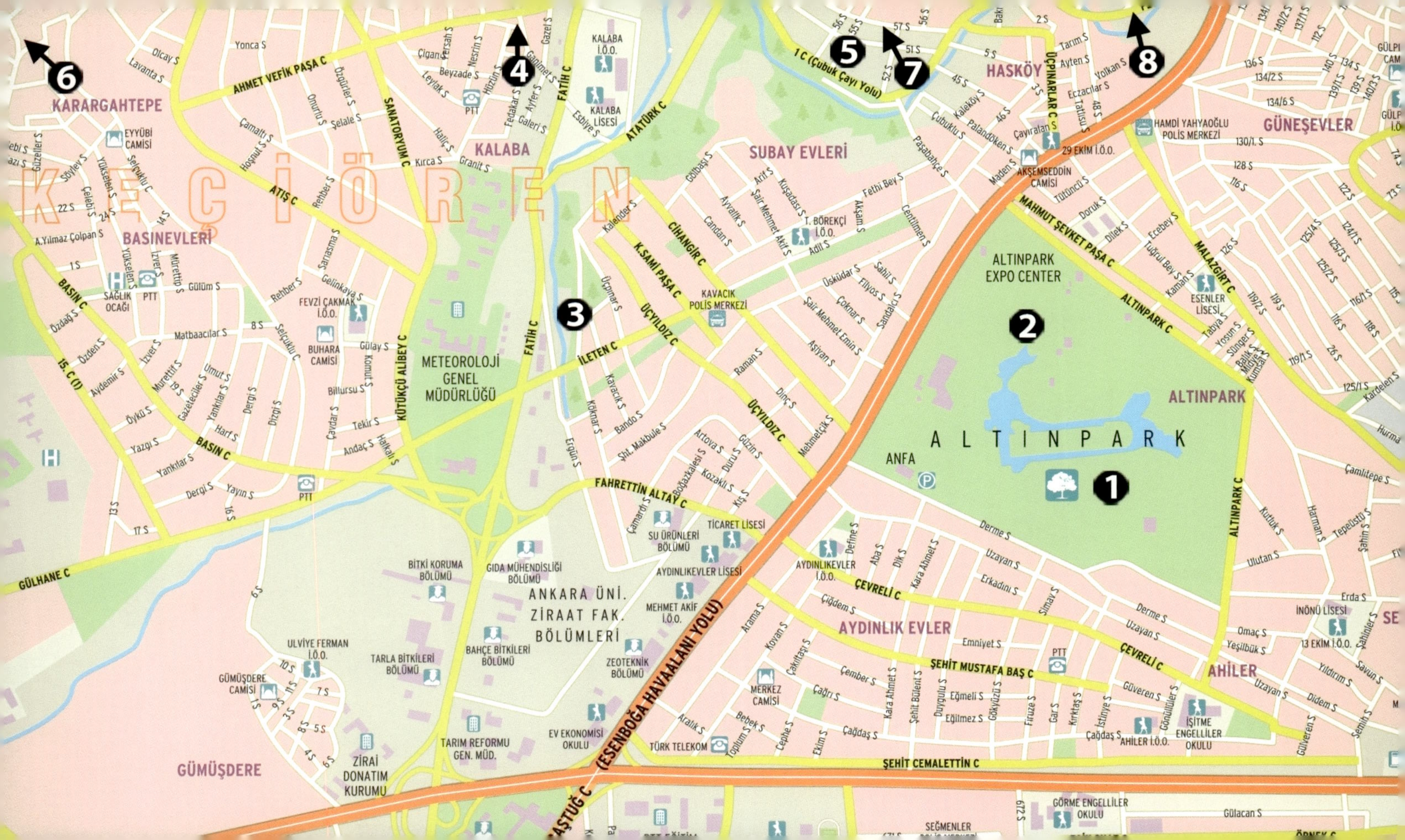
KEÇİÖREN
ALTINPARK
ALTINPARK EXPO CENTER
ANFA
SUBAY EVLERİ
KALABA
HASKÖY
GÜNEŞEVLER
KARARGAHTEPE
BASINEVLERİ
AYDINLIK EVLER
AHİLER
GÜMÜŞDERE
METEOROLOJİ GENEL MÜDÜRLÜĞÜ
ANKARA ÜNİ. ZİRAAT FAK. BÖLÜMLERİ
ESENBOĞA HAVAALANI YOLU
AHMET VEFİK PAŞA C
SANATORYUM C
ATATÜRK C
FATİH C
MAHMUT ŞEVKET PAŞA C
ALTINPARK C
MALAZGİRT C
ÇEVRELİ C
ŞEHİT MUSTAFA BAŞ C
ŞEHİT CEMALETTİN C
FAHRETTİN ALTAY C
ÜÇYILDIZ C
İLETEN C
K.SAMİ PAŞA C
CİHANGİR C
KÜTÜKÇÜ ALİBEY C
BASIN C
ATIŞ C
GÜLHANE C
ÜÇPINARLAR C
1 C (Çubuk Çayı Yolu)
HAMDİ YAHYAOĞLU POLİS MERKEZİ
KAVACIK POLİS MERKEZİ
ESENLER LİSESİ
TİCARET LİSESİ
AYDINLIKEVLER LİSESİ
KALABA LİSESİ
TÜRK TELEKOM
TARIM REFORMU GEN. MÜD.
ZİRAİ DONATIM KURUMU
1
2
3
4
5
6
7
8

North of the City Centre, Keçiören

Keçiören is primarily a residential area and, generally, not a tourist destination. The local mayor has, however, been working to make the area more appealing, especially for children. If you have a few spare hours, or if you're not sure where to take your kids one afternoon, Keçiören might interest you. The area is also home to one of the last vineyard's houses in Ankara, which is open to visitors.

How to get there? (1 to 5)

There are several bus stops on the İrfan Baştuğ Caddesi, near Altınpark: EGO buses 441, 443, 444, 408, 437, 488 go there. Ask for Keçiören ("ke-chee-oer-ren").
Other buses stop on the Fatih Caddesi, close to the funicular. Route numbers 278, 479, 415, 418, 420, 480, 481, 482 and many more. Again, just ask for Keçiören. For more information see www.ego.gov.tr

Bottom station Botanik Parkı, Fatih Caddesi/ Atatürk Caddesi. Parking next to the gas station. Top station next to Cumhuriyet Kulesi, Fatih Caddesi.

route. So you might want to consider taking a return trip on the funicular (as do most people) and then walking (or driving) back up to the castle.

Although the ride up is enjoyable enough, particularly for children, there is not yet anything to see at the top. Cumhuriyet Kulesi and an entertainment complex are planned, housing a shopping mall, an aquarium, a restaurant and a cinema. At the time of writing construction has halted (as it has been for many years) and it is not clear when it will be finished.

At night-time the funicular offers an attractive view, with all the lights of the city visible and landmarks like Atakule and Anıtkabir well illuminated.

4 Estergon Kalesi

Fatih Caddesi, Keçiören. Opening hours: 8:00 – 17:00 Entrance is free.

This castle refers to the Esztergom Castle in Hungary, 50 km northwest of Budapest, which was conquered by *Sultan Süleyman* II in 1543. According to legend his army conquered the castle in just two weeks. This is an important moment in Turkish history –an inroad into European territory (taken from the Christians), and the newly westernmost point of the Ottoman Empire. The story is commemorated in a famous folk song, performed by *Barış Manço*, among others.

The castle is free to visit. It houses an Ethnographic Museum with wax statues representing common Anatolian scenes such as the henna night, the *hamam*, the barber etc. Although a modern build, the castle is nicely constructed and has a vibrant colourful interior. It is also used as a cultural centre, for exhibitions and events.

Inside the castle you'll find two pleasant restaurants. "Osmanlı" restaurant is open for lunch and dinner and serves traditional Turkish cuisine as you might expect. "Ören Köşk" at the very top of the castle (if open) only serves tea and drinks. Next to the castle is a nomad's tent which houses "Özbek Sofrası", an Uzbekistani restaurant (see chapter *Restaurants*).

5 Deniz Dünyası

Atatürk Caddesi 53 Sokak.
Keçiören Tel: 340 53 17
Opening hours: 10:00 – 19:00
Every day except Monday.
Entrance: 3 TL, students 1 TL

Deniz Dünyası has 2 main rooms with 19 normal tanks, 1 underwater tunnel and 1 cylindrical tank. There is not a lot of information available, so it's best to just enjoy the fish. It's not a huge place, but definitely adequate for entertaining small children.

❻ Ankara Bağ Evi

Şehit Hakan Turan Sokak No: 18 Keçiören
Tel: 356 33 93
Opening hours: 10:00 – 17:00. Every day except Sunday. Lunch break between 12:30 – 13:30
Entrance: 2 TL + ID as guarantee.
www.vekam.org.tr

How to get there?

There are not a lot of options as far as buses go. Bus 278 (Şentepe, Siteler) and 289 (Basınevleri Siteler) stop on the Nuri Pamir Caddesi , 10 minutes' walk away. For more information see www.ego.gov.tr

This traditional Ankara Vineyard House is decorated as per the transition between the Ottoman period and the new Republic era. It features items and décor from both times. The guide speaks very good English and can tell you a lot about the house and the area's history.

This area used to be full of vineyards and orchards. Sadly this is one of the few houses to remain but luckily it has been preserved very carefully. The bricks on the exterior walls are original Andesite and Ankara Stone while the interior walls are wooden. As you enter the house you will pass the kitchen, laden with old Anatolian copperware. Ask the guide what it serves for, she will gladly explain.

Moving upstairs, you look into the reception and bedrooms around a central *sofa* (a hall like room). The upper floor was designed for use during winter, the ceilings kept low to keep the rooms warm during the

KOÇ FAMILY

Koç family is important to Ankara and its cultural heritage.

Vehbi Koç was a Turkish entrepreneur and philanthropist and the Vehbi Koç Foundation was set up in his honour. The foundation aims to collate available information about *Vehbi Koç* and Ankara history; for that purpose they have a library and research centre along the same street (No: 9) in another vineyard house, which the family used as summer residence for many years. At No: 18 you'll find old photos of Ankara from their archives, both of the orchard and its surroundings and of the city centre.

It was his daughter, *Semahat Arsel,* who could not bear to see the vineyard house at No: 18 falling into disrepair surely to be replaced by another charmless concrete apartment. *Semahat* restored the house, which had belonged to her father's aunt, in 2006. She then donated the house to the Vehbi Koç Foundation.

Vehbi Koç's only son, *Rahmi Koç,* is today one of Turkey's most famous businessmen. Following in his father's footsteps, he also shows care for Ankara's cultural heritage. He was behind the restoration of the Çengelhan, now a technology museum, where his father opened a shop in 1917. After the completion of the Çengelhan project he turned his foundation to the restoration of the Çukurhan and is now working on the restoration of the Zağfiranhan. For more information see chapter *Hisar.*

cold winter months. The interior decoration shows the coexistence of traditional and modern lifestyle during the era. It has the traditional divans along the walls of the *sofa,* and then a more modern living room with a 78 rpm gramophone. Pay attention to the small details around the interior such as the Ottoman script certificate on the living room wall. It was a present from the Turkish Aeroplane Society to wish the new inhabitants good luck in their new home. Also take a look at the carpet in the sofa, woven by a girl of 15. Her name and the year it was made are woven into the carpet.

The house is also available for reservation for parties, dinners or meetings.

7 Evcil Hayvanlar Parkı

This domestic animals park is fun place for children, but also a pleasant trip for adults. Visit to see a real Angora goat or cat, the symbols of Ankara but not easily found elsewhere in the city. The Angora cat generally has white hair and either green, yellow, copper or blue eyes. It is quite common to see Angora cats with one blue and one green eye. The cat originates from Ankara, but is delicate and not well-equipped for hunting. The same cannot be said of the Angora goat who is well adapted to the climate and terrain of Central Anatolia. It was brought to Anatolia by the Turks in the 13th century and has been bred here ever since. The goat's hair, mohair, was used to make cloth, the famous *sof* (mohair), in the 15th and 16th centuries. It is heat-resistant, can be dyed easily and does not get dirty easily, thus was very sought after and made Ankara a prosperous and important trading city on the Silk Route. Statues of Angora goats are a mainstay of many public areas and parks in Ankara, even at Esenboğa airport.

Besides the special Ankara species here, you'll also find an aquarium, chickens, flamingos, dogs, ponies, donkeys and even an ostrich. In summertime you can take a carriage to drive you around in the park.

How to get there?

There are a couple of bus services passing by the park:bus 479 (Uyanış-AŞTI) and 481 (Uyanış -Pınarbaşı-Ulus-Kızılay) stop on the Aşıkpaşa Caddesi , right out front. For more information see www.ego.gov.tr

Aşıkpaşa Caddesi. Opening hours: 10:30 -21:00. Entrance is free.

8 Gökçek Parkı

There's nothing particularly special about this park, but it's a nice place for a stroll if you happen to be in the neighbourhood. In summertime you can enjoy a tea from *semaver* (Turkish tea kettle) and a *nargile* (waterpipe) on the restaurant terraces in the newly built "old" Ankara house, across the pond.

How to get there?

Bus 410 (Aktepe-Kuyubaşı-Ulus-Kızılay) and 416 (Aktepe-Kızılay) stop on Bursa Caddesi, diagonally opposite the park. For more information see www.ego.gov.tr

Gelen Dost Sokak

Ankara for **Kids**

Ankara for Kids

Ankara is not a particularly child-friendly city and you might have to look around for good places to take your children. The following are some tips to get you started.

Aquaparks

In summertime the best places to go are the aquaparks. For information and addresses see the paragraph "Swimming" in the chapter *"Practical Information"*.

Parks

Ankara has a lot of parks. Most of them have small children's playgrounds. Here are some suggestions:

- Altınpark, İrfan Baştuğ Caddesi (Keçiören), on the way to the airport from Ulus. It has pedaloes, an ice skating rink (in winter time), a mini train, horse carriages and a Science Museum (see also chapter *Keçiören*).
- Mogan Gölü (Gölbaşı lake, 25 km south of the city center)
- Dikman Vadisi (parallel to Hoşdere Caddesi)

- 50. Yıl Parkı (Kızılay)
- Kuğulu Park, Tunalı Hilmi Caddesi (Kavaklıdere), is for younger children who love to feed swans and ducks.
- Lozan Park (next to 365 shopping mall, 451. Sokak), small park, just for a little walk with toddlers.
- Ahlatlıbel (in İncek, 20 km south of the city centre), recreation park, where kids can play balls, skate and kite. Balls and kites are often sold cheaply along the road to the park.
- Eymir Gölü, for biking (see chapter *Practical Information>>Biking*).

Amusement Parks

- Harikalar Diyarı (Wonderland), (Yunus Emre Mah. Ayaş Yolu Cad. 12. km. No: 300 Sincan) with an area of 1 million 320 thousand square meters Harikalar Diyarı is one of the biggest urban parks in Europe. It has several playgrounds, a go-cart track, a mini train, a skate park, a mini golf course and artificial ponds with boats and water bikes.
- Gençlik Parkı (Ulus), access from the Atatürk Bulvarı, near the Opera or opposite the train station) has an amusement park (see chapter *Around the Train Station*).

Zoo

- Ankara Zoo *(AOÇ Hayvanat Bahçesi),* Alparslan Türkeş Caddesi (Çiftlik Caddesi), Gazi Entrance: free. Parking: 5 TL Opening hours: In summer weekdays: 08.30-18.00, weekends 08.30 – 19.00. In winter: every day 08.30-17.00

  Although the zoo does not currently meet European standards either for entertainment or for animal welfare. A new zoo will be built next to it which will conform to the highest standards.
- Domestic Animals Park *(Evcil Hayvanlar Parkı),* (Uyanış Mah., Aşık Paşa Cad. Aktepe-Keçiören). Entrance: free. Opening hours: 10:30 – 21:00

This park has Angora cats, goats, dogs, ponies, donkeys, ostriches, flamingos and chicken. In summer time around the (small) park.

Restaurants

- Both the Uludağ restaurants, on Kırlangıç Sokak in Gaziosmanpaşa and on Çayyolu have nice indoor and outdoor playgrounds for kids.
- Adana Sofrası on 713. Sokak (or 91. Sokak) a side street of Turan Güneş Bulvarı has an indoor playground and great kebabs.
- Kukla Kebap on the junction of 1419. Sokak (3. Sokak), Dr. Sadık Ahmet Cadessi and Ziyabey Caddesi in Balgat, has a small theatrical scene on the wall and in the weekends, at certain times, they have traditional puppet shows (*Karagöz & Hacivat type*).
- Timboo Café and Las Chicas in Kentpark have kids menus, personal DVD players, a selection of kids' movies (for both boys and girls), and a fountain water show outside their balconies set to music.

Art for Kids

CerModern (Altınsoy Caddesi No: 3) organizes art activities called Cer-Çocuk for children aged between 7 and 12. They can join for 50 TL a week or 200 TL a month. Closed on Mondays. For more information see *www.cermodern.org/cercocuk.html* or call 310 00 00.

Shopping Malls

Shopping malls often offer children's entertainment. For the addresses of the shopping malls (see chapter *Practical Information*).

In Kentpark they have small boats on a pond.

Nata Vega has a nice aquarium (see paragraph *Aquariums*).

365 has a playground upstairs with trains and horses.

In the Minasera shopping mall in Çayyolu there is a technology museum for kids over 3 years.

Some shopping malls also have theatres for kids, like Panora and Kentpark. Unfortunately most explanation about program and the play itself are in Turkish.

Aquariums

The Nata Vega shopping mall has an aquarium. You walk through an underwater tunnel. Entrance is 15 TL for adults, 10 TL for children. Free for children under 2 years old.

In Keçiören (Şevkat Mah. 53. Sok. Keçiören Merkez. Buses 404, 415, 418 direction Aktepe) you can find Deniz Dünyası which is smaller with

19 aquariums, 1 tunnel aquarium and 1 cylinder aquarium but also cheaper. Entrance is 3 TL, students 1 TL. Open from 10.00 to 19.00 o'clock, closed on Mondays.

Feza Gürsey Bilim Merkezi

Weekdays 9.00 to 18.00, İrfan Baştuğ Caddesi No: 154 in Altınpark. Tel: 317 99 19 Entrance: 7 TL. Students and teachers: 5 TL www.fezagurseybilimmerkezi.com

A Science Museum where kids can do all kinds of tests and experiments related to physics and the human body. Both fun and educational. All instructions and explanations are written in Turkish and English.

Oyuncak Müzesi

Ankara Üniversitesi Eğitim Fakültesi, Cemal Gürsel Caddesi, Cebeci, Tel: (312) 363 33 50 (extension 32 12) Free entrance Tuesday to Friday but an appointment is required before visiting.

The Toy Museum in Cebeci, houses all kinds of toys made of wood, tin, porcelain, plastic, paper and more. It is the only toy museum in Turkey and has a collection of approximately 2000 toys. The oldest Turkish and foreign toys in the museum are about 50 and 100 years old respectively.

MTA Tabiat Tarihi Müzesi

In the grounds of the building of the Mineral Research Institute (MTA) (Genel Müdürlük Binası) on Eskişehir Yolu, Balgat, Ankara Tel: 287 34 30/1023. Open every day from 09:30 to 17:30

The museum offers a rich collection of mineral and rock specimens collected from geological, mineralogical and paleontological research from all over Turkey. There is also a collection of over 3,000 fossils on display in the museum.

Outside Ankara

Outside Ankara

The main places of interest around Ankara are Hattuşa and Gavurkale.

HITTITES

Modern day Ankara sits in the middle of the old Hittite territory, and in the surrounding areas there are a few interesting Hittite sites to visit. Between 1800 and 1178 BC the Hittites were a powerful people, famous for producing the first written constitution, producing lightweight war chariots and for their Kings who were masters of strategy. They wrote on cuneiform tablets from which historians have been able to learn about their religious beliefs, their methods of administration and their diplomatic relations. One of the most important findings is a peace treaty with the Egyptians, dated from around 1283 BC during the reign of Ramses II.

Hattuşa and Its Surroundings

Hattuşa was the Hittite capital during the late Bronze Age (1500-1000 BC), with a population of around 50,000. Numerous ruins are pre-

served around this UNESCO World Heritage site –bring plenty of water as a lap of the area is a 5 km walk. Besides a few locals selling small trinkets there is little here no places to eat or drink, so most organised tours bring their own supplies.

The Hittites worshipped thousands of Gods and in this city alone 31 structures are defined as temples, the largest remaining of which is the great temple of the storm god Teshup. Besides temples, among the ruins you'll also find the large city walls and gateways. There are a total of 38 structures available to visit. One of the best conserved is the Lion Gate.

If you want to visit Hattuşa under your own steam you might consider staying overnight in nearby Boğazkale but daytrips are also possible. The site can be visited alone but, with no information available, a tour guide will certainly improve your visit. There are a few tour companies running day trips from Ankara (see the website at the end of this chapter for suggestions or ask your hotel if they have a preferred partner). The site is on a high plain, so to avoid the heat it's best to visit in spring or autumn. If you go in summertime be sure to bring a hat or cap.

Other Hittite sites nearby are Alacahöyük (39 km) and Yazılıkaya (2 km) with its open air rock temple. The images of more than 90 Gods, Goddesses, animals and imaginary creatures are carved into the walls.

If you fancy something other than looking around the ruins, there are trekking and mountain biking routes set up in and around the area. English-language guidebooks containing maps and GPS coordinates can be ordered from *culturetoutesinturkey.com/c/hittite-trail* and may also be available from the Çorum municipality.

You can reach Boğazkale/Hattuşa by car. Boğazkale is around 195 km east of Ankara, about a 3 hour drive, and from there you can walk in to Hattuşa. For more information about Hattuşa and its surroundings, as well as links to other travel agencies, see *www.corumkulturturizm.gov.tr/EN/belge/2-28542/transportation.html.*

at Cappadocia. You'll come across monuments, Phrygian inscriptions, Hittite etchings, as well as tombs from the Roman, Seljuk and Ottoman periods. Although the area is becoming better known, it's very likely that you will find yourselves alone in the middle of this amazing world.

One of the highlights is Midasşehir (Midas) in the Yazılıkaya valley. As you arrive here you will probably be noticed by the guard. If you don't see him, he'll be at the museum next to the grand monument. He is very friendly and will guide your around the site, showing you the Midas monument, the water cisterns, tunnels, altars and cave houses. Tickets are 3 TL. There is also an interesting book about the area available to buy. He doesn't want to take money but you can support him by buying a book about the place or a little souvenir from his shop.

On your way you could drop by Seyitgazi where a convent/castle is currently under restoration. The building belonged to and was extended by the Romans, Byzantines and Ottomans in succession.

For more information about the Phrygian Valley see *www.frigvadisi.org/default-en.aspx*

Kızılcahamam (Thermal Baths & National Park)

For those who enjoy hiking through nature, Kızılcahamam is one of the best escapes from the bustle of Ankara. It's around a 1.5 hour drive and if you pass through the small town, one of the oldest settlements in Anatolia, you'll reach the National Park on the other side.

In summer you'll find a lot of people out enjoying the weather and a barbecue, but if you walk a little bit further you will find yourself almost all alone in some beautiful surroundings for hiking. There are a number of trails to follow and if you want some company there are several organised walking groups at the weekends. Check *www.alternatifrekking.com* or *www.artiyasam.com* if you want to join a hike. The forest has a very diverse landscape, from Anatolian steppes to forests of Black Sea pine trees. Wild boars, bears, foxes, jackals, squirrels, rabbits and hundreds of bird species call this area their home.

There are other interesting locations around Kızılcahamam. Taşlıca Village (17 km southeast) has some peculiar eroded rock formations. Mahkeme Ağcin village plays host to an underground city, churches built of tuffs and the Alicin Monastery which, like the Sumela Monastery in Trabzon, seems glued against the rocks. General consensus has named it a monastery but some locals believe the caves were actually carved by a bandit called Alicin in the 19th century. It's unclear what period they actually belong to –they also might have been shelters carved during the Roman period. If you have a GPS device you can find the caves at 40.324544 (40° 19′ 28.36″ N), 32.456836 (32° 27′ 24.61″ E). Be sure to look up –they're up at a height of 70 metres. Unfortunately you cannot visit the cave interiors.

For more ancient sights in and around Kızılcahamam see *www.kizilcahamamgezi.com/Historical_Buildings_in_Kizilcahamam.htm*

Aside from the National Park, Kızılcahamam is known for its thermal baths which have been used since Roman times. The baths are said to heal rheumatic and digestive issues, kidney problems and bone and joint diseases. The Asya Thermal Resort (*www.asyatermalotel.com.*

tr) and Patalya Resort Hotel (*www.patalyahotel.com.tr*) are the most famous hotels in the area.

It's best to drive to give you freedom to explore the area, but small buses for the National Park leave from the Etlik Garaji (Eski Terminal) at Etlik Caddesi, from Migros at Ankamall or from opposite the Atatürk Kültür Merkezi on Hipodrom Caddesi. A ticket is 7 TL. A bus departs every 20 minutes between 6:45 and 20:00. After 20:00 there are buses at 20:45, 21:30 and 22:30. It is a 1 hour journey to Kızılcahamam.

Buses back to Ankara leave the Municipality Bus Terminal *(Belediye Otobüs Terminali)* every 20 minutes between 6:00 and 18:00. After 18:00 they're every half hour until 20:30.

Cappadocia

Cappadocia is about 300 km. (4 hour's drive) southeast of Ankara and is a popular destination because of its historical, cultural and unique geological features. Parts of Cappadocia, like the Göreme National Park, feature on the UNESCO World Heritage List.

Cappadocia's amazing landscape was formed by the precipitation of lava and ash from the volcanos 40 million years ago. Water and wind eroded the soft tuff (or volcanic) rocks for millions of years, different rocks at different rates, creating the whimsical forms found today. Mankind has also left its mark over previous millennia. People realised the stone was soft enough to carve houses, churches, even whole underground cities, living there for hundreds of years and decorating their caves with interesting paintings.

Göreme National Park is the best place to see all of this as it's surrounded by the villages of Ürgüp, Göreme, and Uçhisar. These villages all feature cave homes, now made into hotels, and daily tours run all year round. You don't have to purchase a tour from one of these villages; you can also buy tickets for trips straight from Ankara in Kızılay. Nevşehir Seyahat is one of several companies running daily bus trips

from Ankara to Cappadocia. A one way ticket cost around 35 TL. See *www.nevsehirlilerseyahat.com.tr* (Turkish only) or call them at 0384 444 50 50.

Cappadocia is the busiest area in the world for commercial balloon flight. Every morning at sunrise almost 100 hot air balloons take off to fly over the National Park. Joining one of them is a breath-taking experience; a little pricey at somewhere around the €150-€200 but many hotels can get you a discount and it's definitely one of those 'once in a lifetime' things to do.

For a proper visit, to take everything in, you should spend 2 to 3 days here. There are many books devoted to Cappadocia available if you want to learn more. Also available at the many souvenir shops in Cappadocia.

Thermal Spas and Hotels

There are several thermal spas in and around Ankara. These are a few notable examples:

Ankara

No:19 Boutique Hotel
Birlik Mah. 457. Sokak No: 19 Çankaya
Tel: 495 18 19 / 11 35
www.no19hotel.com/english.php

Bilkent Otel ve Konferans Merkezi
Üniversiteler Mah. 1599. Cad. No: 6 Bilkent
Tel: 266 46 86
www.thesanitas.com/en/ankara-bilkent-hotel-sanitas-spa.html

Kızılcahamam

Asya Thermal Resort
İsmetpaşa Mahallesi Kızılcahamam
Tel: 736 40 00
www.asyatermalotel.com.tr

Patalya Resort Hotel
Soğuksu Milli Parkı Kızılcahamam
Tel: 736 02 00
www.patalyahotel.com.tr

See the information under the chapter *Kızılcahamam* how to go there by bus.

From the bus stop the Patalya Resort Hotel is an approximate 10 minute taxi journey. The Asya Thermal Resort is a 15 minute walk, or 5 minutes by taxi.

Ayaş

Ayaş İçmece ve Kaplıcaları
Ayaş Beypazarı Yolu 23. Km (83 km from Ankara) Ayaş
Tel: 718 31 01
www.ayasicmeceleri.com

Hitit Ayaş Termal Hotel
Çoban Hamam Mevkii
Çağa-Güdül (20 km from Ayaş, 80 km from Ankara)
Tel: 473 17 90
www.hititayastermal.com.tr

Check for buses to Ayaş at the AŞTI bus terminal at Konya Yolu (Mevlana Bulvarı).

Afyon

Güral Afyon Wellness & Convention
Izmir Karayolu 7. km Afyon
Tel: (0272) 220 22 22
www.guralafyon.com/en

Oruçoğlu Thermal Resort
Afyonkarahisar Kütahya Karayolu 14. km Afyonkarahisar
Tel: (0272) 251 50 50
www.orucoglu.com.tr/eng

There are several spa hotels in Afyon. For more suggestions see *www.tatilbudur.com/termal-oteller/afyon_termal-oteller.html, and www. tripadvisor.com* or your favourite hotel booking website.

Buses to Afyon depart the AŞTİ bus terminal at Konya Yolu (Mevlana Bulvarı). It takes between 3 and 3.5 hours. At the other end, taxis to most hotels take around 15 minutes.

Duatepe & Alagöz

Duatepe was an observation hill during the Battle of Sakarya in 1921, when the Turkish were fighting off an attack by the Greeks. The battle went on for 21 days from 23rd August until 13th September on the banks of the Sakarya river, near Polatlı. It was the first hill captured back from the Greeks and thus seen as the turning point in the Greco-Turkish war.

The final counterattack, which began on 10th September, was made under the command of *General Mustafa Kemal Paşa*, later to receive his modern name *Mustafa Kemal Atatürk*. The monument at Duatepe symbolises the change for Turks from a life spent under foreign oppression to an independent republic of Turkey under *Atatürk*'s leadership.

There are several sculptures on the hill. The sculpture of *Atatürk, İnönü* and *Fevzi Çakmak* marks the unity of the command team during battle. The sculpture of the women represents the contribution of Anatolian women during the war. The sculpture of *Atatürk* and his assistant watching the theatre through binoculars symbolises the upcoming victory.

Even if you're not particularly interested in the history, Duatepe is worth visiting for the amazing view.

On your way back to Ankara you could stop by at Alagöz on the Ankara-Eskişehir road. Next to the train station you'll find the house used as headquarter by commanders during the battle and where the plans for the counterattack were made. It's now a small museum. Opening hours are 9:00 until 17:00 (until 16:00 in winter). If the museum appears closed, try waiting around a bit for someone to show up. There are some artefacts on display outside: more sculptures, a plane and old cannon.

Çubuk I - II, Karagöl, and Mavi Göl

The twin Çubuk reservoirs ensure Ankara's water supply even during dry periods. These artificial lakes around Ankara are also a good place for a walk.

The first Çubuk reservoir is out along the way to the airport – *Atatürk* used to row here. It is still open to public but unfortunately it is rather neglected. If you want to find some past glory of the early days of the Republic, you can find it at the Baraj Caddesi, north of Keçiören (40° 0′ 21″ N, 32° 55′ 49″E).

Mavi Göl, on the east ring road to the airport, from the city 25 km before you reach first Çubuk is better looked after. If you want to row, this is the place.

The second reservoir is past the airport, about an hour and 40 minute drive out of Ankara. Follow signs for Çubuk and Karagöl northwards on the road to the airport. The area is much quieter than Mavi Göl –it's less popular meaning fewer BBQs and picnic tables and more unspoiled nature. It's a lovely spot for a walk, although it can be tricky

to find the entrance to the designated track. Get to highest point, where you'll find a small house housing the public toilets. From here, walk past the small area of tables and into a valley to follow the walking path.

Beypazarı

Beypazarı is approximately 100 km northeast of Ankara, on average a 90 minute drive. It is one of the nicest and most popular getaways from Ankara –not just the village but also its surroundings, like the İnözü Valley, are lovely places worth visiting.

Beypazarı means gentlemen's bazaar, referring to the markets and fairs that were previously held in this cute Ottoman village in a time when the village was one of the stops on the "Silk Route". Many of the traditional houses have been restored and the 3500 white painted and wooden framed mansions and houses form the village's main attraction. On Alaaddin street, İmaret Square and the Suluhan Kervansaray you get a real sense of the history, thanks not only to this lovely Ottoman architecture but also to the many local vendors selling their wares. Traditional handicrafts like copperware, gold and silver filigree embroidery *(telkari)* and textile embroidery are still on show all around you. The *bindallı* is a famous item of note –a long velvet robe, embroidered with silver or gold threads, that is worn over clothing with a broad golden belt.

The top of the Hıdırlıktepe hill provides a fascinating panoramic view over the old town and the surrounding countryside. You can climb this hill, west of the old town, on foot directly from the city centre or you can drive to the top. The hilltop view over Beypazarı really is wonderful and a must see.

The best way to take in the village, though, is to just stroll about the small cobbled streets. If you want to learn about life in an old Ottoman house, head for the Yaşayan Müze on Çınar Sokak. Here you'll find traditional Ottoman crafts being performed by students, and visitors participate too –perhaps especially interesting for children. Sometimes you can watch a performance of the traditional Karagöz and Hacivat shadow puppets, a well established tradition in Turkey. Another interesting museum, housed in an authentically restored mansion, is

the combined Tarih ve Kültür Müzesi and Kent Tarihi Müzesi. Here you can see traditionally furnished rooms, with plenty of old utensils and costumes from the Ottoman era on display.

On the village square you'll find a big carrot statue; not what you'd expect in a town square perhaps, this giant vegetable celebrates the Beypazarı's most (and perhaps only) famous export. 60 percent of the carrots eaten in Turkey are grown here, possibly many carrots eaten abroad too. Every year at the end of June the village hosts a carrot festival, and carrots are so loved here that the locals even produce a carrot flavoured variant of the famous *Turkish lokum,* more commonly known as Turkish Delight. It is probably the only place in Turkey where you can try this, or at least the only place you'll get it freshly made, so don't miss out, and don't leave without tasting the fresh carrot juice either.

The village benefits from nature in another way too –natural thermal springs flow from outside Beypazarı in Dutlu (20 km to the south-east) and Kapullu (30 km to the south). Tahtalı Termal is particularly reviled. It is said that the hot spring water here cures afflictions ranging from dermatological disorders to nervous system diseases. Whether or not that is true, a visit to the spring is relaxing and a special experience

Beypazarı is most easily accessed by car, but there are also daily tours departing from Ankara. Ask a travel agency for details. Public buses also travel to Beypazarı daily, every 30 minutes between 7:00 and 21:00, from the bus stop next to Ankamall. Tickets cost around 8TL.

For more information see *www.ankaracityguide.com/Beypazari.htm*

General Information: **Turkey** and **Ankara**

Weather

Snow on Elmadağ

Turkey is a large country, so the climate is influenced by both the surrounding seas and the interior mountains and differs greatly between the regions. Ankara is centrally located and therefore has a continental climate, with cold snowy winters and hot dry summers. The dry air coupled with Ankara's high altitude mean that, despite high daytime temperatures, evenings and nights during the summer months remain cool. The annual average precipitation is fairly low, but is spread across the whole year. During winter fog often occurs in the night and morning, and heavy snow is possible.

The best times to visit Ankara are in spring, summer and autumn. Although summer days can be hot, the cool nights make life much more bearable. Also remember that some restaurants, cafés and public areas are open only during the summer season.

	Jan	Feb	Mar	April	May	June	July	Aug	Sept	Oct	Nov	Dec
High	1	4	10	15	20	24	27	28	24	18	10	4
Low	-6	-5	-1	3	6	9	12	12	8	3	-1	-3
Rainy	8	8	11	17	17	13	7	5	5	10	11	10
Snowy	13	10	6	1	-	-	-	-	-	-	3	9
Sunlight	3	4,5	5,5	7,5	9	11	12	11,5	9,5	7	5	3,5

Table: All averages of temperature
Source: www.weatherbase.com www.ankara.climatemps.com

Currency

The currency in Turkey is the Turkish Lira, commonly abbreviated as TL but also referred to as TRY and newly represented by the symbol ₺.

A 1 lira coin very much resembles a 1 euro coin. 1 TL is worth 100 kuruş, but be aware that any amount less than 5 kuruş is very rarely given in change (prices are often rounded up or down at the time of payment). Turkish banknotes have 6 values: 200, 100, 50, 20, 10 and 5. Unfortunately fake banknotes are in circulation and sometimes a cashier might refuse your banknote. As anywhere, always be sure to check your change.

The old lira was valid until 2008. Make sure you do not get old lira coins as exchange (huge numbers will be a quick indication of this). The lira is worth 1 million old lira, and a lot of people, particularly older folk, still refer to amounts with "million" after the true value. They hardly ever really mean a million new Turkish Lira.

Over the past few years the exchange rate has generally been between 2-2.9 TL to the Euro. The US Dollar has fluctuated between 2 TL in wintertime and 1.65 TL in summertime. Rates are generally better in winter.

ATMs (*Bankamatik*) can be found everywhere in Ankara, usually outside banks but sometimes in little booths by the road. Your bank might charge you for taking out money, please consult them for fees.

Credit cards are widely accepted, except in the very smallest restaurants and shops. These kind of small enterprises often prefer to take cash and in some cases where the venue does accept credit cards you might be charged less if you pay with cash. For large purchases you will be asked if you want to pay in instalments (*taksitli*). It is always cheaper, as in other countries, to pay direct (*peşin*, *nakit*, or most simply "*tek çekim*").

You can change money at exchange offices *(döviz bürosu)*. They offer the best rates and are trustworthy. Updated rates are usually displayed on an electronic board. A couple of exchange offices: Ertan Döviz on Tunalı Hilmi Caddesi (No: 94) and Özaltın Döviz on Uğur Mumcu Caddesi (No: 38/A)

You might also be able to change currency in your hotel, but in most cases this is (much) more expensive.

Public Transport

Travel by Bus Long Distance

As well as transport in the city, buses (or, more specifically, coaches) are frequently used for long distance journeys in Turkey. These long distance coaches are a comfortable and cheap alternative to flying. The best known agencies are Kamil Koç, Varan, Pamukkale and Ulusoy. You can buy tickets online or at ticket offices. There are offices situated on Tunalı Hilmi Caddesi and on Turan Güneş Bulvarı and at several other places. Try looking on the websites for more information.

www.ulusoy.com.tr (Turkish and English)
www.kamilkoc.com.tr (Turkish only)
www.pamukkale.com.tr (Turkish only)
www.varan.com.tr (Turkish only)
www.nilufer.com.tr (Turkish only)

Most buses leave from the bus terminal (AŞTİ) at Konya Yolu (or Mevlana Bulvarı). Tickets can also be purchased at the desks there.

Travel by Bus within the City

Within the city there are two types of buses: public and commercial. The public buses, run by the municipality, are called *Belediye Otobüsü* and are mostly blue/white (occasionally red) with EGO written on the sides. To use these buses you need an Ankara card, which can be bought at kiosks with the Ankara kart logo or at the SmartBanko or MiniBanko machines, which can be found in the metro stations. For

a list of selling points see *www.ankara-kart.com.tr/uye-isyerleri*. You need to add value to the card, which can be done at the kiosks or at the Banko machines. You can also use the card for the metro. A single journey at the time of writing is 1.75 TL (within the city). A single normal (disposable) ticket is 2.60 TL. To go outside the city (e.g. Esenboga airport or Elmadag) you pay more.

Information about the EGO bus routes and their timetables can be found at *www.ego.gov.tr.* Click in the left menu on "*Şehir içi ulaşım web bilgi sistemi*". A new window with the EGO bus routes open. Click in the left menu on the fifth option "*Nasıl gi-derim?*", type in from where (*Nereden*) to where (*Ner-eye*) you want to go. An EGO app is available for iPhones and android devices (search for EGO Ankara). Bus routes are not available at the bus stops. Unfortunately all in-formation is only provided in Turkish.

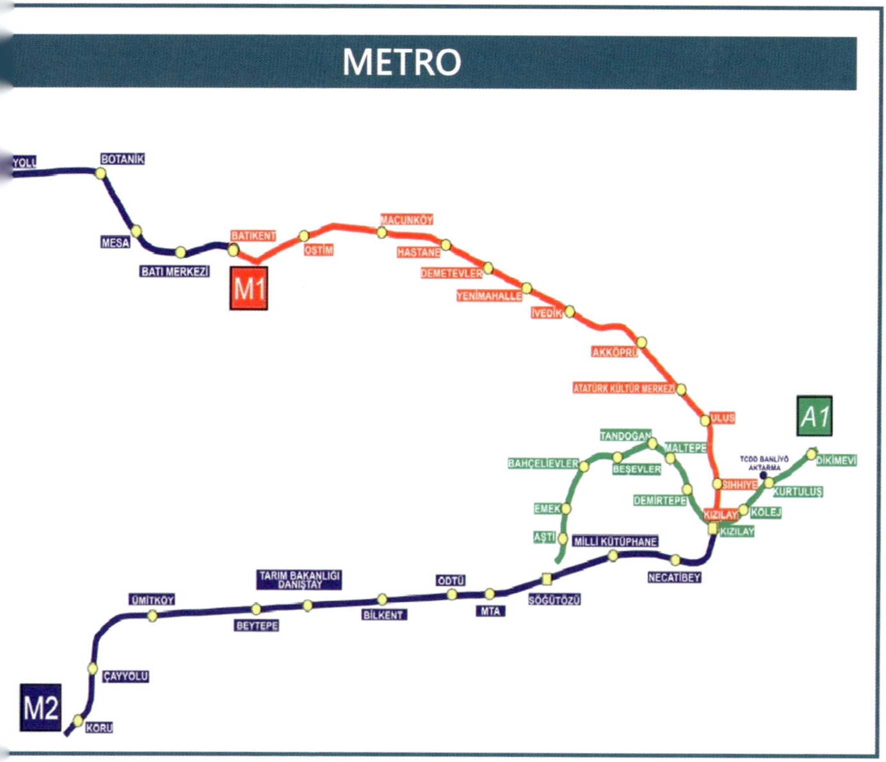

The privately run buses are called *Halk Otobüsü* and are usually referred to as the *Mavi Otobüs* (blue bus since they are blue). These buses only accept cash. You buy a ticket from the conductor who will be usually sitting in the middle of the bus in a small booth. Tickets are 2 TL per ride at the time of writing. They mostly follow the exact same routes as the EGO buses, sometimes doubling up to track the course of two EGO routes (many EGO buses turn around at Kızılay, some of the matching blue buses continue on another route).

Metro

Ankara's metro system will be greatly extended in the coming few years, but for now there are 2 routes through the city: Ankaray and Metro. The sole connection between Metro and Ankaray occurs at Kızılay station. The fare for a single journey on either line is the same as the EGO bus and the same EGO card tickets are used here. Route maps can be obtained from any underground station, EGO cards from the stations or over ground kiosks. Working hours are 06:00-00:00.

The Metro line runs from AŞTİ Batıkent (in the north of the city), and from Çayyolu (in the west of the city) to Kızılay, the modern-day centre of Ankara.

Ankaray line runs from (Ankara Intercity Bus Station), the coach terminal, in the west, passes through Kızılay and ends in Dikimevi.

Dolmuş

Dolmuş buses are small blue minibuses, a sort of collective taxi which follows a specific route. The routes are normally displayed on signs hanging inside the windscreen and printed on the sides. The routes can sometimes differ due to heavy traffic or road closures. The driver will usually ask if anyone needs a certain stop, and skip it if nobody replies. This is rare, but pay attention. You can hop on and hop off of a dolmuş wherever you want. Hail a dolmuş by sticking out a hand, and

get off wherever you want by asking the driver in Turkish: "*inecek var*". You pay the driver as soon as is practical after you get on. Fares within the city are mostly fixed at 2 TL; some very long journeys may be more and fares will be displayed somewhere in the front of the vehicle. If you are sitting at the front behind the driver be prepared to pass the money to the driver from passengers behind you. You will be expected to handle change too and it can get tricky. Try sitting at the back!

The municipality fixes the relatively cheap fares. This is a very practical means of transportation and much cheaper than a taxi, although you have to be familiar with the different areas in Ankara and learn the various routes these buses take. In busy areas (Kızılay, Ulus, etc.) you will find dolmuş terminals.

Train

If you want to travel out of Ankara, the train now offers a good alternative to coaches and aeroplanes. There are new high speed trains to İstanbul, Konya, and Eskişehir. For more information about trains see *www.tcdd.gov.tr.*

Airport

Ankara has one large airport (Esenboğa Havaalanı) with both a national and international terminal.

The cheapest way to get to the airport is by Havaş coach, which leaves from the AŞTİ bus terminal. You can buy your ticket on the bus for 10 TL and the journey to the airport will take around an hour. Coaches depart every half hour between 2:00 AM and 10:00 PM and are departures overnight are adjusted daily according to aircraft arrivals and departures. You can also board Havaş at Atatürk Kültür Merkezi (Culture Centre) near Kızılay, which might be more convenient.

It goes without saying that Havaş buses also go the other way around, from the airport to the city centre. For more information see *www.havas.net/en/shuttle-parking/ankara.*

Taxi

Taxies are pretty cheap when compared to most European countries, and in Ankara (as opposed to İstanbul) they are still reliable and trustworthy. The meter starts at 2.70 TL. Most taxi drivers only speak Turkish so make sure the driver understands where you are going –try showing it on a map or in this guide! The drivers tend not to use GPS systems and often do not know all the streets, so they frequently use their phones/radios or pull alongside other cars to ask colleagues. Do not worry about this. It is common practice and in almost all cases you will end up in the right place.

Etiquette

Turkey is more conservative than most Western countries. Although there are a lot of modern young people, Turkish people overall will dress more conservatively. If you visit the modern or student quarters of the city, there will be no problem. But to avoid problems and staring please keep in mind to dress appropriately while going to the more traditional neighbourhoods like Ulus.

Tipping

Taxi drivers do not expect a tip and even round down the amount sometimes. If you round up or give 1 or 2 TL extra they will appreciate it however. As for the attendants at petrol stations, if they clean your windscreen or some similar extra service, 1 or 2 TL will be appreciated (and in this case somewhat expected).

At other places like restaurants, *hamams* and hair dressers you can give a discretionary tip of about 10%.

Smoking

Smoking is forbidden in public places but most restaurants and café's offer outside (in many cases covered) smoking areas. In the winter these are often heated by outside heaters. Smoking is very common in Turkey.

Health

In Turkey it is advisable not to drink water from the tap –indeed a large proportion of locals only drink bottled water. The tap water is quite highly chlorinated –you can smell it. Bottled water is available everywhere and is very affordable. Large bottles offer better value, and huge 19 litre bottles are available in supermarkets.

If you need medical attention, try to go to a private hospital (*özel hastane*) if you can afford it. Compared to Western-Euro-

Bangladesh
Birlik Mah. 391. Cad. No: 16 Çankaya
Tel: 495 27 19-495 27 20

Belarus
Abidin Daver Sokak No: 17 Çankaya
Tel: 441 67 69/70

Belgium
Mahatma Gandi Cad. No: 55 Gaziosmanpaşa
Tel: 405 61 66

Bosnia
Turan Emeksiz Sok. Park Blokları B-Blok
No: 3/9-10 Gaziosmanpaşa
Tel: 427 36 02/03

Brazil
Reşit Galip Caddesi İlkadım Sokak No: 1
Gaziosmanpaşa
Tel: 448 18 40

Bulgaria
Atatürk Blv. No: 124
Kavaklıdere
Tel: 467 20 71-427 51 42

Canada
Cinnah Cad. No: 58
Çankaya
Tel: 409 27 00

Chile
Reşit Galip Cad. Hirfanlı Sok. No: 14/1-3
Gaziosmanpaşa
Tel: 447 34 18

China
Gölgeli Sok. No: 34 Gaziosmanpaşa
Tel: 436 06 28

Croatia
Kelebek Sokak No: 15/A Gaziosmanpaşa
Tel: 446 08 31-446 94 60

Cuba
Şölen Sok. No: 8 Çankaya
Tel: 442 89 70

Czech Republic
Kaptanpaşa Sok. No: 15 Gaziosmanpaşa
Tel: 405 61 39/41

Denmark
Mahatma Gandhi Cad. No: 74
Gaziosmanpaşa
Tel: 446 61 41

Egypt
Atatürk Blv. No: 126
Kavaklıdere
Tel: 426 10 26-468 22 40-426 61 32

Estonia
Gölgeli Sok. No: 16
Gaziosmanpaşa
Tel: 405 69 70

Finland
Kader Sok. No: 44
Gaziosmanpaşa
Tel: 457 44 00

France
Paris Cad. No: 70 Kavaklıdere
Tel: 455 45 45

Georgia
Oran Diplomatik Site Kılıç Ali Sok. No: 12
Tel: 491 80 30/31

Germany
Atatürk Blv. No: 114
Kavaklıdere
Tel: 455 51 00

Greece
Zia Ür-Rahman Cad. No: 9-11
Gaziosmanpaşa
Tel: 448 03 87-448 06 47

Hungary
Sancak Mah. Layoş Koşut Cad. No: 2
Yıldız-Çankaya
Tel: 442 22 73

India
Cinnah Caddesi No: 77/A
Çankaya
Tel: 438 21 95/98

Indonesia
Abdullah Cevdet Sokak No: 10 Çankaya
Tel: 438 21 90

Iran
Tahran Cad. No: 10 Kavaklıdere
Tel: 468 28 20/21

Iraq
Turan Emeksiz Sok. No: 11
Gaziosmanpaşa
Tel: 468 48 34-468 74 21

Ireland
Uğur Mumcu Cad. MNG Binası No: 88
B Blok Kat: 3 Gaziosmanpaşa
Tel: 459 10 00

Israel
Mahatma Gandhi Cad. No: 85
Gaziosmanpaşa
Tel: 459 75 00

Italy
Atatürk Blv. No: 118 Kavaklıdere
Tel: 457 42 00

Japan
Reşit Galip Cad. No: 81
Gaziosmanpaşa
Tel: 446 05 00

Jordan
Dede Korkut Sok. No: 18 Mesnevi
Çankaya
Tel: 440 20 54

Kazakhstan
Oran Diplomatik Site Kılıç Ali Sokak No: 6
Çankaya
Tel: 491 91 00

Kosovo
Hirfanlı Sokak No: 14/2
Gaziosmanpaşa
Tel: 446 70 54

Korea
Alaçam Sokak No: 5 Cinnah Caddesi
Çankaya
Tel: 468 48 21/22/23

Kuwait
Reşit Galip Cad. No: 110
Gaziosmanpaşa
Tel: 445 05 76/80

Kyrgyzstan
Murat Mah. Boyabat Sok. No: 11 Eren Apt.
Gaziosmanpaşa
Tel: 446 84 08/9

Latvia
Reşit Galip Cad. No: 95
Gaziosmanpaşa
Tel: 405 61 36/38

Lithuania
Mahatma Gandi Cad. No: 17/8-9
Gaziosmanpaşa
Tel: 447 07 66

Macedonia
Karaca Sok., No: 24/5-6
Gaziosmanpaşa
Tel: 439 92 04/08

Malyasia
Mahatma Gandhi Caddesi No: 58
Gaziosmanpaşa
Tel: 446 35 47/48

Mexico
Kırkpınar Sokak No: 18/6
Çankaya
Tel: 442 30 33-442 23 82-442 25 07

Moldova
Kaptanpaşa Sok. No: 49 Gaziosmanpaşa
Tel: 446 55 27

Mongolia
Koza Sokak No: 109 Gaziosmanpaşa
Tel: 446 79 77

Morocco
Reşit Galip Cad. Rabat Sok. No: 11
Gaziosmanpaşa
Tel: 437 60 20/21

The Netherlands
Hilal Mah. Hollanda Cad. No: 5 Yıldız
Çankaya
Tel: 409 18 00

New Zealand
Kızkulesi Sok. No: 11 Gaziosmanpaşa
Tel: 446 33 32

Norway
Kırkpınar Sok. No: 18/3-4 Gaziosmanpaşa
Tel: 405 80 10

Oman
Mahatma Gandhi Cad. No: 63
Gaziosmanpaşa
Tel: 447 06 30/31

Pakistan
İran Cad. No: 37
Gaziosmanpaşa
Tel: 427 14 10/14

Palestine
Filistin Sok. No: 45
Gaziosmanpaşa
Tel: 436 08 23/24

Philippines
Mahatma Gandhi Cad. No: 56
Gaziosmanpaşa
Tel: 446 58 31-447 03 50

Poland
Atatürk Blv. No: 241 Kavaklıdere
Tel: 457 20 00

Portugal
Kuleli Sok. No: 26 Gaziosmanpaşa
Tel: 405 60 28

Qatar
Oran Diplomatik Site Bakü Sok. No: 6
Tel: 441 13 64/6

Romania
Bükreş Sok. No: 4 Kavaklıdere
Tel: 466 37 06

Russia
Karyağdı Sok. No: 5 Kavaklıdere
Tel: 439 21 22

Saudi Arabia
Turan Emeksiz Sok. No: 6 Gaziosmanpaşa
Tel: 468 55 40/42

Serbia
Paris Cad. No: 47 Kavaklıdere
Tel: 426 02 36

Slovenia
Kırlangıç Sok. No: 36 Gaziosmanpaşa
Tel: 405 42 21/22

South Africa
Filistin Sok. No: 27 Gaziosmanpaşa
Tel: 405 68 61

Spain
Abdullah Cevdet Sok. No: 8 Çankaya
Tel: 440 21 69

Sudan
Mahatma Gandi Cad. No: 48 Gaziosmanpaşa
Tel: 446 63 27/28

Sweden
Katip Çelebi Sok. No: 7 Kavaklıdere
Tel: 455 41 00

Switzerland
Atatürk Blv. No: 247 Kavaklıdere
Tel: 457 31 00

Syria
Sedat Simavi Sok. No: 40 Çankaya
Tel: 440 96 57/58

Taiwan
Rabat Sok. No: 16
Gaziosmanpaşa
Tel: 436 72 55

Tajikistan
Mahatma Gandhi Cad. No: 30
Gaziosmanpaşa
Tel: 446 16 02

Thailand
Koza Sok. No: 87 Gaziosmanpaşa
Tel: 437 43 18-437 52 48

Tunisia
Oran Diplomatik Site
Ferit Recai Ertuğrul Cad. No: 19
Tel: 491 96 35/36

Turkmenistan
Koza Sok. No: 28
Gaziosmanpaşa
Tel: 441 71 22/23/24/26

United Arab Emirates
Turan Güneş Blv. Yüksek Sancak Mah.
571 Cad. 608 Sok. No: 3 Çankaya
Tel: 490 14 14

Ukraine
Sancak Mah. 206. Sok. No: 17 Yıldız
Çankaya
Tel: 441 54 99

United Kingdom
Şehit Ersan Cad. No: 46/A
Çankaya
Tel: 455 33 44

United States of America
Atatürk Blv. No: 110
Kavaklıdere
Tel: 455 55 55

Uzbekistan
Sancak Mah. 549. Sok. No: 3 Yıldız
Çankaya
Tel: 441 38 71

Vatican
Birlik Mah. 428. Cad. No: 37 Çankaya
Tel: 495 35 14

Venezuela
Cinnah Cad. No: 78/2 Çankaya
Tel: 439 31 98-438 71 35

Vietnam
Çayhane Sok. No: 34 Gaziosmanpaşa
Tel: 446 80 49

Yemen
Mahmut Yesari Sok. No: 10 Çankaya
Tel: 447 68 61

Holidays

There are two types of public holidays in Turkey. The non-religious holidays have the same date every year while the Islamic ones follow the Muslim lunar calendar and therefore shift dates. It is common that a half day before a major public or religious holiday is given off as well to prepare the feast.

Non-religious Holidays

1 January	New Year's day
23 April	National Sovereignty & Children's Day (anniversary of the establishment of the Turkish Grand National Assembly)
19 May	Youth & Sports Day (commemorates the beginning of the War of Independence)
30 August	Victory Day (celebrates the victory over the invading Greek forces during the War of Independence)
29 October	Republic Day (commemorates the proclamation of the republic in 1923 by *Atatürk*)

On 10 November at 9:05 o'clock *Atatürk*'s passing is commemorated with a 2 minute silence. People and traffic (even on highways) stand still for 2 minutes throughout Turkey, which is quite a sight to behold.

Religious Holidays

As the Islamic holidays follow the Muslim calendar and the dates differ every year, shifting by 12 days. During *Ramazan* (Ramadan), all Muslims fast during the day, apart from pregnant or nursing women, young children, the infirmed, the aged and travellers. After sunset and before sunrise people can eat and drink. It might be hard in some conservative areas to get food or drinks during the day throughout *Ramazan*. You might also be asked to take food or drinks out of sight. It might be slightly crude to walk along the streets in these areas eating or drinking. In 2013 *Ramazan* started on 9th of July.

Şeker Bayramı

This feast celebrates the end of *Ramazan* and lasts for 3 days. During this time children go from door to door to ask for candies and sweets (much like American children might do during Halloween). People visit friends and families with gifts of home-cooked food, sweets, and chocolates. In 2013 *Şeker Bayramı* was celebrated on 8th of August.

Kurban Bayramı

This is the feast of the Sacrifice. It commemorates the sacrifice İbrahim was willing to make for God of his son İsmail. Instead God allowed him to sacrifice a sheep. During this feast families slaughter an animal or more often purchase an animal to be slaughtered in their name. Sometimes a few families will get together to purchase an animal. The meat is butchered and divided among the families and poor or needy people in the neighbourhood. After that they prepare a feast. You will not see much of this in the modern parts of the city but out in the countryside and in some more traditional areas you might see people in their yards or gardens butchering a sheep or cow. If that is not for you, avoid such areas on the first day of the feast. It is a 4 day holiday, and in 2013 it was celebrated between the 14th and 18th of October.

Ankara Festivals

Ankara Jazz Festival (February)

A festival organized by the Ankara Jazz Society and the Leo Organization for Jazz lovers. It takes place across several different venues.

Ankara Film Festival (March)

An annual film festival, featuring documentaries and film house quality screenings. The festival supports young and up-and-coming directors, actors and actresses. (For more information see *www.filmfestankara.org.tr/en*)

International Ankara Music Festival (April)

A yearly festival, running since 1981 and including symphonic and chamber music, tap dance, musical comedies, guitar performances and song recitals among other things. The festival brings together talented artists and musicians from around the world. (For more information see www.ankarafestival.com/en)

Flying Broom International Women's Film Festival (May)

The festival aims at making women more visible in the cinema industry and promoting women's contributions to the field. Every year films from different countries are screened. Besides special film selections, there are panel discussions, films readings and exhibitions. (For more information see www.*festival.ucansupurge.org/english/index.php*)

International Asia-Europe Biennial (May-June)

Held bi-annually to celebrate the city's ties between Europe and Asia. This notable fair presents culture, food, music, song, and dance and highlights long-established intercontinental trade links.

Shopping Festival (June)

The first Ankara Shopping Festival ran from the 8th of June until the 1st of July in 2012. Whether it will become a yearly tradition is unknown, but seems likely. During the 2012 Shopping Festival various shows and entertainments took place within the shopping malls and busy shopping streets. In the evenings, concerts were held. Most if not all shops in the applicable districts offered special discounts. (For more information see *www.ankarashoppingfest.com.tr*)

Open Air Cinema (June-September)

From June to September an open air screen shows movies every Tuesday at 9:00 PM outside the Cer Modern art gallery. Tickets are 10 TL per person. (For more information see *www.cermodern.org/sinema-eng.html*)

Bilkent International Anatolian Festival (August)

Set up by the university's Music and Performing Arts Faculty, this event attracts thousands of music lovers and performers to the city. An innovative program includes classical orchestral music, alternative acts and traditional regional folk music and dancing. (For more information see *www.bilkent.edu.tr*)

Sports

Ankara is not exactly a haven for sport lovers. Even joggers will not have a particularly easy time on the pavements and streets. But there are a few things to be found.

Outdoor Fitness

In many of the parks or sometimes just along the side of the road you can find a kind of outdoor gymnasium –hardy metal equipment, mostly very simple but quite effective. Ankara's fitness fanatics dress up for the occasion in their best new tracksuits and you will see running the track or exercising on the machines. As fitness centres are expensive in Ankara, this is a good alternative as long as it is not snowing. The outdoor equipment is also very popular among older people during the daytime, keeping spry.

Skiing and Sledging

When there is enough snow you can ski on Elmadağ, which is just around half an hour's drive from the city centre. It has only one drag-lift and main piste but it is perfectly adequate for a bit of fun. The highest point is 1850 metres going down to 1500 metres at the base. Skis can be rented on-site at a very reasonable rate. You must buy tickets to use the lift, again quite inexpensive.

Sledges can be rented too, and during the winter weekends it can be very crowded on the lower portion of the slope with families (mainly kids) sledging at death-defying speeds. Driving back to Ankara you can end up in a traffic jam because people parking their cars at the side of the road and BBQing in the snow. It is a very typical winter past-time which might sound odd but is surprisingly enjoyable. Try to go early and leave before lunch-time, which is when the area starts to get very busy.

Ice Skating

There are several ice skating venues in Ankara:

- Gençlik ve Spor İl Müdürlüğü Buz Pateni Sarayı (Belpa)
  Akdeniz Cad. No: 57, Bahçelievler

  Entrance fee: 9 TL weekdays, 10 TL weekends.
  Open from 10:00 – 22:00. Website: *sgspor.com/index.php*

- Acity Outlet Alışveriş Merkezi
  İstanbul Yolu 5. km. Fatih Sultan Mehmet Bulv. No: 244 Ostim

  Entrance fee: 9 TL weekdays, 10 TL weekends.
  Open from 10:00 – 22:00. Website: *sgspor.com/index.php*

- Ankara Optimum Outlet Buz Pisti, Yeşilova Mh. Ayaş-Ankara Yolu Bulvarı (Ayaş Yolu) No: 93 Tel: 281 05 81

  Entrance fee (45 minutes): 11 TL weekdays, 12 TL weekends, 17 TL for a private lesson of 30 minutes.
  Open from 10:00 – 22:00. Website: *www.funonice.net*

- Kızılay, Kurtuluş Parkı: Ice skating rink, only in wintertime.

- Keçiören, Altınpark: Ice skating rink, only in wintertime.

Cycling

It's very uncommon, although growing, to see people riding bikes in Ankara. It is rather dangerous to ride on the roads as cars do not tend to take much care and there are no cycle lanes available. The only nice biking area is around Eymir Gölü. You can rent bikes at the parking area just outside the main entrance. The lake is a nice natural area and only a few cars are allowed to drive in (you must pay a fee or be a METU university member). Be careful of the stray (wild) dogs around the lake.

Eymir Gölü can be reached from Turan Güneş Bulvarı. Coming from the city centre drive in the direction of Panora Shopping Mall; when you get to the TRT building, turn left. There is a sign that reads Eymir Gölü. Follow the road next to the TRT downhill. You will have a marvellous view from there but pay attention because the road is very steep and narrow. The entrance is at the bottom of the road, on the right. The bikes can be hired at the car park on the left.

Hiking and Running

Not just for cycling, Eymir Gölü is also a nice place to go for a gentle hike or a run. The lake's circumference is approximately 11 kilometres.

Running fans often use the lake for their work out. During the weekends you will see runners in groups, mostly in the morning. Occasionally half marathons are organised to take place here.

As with for biking, be wary of stray dogs milling around.

If you want to go on a bigger hike, the best place to go is Soğuksu Milli Parkı in Kızılcahamam, some 1.5 hour drive out of Ankara. Organised hiking treks take place every weekend.

Swimming

There are a few public swimming pools in Ankara. The public ones are mostly aquaparks, with water slides and such. Access fees to swimming pools are quite expensive.

Aquapark, İncek

The biggest one is probably Aquapark, on the İncek Bulvarı, behind Olympic Park Hotel. It also has slides. It is only open from June until September from 10:00 to 18:00 during weekdays and until 19:00 on weekends. Entrance fee is 30 TL on weekdays, 35 TL on Saturday and Sunday. Kids until 6 years for free, from 7-12 with 20% discount. Entrance for men only (without family or female company) is not possible.

There is a free transport from the corner of Kumrular Sokak in Kızılay to the Aquapark, in front of Ümitköy Galeria at 10:30 and 11:30 on weekdays, at 10:30, 11:30 and 12:30 on weekends. There is transportation back to the city centre between 17:00 and 18:00.

Çiçek Aqua Park, Sincan

Another aquapark, Çiçek Aqua Park, is situated in Sincan on Eskişehir Yolu 32. km (Aşağıyurtçu Köyü Çıkışı, Çiçektepe Köyü Girişi). Entrance fee is 30 TL on weekdays, 35 TL on Saturday and Sunday. Kids until 5 years for free, from 5-12 50% discount.
www.cicektepeaquapark.com (only Turkish).

Within Atılım University grounds is Atılım Garden. It is also situated on İncek Bulvarı. A nice place to have a Sunday's brunch and afterwards to take a dip in their pool. Entrance to the pool is around 25 TL per person.

Most sports clubs also have normal swimming pools. Sometimes they allow people to use it if you pay a day entrance or a special pool-only fee.

Sports Clubs

- Dorupark Sağlıklı Yaşam, Yeni Atabilge Sitesi Çayyolu 2 Yaşamkent
- Sports International Bilkent, 1. Cadde Bilkent
- Base Life Club, Angora Cad. No: 209/10 Beysupark Çayyolu
- Sporthill, Ahlatlıbel Mah. Güneykent Sitesi 52. Cad. No: 5/A İncek

There are many more than those listed above. Many shopping malls also integrate some kind of sports centre/fitness club as do some bigger hotels.

Horse Riding

- Ankara Atlı Spor Kulübü, Çiftlik Cad. No: 22 Beştepe
  www.aask.org.tr
- The Pony Club, Tolga Köksal Aydın (English speaking)
  Tel: 215 67 58 e-mail: *pony@aask.org.tr*

Shopping

If you want to shop for authentic souvenirs, the best places are Hisar (Ulus), the area within or around the citadel, and on Çıkrıkçılar Yokuşu (see chapter *Hisar*).

Modern shopping streets can be found in Kızılay, such as on Atatürk Bulvarı around Kızılay Square (see chapter *Kızılay*), the area around the Sheraton hotel and the small shopping mall Karum, the area around Kuğulu Park and all along Tunalı Hilmi Caddesi.

Ankara has the highest amount of shopping centre leasable area per capita in the country, more than İstanbul. This is stimulated by the municipality. The yearly shopping festival is an example of the city's desire to be a shopping destination but you can see it plainly by the sheer number of shopping malls. Most of them are found along the main western arterial road, the Eskişehir Yolu. Armada, CEPA, Kentpark and Gordion are found along this street, in some cases very close to one another. The current largest, with over 300 shops, is Ankamall on the Mevlana Bulvarı (or Konya Yolu). This is also the only mall accessible by metro: Akköprü station on the Metro line.

The shopping malls mostly carry the same national and international brands. They are also the main homes of other entertainment venues such as cinemas, bowling alleys, food courts, play centres and small playgrounds or other entertainment for kids. Nata Vega shopping mall on Doğukent Bulvarı (east of the city, next to IKEA) even has a large aquarium.

Cinemas

As stated previously, most cinemas are to be found within shopping malls. At most of these cinemas, international films are shown in English (or their original language) with Turkish subtitles. Occasionally films will be dubbed, usually marked *"dublaj"* on the poster but it is a good idea to check. There are cinemas in Ankamall (including an IMAX screen), CEPA, Kentpark, Panora, Bilkent Center, Optimum and Nata Vega/Anatolium, as well as other smaller malls. The mall cinemas are generally well maintained and of high standards.

In Kızılay next to Kocatepe Camii you can find the Kızılırmak cinema and the cosier Büyülü Fener cinema. Disadvantage of some of the cinemas is the poor sound insulation between rooms.

To check the latest screenings see *www.intersinema.com/ankara-sinemalari/* (Turkish only).

Nightlife

As Ankara has several universities, and thus thousands of students, it also has plenty of cafés, bars and clubs. There are no "super clubs" here, more popular are live music venues, but there are a few dance music places to be found. The nicest cafés can be found in Yüksel Caddesi and around (see chapter *Kızılay*) and Bestekar Sokak, near Tunalı Hilmi Caddesi (see chapter *Kavaklıdere*). If you are looking to dance into the night, try places like Eski Yeni (electronic music) or Pasaj (usually live bands). Both are near Kızılay.

Restaurants

Food is an important part of the Turkish culture and you will find outlets everywhere. Most restaurants offer fairly traditional Turkish cuisine with the main exception of the restaurants in Gaziosmanpaşa and Çayyolu and to a certain extent 7. Cadde in Bahçelievler. Most expats go to these areas if they have an appetite for something else. Çayyolu features an avenue of restaurants, outside the main city. Closer to the city centre, Gaziosmanpaşa (mostly Filistin Sokak and the surrounding streets) offers the most restaurants with foreign cuisine.

Restaurant suggestions per area are made in chapter *Restaurants*.

Hamams

When visiting Turkey, it would be a waste not to visit a *hamam* (Turkish bath). Hotels often have their own *hamams,* but the oldest and most authentic ones can be found in Ulus. A proper Turkish *hamam* is, contrary to popular belief, not a comprehensive spa or wellness experience. The *hamam* is a bathhouse pure and simple, but nonetheless very relaxing.

In all *hamams* you have to wear either swimming gear or at the very least underwear. Men and women have their own entrances and *hamam* areas. You will start by taking a shower and then moving to the sauna or steam room until your skin is warm and ready to be scrubbed. The staff of the *hamam* will tell you when you are good to go. Then it is time to take your position on a marble platform and let the staff give you the treatment you asked for. They will always wash and scrub you and if asked will give you a massage or any other treatments they offer. A typical *hamam* session takes about an hour.

You will pay a standard entrance fee for the use of the *hamam*. For every treatment, like scrubbing (*keselenmek*) and massage (*masaj*), a fee is added to your total. There should always be a clear price list with the treatments listed. If you cannot see one displayed, ask for a copy. Sometimes you will also pay for towels, bathrobes and the soap, a fee you can save if you bring your own. When you leave the *hamam* you will be billed what you owe. A normal visit costs between the 30 and 40 TL and it is fairly customary to tip the man or woman who gave you the treatment 5-10 TL. You can do this at the end.

Şengül Hamamı

This *hamam* was probably built in the second half of the 15th century. Inside, the bath is constructed entirely from white marble and features Ottoman patterns and a beautiful dome with holes in a star pattern.

Denizciler Caddesi,
Acı Çeşme Sok. No: 3 Ulus
www.sengulhamami.com.
Opening hours: Daily between
6:00 – 24:00 (men's section)
6:00 – 20:00 (Friday 22:00) (women's section)

Around the central massage platform there are private areas which make it a cosy *hamam*. They also offer a special coffee treatment here. You will smell like a coffee bean for hours, which may or may not excite you, but regardless make sure you do not wear your brand new bikini if you chose this treatment as it might leave some stains on light textile. It is, however, very relaxing and leaves you with baby soft skin.

Tarihi Karacabey Hamamı

Tarihi Karacabey Hamamı, opposite the clock tower in Hamamönü, dates from 1444. It is the oldest *hamam* in Ankara, with beautiful architectural domes. This *hamam* was restored in 1988, and then refurbished and modernised in 2012. All marble in the steam baths and the wet areas was renewed in such a way that the authentic atmosphere was not affected. They have a men's and women's section here and offer a wide range of different treatments. The male dressing area has a barber, where you can get a real Turkish style shave.

Talatpaşa Bulvarı No: 101 Hamamönü,
www.tarihikaracabeyhamami.com
Opening hours: Daily between 5:30-24:00 (men's section)
7:30-20:00 (women's section)

Eyne Bey Hamamı

Adnan Saygun Caddesi No: 11
Ulus www.eynebeyhamami.com
Opening hours: 24 hours a day

This *hamam,* dating from 1502, is open 24 hours a day but is open to men only. It is quite a large venue, with a swimming pool and a plethora of staff for massages and scrubbing. Lots of local men, of all ages, visit for a shower, a quick Turkish bath and a scrub. It can get quite crowded at times. The staff can be pushy, trying to offer extra treatments or asking for extra money. Arranging the price in advance for a fixed treatment is strongly recommended.

Practical websites with information about Ankara

www.worldtravelguide.net/ankara (for trips and tours)
www.madeeasierguides.com/index.html
www.members.virtualtourist.com/m/a0e8a/1c4b87/4

Restaurants

Restaurants

Restaurants and café's change often, especially in the Gaziosmanpaşa area, but here are a few of our favourites. We've mostly chosen places that have been around a long time, for the reason just mentioned. Restaurants are listed by area.

This list is by no means exhaustive. There are many more good eateries in Ankara.

If you have a suggestion for future inclusion please e-mail the details to guideankara@gmail.com.

Food

Here are some translations of common words that might help you when eating out or going drinking:

Drinks

Ayran	A drink made from yoghurt and water and, usually, salt. More refreshing than it sounds, commonly served with kebab dishes.
Çay	Tea. It can be strong, ask for *açık çay* for a weaker one.
Semaver	The two-stage Turkish tea pot. On top is a pot of strong tea and below is boiling water. Pour a measure of tea and dilute according to your taste.
Kahve	Coffee. Usually this will be instant Nescafe or similar. Ask for *sütlü kahve* if you want milk or *sade* if you want black coffee.
Bira	Beer. Usually Efes, the national brand and thoroughly drinkable.
Şarap	Wine. Ask for *kırmızı* for red, *beyaz* for white. Turkish wines are perfectly good. Do not be surprised however if they serve red wine chilled.
Rakı	The Turkish national spirit –an aniseed– based liquor, very similar to Pernod or indeed Ouzo (but best not to bring that up).

Food

Gözleme	Savoury pancakes sandwiched together, generally filled with cheese (*peynirli*), spinach (*ıspanaklı*), potatoes (*patatesli*) or minced meat (*kıymalı*).
Tost	Toasted sandwiches. Most commonly made with cheese (*peynirli*), sucuk (*sucuklu*) or both (*peynirli-sucuklu or karışık*).
Börek	Pastries often containing cheese and sometimes spinach.
Meze	Appetizers. There is a vast variety but common dishes include filled vine leaves (with minced meat and rice), mashed aubergine, crushed tomato and spices, humus, seaweed... Olive oil is often added in abundance and is very much part of the food, don't be scared if dishes look oily.
Mantı	The Turkish equivalent of ravioli, served hot with yoghurt and spices. Sometimes with a chilli sauce on top of the yogurt.
Balık	Fish. Often restaurants will serve only fish, and these are the places to go since they'll usually cook and serve it wonderfully. Generally the fish is served by itself with just salad or rocket leaves. Start with *meze* (see above).
Kebap / Kebab	*Şiş kebabı* Shish (pronounced the same way) kebab – meat grilled on a skewer. Most places will offer lamb (*kuzu*), chicken (*tavuk*) or liver (*ciğer*), sometimes beef (*dana*). *Döner kebabı* Meat cooked on a vertical spit, sliced off and either served on a plate with rice or chips (döner *servis*), or inside bread with salad (*döner ekmek*). *Adana kebabı* Minced meat grilled on a skewer, a bit like a long meatball (*köfte*, see below). Can be spicy, the *Urfa kebabı* is similar with more chilli if you prefer such things. Almost all regions of Turkey have their own speciality *Kebap*, try the local one!

Çiğ köfte	A common Turkish food which in the past was made from raw meat and spices. Today the raw meat variety is almost nowhere to be seen, particularly in cities. The vast majority of sellers produce a vegetarian version made from lentils, bulgur and herbs. It's eaten rolled in a lettuce leaf with a squirt of lemon juice.
Pide	Flatbread pizza.
Kokoreç	A large sausage, a bit like a döner, made from lamb's intestines, grilled on a spit then finely chopped and mixed with herbs and spices. It's usually eaten in a sandwich but sometimes served with chips and salad on a plate. A popular street food, but best bought only from reputable vendors.
Köfte	Minced or ground meat, usually beef or lamb (sometimes both), mixed with spices and/or onions and made into a meatball. Very popular. Served either on a plate with rice/chips/salad, or in a sandwich.
Makarna	Pasta.
Pasta	Cake. (Careful with this one not to mix it up with makarna!)

Establishments

Lokanta(sı) *Sofra(sı)*	Small restaurants serving Turkish cuisine.
Meyhane	A tavern, usually quite "local" places and sometimes best avoided. Stick to "bars" or "pubs" if you're not overly adventurous. However there are some good ones. See our suggestions.
Gazino	A form of "adult entertainment" bar, generally quite shady and definitely best avoided.

Hisar

Café Eski Ankara

This café is just across from the entrance to the Pirinç Han. In winter time the inside area provides a nice shelter from the cold weather. It offers (as do almost all of the surrounding restaurants) *gözleme* and other traditional Turkish food, and tea and coffee. It also offers a very nice view over Ankara. The staff is very friendly.

Café Eski Ankara, Pirinç Sokak No: 7/C Tel: 311 84 83

Kirit Café

Kirit Café is a very pleasant café teahouse, also serving Turkish food with a modern twist. Many of their menu items are made from organic products. They also buck the local trend by serving well-made Italian coffees and all sorts of teas, rather than just Nescafé and Turkish tea. They also sell felt hats, bags and slippers inside. A very nice place to stop if you're walking through.

Kirit Café, Koyunpazarı Sokak No: 60 Tel: 324 09 31

Çengelhan Brasserie & Café

This brasserie is a bit classier than the surrounding restaurants, and you will pay more for the privilege, but the location within the Çengelhan and its museum (admission free if you're a restaurant customer) is absolutely worth it. Both local and international dishes are offered, as well as some lovely local wines. There is also a spacious terrace overlooking the Ankara Citadel, excellent in spring or summer. A great place to visit, unless it's Monday (they are closed).

Çengelhan Brasserie & Café, Necati Bey Mahalesi, Depo Sokak Çengelhan Rahmi Mustafa Koç Müzesi No: 1 Tel: 309 68 00 cengelhan_brasserie@divan.com.tr.

www.divan.com.tr/ENG/Hotel-Destinations/Divan-Cukurhan/Food-and-Beverage

In the Citadel

AND Café

The entrance to AND café is through one of the remaining original citadel gates. This café's biggest draw is its fantastic location, up on top of the citadel with panoramic views over the city. The kitchen offers the standard traditional Turkish dishes, beer and wine are also served (which can be rare in this area).

AND Café, (end of) Kale Kapısı Sokak Tel: 312 79 78

Kınacızade Konağı

As well as being a restaurant, Kınacızade Konağı is also something of a museum (see chapter *In and Around the Citadel* for an explanation). It offers food from the traditional Turkish kitchen –gözleme is particularly nice, great for a light lunch.

Kınacızade Konağı, Kale Kaspısı Sokak No: 28 Tel: 324 57 14
www.kinacizadekonagi.com

Zenger Paşa Konak Restaurant

Like Kınacızade Konağı, this is another combined museum/restaurant. The first two floors feature displays of traditional Turkish clothing and furniture. The restaurant is on the third floor. As per most of the other restaurants within the citadel the kitchen serves Turkish cuisine. This is a good place to eat freshly made *mantı* (Turkish ravioli, served with yogurt and spices). Fixed price menus are available here too. Dearer than other nearby restaurants, again, but with a lovely view over Ankara.

Zenger Paşa Konağı, Doyran Sokak No:13 Tel: 311 70 70
www.zengerpasa.com

Hamamönü

In the summertime, Hamamönü's outdoor terraces are a great place to sit and enjoy a meal. Indeed, it becomes one of the liveliest places in Ankara. In Sanat Sokak (art street) owners set out stools in the square. Sit here and enjoy a *gözleme* and a cup of tea in the sunshine.

Two other favourites, restaurants in restored mansions, are:

Lezzet-i Tarih

This restaurant has possibly the best view over Hamamönü. It offers traditional Turkish cuisine as well as a large range of breakfasts (very nice on a sunny morning). Also a nice spot just to stop for a cup of tea or a Turkish coffee.

Lezzet-i Tarih, Mehmet Akif Ersoy Sokak No: 3
Tel: 312 71 71 and 312 73 37 www.lezzetitarih.com

Hanzade Konağı

Despite being in an old restored building, Hanzade Konağı has a very modern, clean interior. The menu offers *tosts* (toasted sandwiches), salads, hamburgers and breakfast platters, as well as meat and fish dishes. They also serve a nice range of *börek* (pastries).

Hanzade Konağı, Hacettepe Mahallesi, İnanlı Sokak (little street across from the Taceddin Camii) No: 5 Tel: 309 99 09 www.hanzadekonagi.com

Kızılay

Atatürk Bulvarı and Gazi Mustafa Kemal Bulvarı, the main streets, are home mainly to fast food restaurants (both Turkish and the familiar international brands). Venture into the side streets, the pedestrian area east of Atatürk Bulvarı, and you will find small restaurants offering Turkish food.

Sakarya Caddesi offers mainly traditional Turkish establishments. Some restaurants have live Anatolian music performances in the evenings. These can be quite loud, be warned.

Yüksel Caddesi offers a lot of student-y pubs, bars and restaurants. Most will offer Turkish food but, thanks to the students' demands, more and more international food is arriving. Selanik 2 Caddesi is a very "sweet" little street populated with ice creamstores and patisseries.

FLZ Café and Restaurant

This restaurant offers a nice view over of Ankara's busiest squares, and one of few local green areas (Güvenpark). The entrance is on Gazi Mustafa Kemal Bulvarı. It is in the same building as the "YKM" department store, find the lift labelled FLZ.

The menu offers sandwiches, salads, pizza, pasta, light snacks and a variety of meat and fish main dishes. Between 19:30 and 23:30 there is often live music. The restaurant is open from 8:30 in the morning until midnight.

FLZ Café and Restaurant, Gazi Mustafa Kemal Bulvarı YKM Building No: 3 D: 8 Tel: 418 22 33 www.flzrestaurant.com

Tavukçu Lokantası

This is one of Ankara's oldest rakı restaurants. *Rakı* being the national aniseed-based liquor (similar to Ouzo or Pernod). The venue was very popular back in the 1980s and, while it might look a bit old and tired, it is still a fantastic place to eat mezze, fish, chicken or liver and of course to drink *rakı*. They even offer fresh goat brains, for those who want to try something a little different. As dessert you'll be served fresh fruit.

Rakı is commonly served with fish and compliments it well. You cannot leave Turkey without trying it!

Tavukçu Lokantası, İnkılap Sokak No: 25/A Tel: 425 30 17

Around the Train Station

Between Atatürk Bulvarı and Anafartalar Caddesi, especially on Denizciler Caddesi, there are plenty of *Lokanta(sı)* or *Sofra(sı)* –smaller restaurants, generally offering Turkish food and often focusing on a specialty such as *kebap* or *çiğ köfte*.

DİVAN Cafeteria CERModern

Divan, next door to the CERModern art gallery, is a good stop for tea, lunch or a buffet brunch (on Sundays). It offers salads, sandwiches, pastas, pizzas, main dishes, as well as a wide range of cakes and sweets. When the museum is open in the evening Divan also opens for dinner.

During nice weather there is a terrace out front. It's a lovely place to sit; on busy days it can be hard to get the waiting staff's attention though.

Divan Cafeteria CERModern, Altınsoy Caddesi No: 3 Tel: 310 90 11

Tea Gardens in Gençlik Parkı

There are several of these scattered around the park. You will be given a semaver from which you can pour your own teas. Use the upper pot to pour a little bit of strong tea in your glass and then dilute it with the water from the tap on the lower pot. You may need to wait until the tea is brewed. Your waiter will be happy to help out.

The tea gardens do not generally offer meals. Some more enterprising ones might serve tost or hotdogs.

Atatürk Orman Çiftliği

Most of them on the Alparslan Türkeş Caddesi (Çiftlik Caddesi) and Silahtlar Caddesi offer *kebap, köfte* and other traditional Turkish dishes. The area has a lively atmosphere and friendly waiters and chefs. Turkish people often descend upon this area at the weekends, either for a big breakfast in the morning or a dinner and some live music in the evening.

Yeni Çiftlik Restaurant

Most restaurants in Ankara are best to visit in summertime but this one is also cosy during winter. Unless it's snowing, a chef will generally be preparing *köfte* and other grilled meats and will try to lure you in. Give in to his charms and enjoy some lovely food and warm hospitality. On Tuesdays, Wednesdays, Fridays and Saturdays there is live music in the evening, starting at 19:00.

Yeni Çiftlik Restaurant, Çiftlik Caddesi No: 78 Tel: 211 05 32
www.yeniciftlikrestaurant.com

Mehmetzade Köftecisi

This old train station will immediately draw your attention as you walk through the area. The station was built in 1926 and was in service until 1992, with architecture that mixes Ottoman style features and Western building practices of its time. After a renovation it now serves as a restaurant, offering all sorts of *kebap* dishes and other Turkish food.

Mehmetzade Köftecisi, AOÇ Gazi Tren İstasyonu Binası, Silahtar Cad. No: 220 Tel: 211 11 22 and 211 21 61
www.istasyonrestoranlari.com/mehmetzade

Bahçelievler and Beşevler

This is a student neighbourhood, so the choice of food is wider than just Turkish cuisine. 7. Cadde (also known as Aşkaabat Caddesi) has a mix of fast-food outlets and sit-down restaurants. You'll also find the famous Sim ice cream shop, selling speciality chewy Turkish ice cream (see chapter *Bahçelievler*). Beşevler's 3rd street (3. Cadde, also known as Azerbaycan Caddesi) and 2nd Street (2. Cadde, also known as Prof. Muammer Aksoy Caddesi) offer an almost constant run of restaurants and bars.

7on Heaven Café and Bistro

This bistro gives you a nice view over 7. Cadde. The interior is modern Turkish and the menu offers wraps, sandwiches, fast food, pasta and international dishes. If you fancy something other than Turkish food this place is a good option.

7on Heaven Café and Bistro, 7. Cadde 70. Sokak No: 13/1-2
Tel: 222 07 08 and 222 07 38 www.7onheaven.com

Roka Köfte

Roka Köfte is down a side-street, away from the bustle of the main road. It's a small restaurant with an open terrace where students and local office workers often come to eat. It offers a small menu but you come here for one thing: *Köfte*. Be prepared for a slightly different experience –a huge selection of salad thrown (almost literally) directly onto the table (on a fresh clean table mat), followed by tasty meatballs and fresh bread, for a very reasonable price. Drink *ayran* for the full experience. This is a great place for a simple but delicious meal.

Roka Köfte, 7. Cadde, 22. Sokak No: 4/A Tel: 222 19 13
www.rokakofteci.com

Çankaya

Café de Paris

Abdullah Cevdet Sokak runs parallel to Çankaya Caddesi, the main road passing the Atakule tower and Botanik Parkı, and is home to a very sweet and intimate restaurant. In times gone by it had only one menu –salad to start followed by 'steak frites' with sauce de Paris, and a delicious chocolate soufflé for dessert. Recently they have expanded their offerings but this excellent menu is still available. They have a good stock of fine wines but remember taxes on wines in Turkey are 400% so do not forget to ask for the price first.

Café de Paris, Abdullah Cevdet Sokak No: 30/A Tel: 440 51 23
www.cafedeparis.com.tr

Fige

Another restaurant close to the Atakule, in the heart of Çankaya. The comprehensive menu offer both Turkish and world food. Meat dishes are around 35 TL, wraps and chicken 20 to 25 TL. On Sundays there is an extensive breakfast for 35 TL; for lunch there is an open buffet at 20 TL. Weekend evenings feature live music.

Fige, Abdullah Cevdet Sokak No: 15 Tel: 438 07 50
www.fige.com.tr

Farabi Sokak

Farabi Sokak, the connection between Atatürk Bulvarı and Cinnah Caddesi, is home to several restaurants and a popular spot for lunch. Most restaurants serve modern Turkish and Western dishes. Liva, Liva Light and Sandviç Evi are good places for a salad, a sandwich or a quick kebab lunch.

There are also a couple of popular meyhanes along Farabi: Kalender Zebra and Hollywood Meyhane. These are cosy eateries that become more lively later in the evening. They offer fixed menus for a reasonable price: *meze* to start, and a main meat or fish dish. You can choose for limited or unlimited alcohol next to your meal. Of course this will affect the price.

Kalender Zebra, Farabi Sokak No: 32/A Tel: 466 14 01
www.kalenderzebra.com

Hollywood Meyhane, Farabi Sokak No: 23
Tel: 468 12 15 and 467 39 85 www.myhane.com

Newcastle Pub

If you're pining for a "traditional British pub", this is about as close as you'll get in Ankara. The décor is fairly authentic (wood panelling et al) and they have a decent variety of beers on tap and in bottles, including otherwise elusive Draft Guinness. The pub kitchen serves snacks and hotdogs. With the high tables, large screen TVs showing world football, and the smell of fish and chips in the air, you could almost be in the UK. This pub is a popular place for diplomats and expats, as well as local students and businesspeople.

Newcastle Pub, Üsküp Caddesi No: 7/C Tel: 466 05 75
www.newcastle.com.tr

Manhattan

Directly next door to the Newcastle, this is a club rather than a bar. Located in a basement, with a prominent stage for live music, it's an interesting place for rock, jazz and blues lovers. Manhattan offers an interesting variety of performances –they don't shy away from some pretty experimental performances.

Manhattan, Üsküp Sokak No: 7 Tel: 427 62 63
www.manhattan.com.tr

November Pub

November is another western-style bar, opposite the Newcastle and Manhattan. It's another popular hangout for expats and diplomats. There's a "beer garden" style terrace out front and extending around the side. The kitchen serves both Western and Turkish food, which is tasty and of good quality.

November Pub, Üsküp Caddesi No: 24 Tel: 467 67 06
www.november.com.tr

Gaziosmanpaşa (GOP)

Here's a selection of long-established restaurants in Gaziosmanpaşa. Things change frequently, especially in this fairly upmarket area, so keep your eyes open for new or moved venues. If you're brave enough, ask the locals for the current hot spots!

Please note that in this area prices tend to be higher than average. Alcoholic drinks can be particularly expensive. It's a good idea to check the menu beforehand, or ask if there's no price list available.

Restaurants

Trilye

According to *tripadvisor.com* this is the highest voted restaurant in Ankara. It's a pretty classy fish restaurant where undoubtedly the best place to sit is in the large indoor garden, open all year round. The *meze* dishes here are an absolute must-try. The prices are a bit on the high side, but the great food, good service and nice atmosphere validate the price tag. If you decide to give this place a try, making a reservation is strongly recommended.

Triliye, Hafta Sokak No: 11/B (entrance at İzci Sokak) Tel: 447 12 00
www.trilye.com.tr

Balıkçıköy

Balıkçıköy operates a chain of three seafood restaurants in Ankara, one of them in Gaziosmanpaşa (the other two branches are on Tunalı Hilmi Caddesi and in Çayyolu). They are popular and tend to be very busy. A meal begins with *meze* followed by your choice of fish. The relaxed Mediterranean setting and good service make for an enjoyable experience. Reservation is recommended.

Balıkçıköy, Kırlangıç Sokak No: 3 Tel: 428 00 47
www.balikcikoy.com

Kafes Fırın

Whilst the Turkish are famous for their love of bread, finding a good bakery in Ankara is harder than you'd think. Kafes Firin is possibly the best the city has to offer. Besides breads, sandwiches and pastries, it also offers salads and take-home prepared meals. With diverse offerings and a friendly English-speaking manager, this place is very popular with foreigners and diplomats. It's also, in case you couldn't tell, one of our personal favourite places to eat. Much of this book was written over coffee and pastries sat in this café.

Kafes Fırın, Filistin Sokak No: 31/A Tel: 447 01 83-93
www.kafesfirin.com

The House Café

The House Café, despite its singular name, is a chain of trendy restaurants. Perhaps their flagship is at the corner of Filistin Sokak and Nenehatun Caddesi, and is very much a place to be seen dining. They serve breakfast, lunch, dinner and stay open late for beers, cocktails and wines. The covered terrace protects from bad weather but can be opened when the sun's out, making it an attractive place all year round. The food and service are of a high standard and the menu is available in English –if you look like an "outsider" you'll likely be given this automatically.

The House Café, Nenehatun Caddesi No: 74 Tel: 446 46 88
www.thehousecafe.com

Günaydın

Another chain, Günaydın has three different restaurants in this area. A paradise for carnivores, Günaydın restaurants prepare high quality meat very well. Günaydın Steakhouse, on Arjantin Caddesi, serves all the favourite cuts of steak cooked expertly. Günaydın Burger, on the corner of Filistin Sokak and Nenehatun Caddesi, serves a large range of hamburgers. For lovers of Turkish cuisine, try Günaydın Kebab on Attar Sokak. As the name implies, the menu predominantly features *kebap* based dishes.

Günaydın Steak House, Arjantin Caddesi No: 18 Tel: 468 53 53
Günaydın Burger, Filistin Sokak No: 8 Tel: 447 42 43
Günaydın Kebab, Attar Sokak No: 6 Tel: 466 76 66
www.gunaydinet.com

SushiCo

SushiCo is a very stylish Japanese-Asian restaurant with a large semi-covered garden, open even during colder periods (with external heaters set to blazing). The menu, which is translated into English, is full of a huge range of pan-Asian dishes: Thai curries, Chinese noodles, Japanese sushi and bento, and more.

SushiCo, Attar Sokak No: 10 Tel: 426 25 26 www.sushico.com.tr

Big Chefs

A popular modern restaurant chain, with an extensive international menu printed in English. Despite being a large restaurant, with multiple floors and a large garden area, Big Chefs offers a cosy atmosphere. The service is efficient and most waiting staff speak English.

Big Chefs, İran Caddesi No: 35 Tel: 436 74 54 www.bigchefs.com.tr

Cafemiz

The romantic decor, with angels, chandeliers and pink and white furniture might be too much for some, but the good menu should be enough to tempt you in. At the weekends it offers an elaborate breakfast buffet. For dinner, as well as salads, burgers and the other usuals, you can order your own custom combination of pasta, vegetables and sauce.

Cafemiz, Arjantin Caddesi, No: 19 Tel: 467 79 21
www.cafemiz.com.tr

Mezzaluna

This beautiful restaurant, with large open terrace, is almost always busy. Specialising in pizzas, it has a wide ranging menu also offering pastas, salads and Italian desserts. The wine and liquor list is also pretty extensive. Good quality food and service.

Mezzaluna, Turan Emeksiz Sokak No: 1 Tel: 467 58 18
www.mezzaluna.com.tr

Köşebaşı

This restaurant's name means "Street Corner", and this is one of a renowned chain of Turkish restaurants with branches all over Turkey and abroad. An established chain like this might be a good place to get first acquainted with Turkish cuisine. This branch is a luxurious, stylish restaurant, with excellent staff. The menu includes a range of Turkish appetizers and an array of different *kebap* and *köfte* dishes. There is also a large outdoor terrace. Köşebaşı is, as you might have imagined, located on a corner.

Köşebaşı, Kuleli Sokak No: 32 Tel: 446 59 59 www.kosebasi.com

Quick China

Quick China offers more than just Chinese food. Its elaborate menu also contains sushi, Thai and Japanese food. The food is delicious and the atmosphere both inside the restaurant and outside in the garden is calm and relaxing –a lovely hideaway from the business around it. This is definitely one of the authors' favourites.

Quick China, Uğur Mumcu Sokak No: 64/B Tel: 437 04 03
www.quickchina.com.tr

Kahve Dünyası

This must be the only place in Ankara, perhaps indeed Turkey, where you cannot get a cup of tea. Kahve Dünyası means "Coffee World" and that is what they serve here: coffee, coffee and more coffee, in all its variants. If you're pining for a Cappuccino, or you're fed up with Turkish coffees and Nescafés, this is the place to get your fix. Kahve Dünyası is also chocoholic friendly –some chocolate comes free with every cup.

Kahve Dünyası, Uğur Mumcu Caddesi No: 71
Tel: 437 99 56 and 437 99 57 www.kahvedunyasi.com

Casa di Vino

This restaurant offers a wide range of world dishes. As the name might suggest it's also a sensible destination if you fancy a glass of wine. Elegant décor and good offerings from the kitchen and bar make it a worthwhile venue.

Casa di Vino, Uğur Mumcu Caddesi No: 12/6 Tel: 446 20 51

Bars – Clubs

Victoria Club

This is a "proper" club, not just a bar with loud music. A strict door policy means it might not always be easy to get in, unless you're on the guest list. Patrons consist mainly of wealthy locals, VIPs and expats. An evening can be expensive, but it's an interesting experience which can last well into the night.

Victoria Club, Umurbey Sokak No: 6 Tel: 448 00 06
www.victoriaclub.net

Mickey's

This is a popular bar for expats and diplomats with a decent cocktail list as well as the usual mix of local and foreign beers and wines. Pub snack style food is served out of the kitchen. They have a terrace in front which is busy almost every single day of the year thanks to its outdoor heating.

Mickey's, Arjantin Caddesi No: 17 Tel: 466 43 26

Copper Club

The Copper Club, inside the Sheraton Hotel, is styled (and priced) for the "upper echelon". A jazz club theme, with dim lights, red benches and designer chairs, plays host to regular themed parties attended by mainly wealthy businessmen, diplomats and hotel guests. It is expensive, but stylish.

Copper Club, Noktalı Sokak No: 1 (inside Sheraton Hotel)
Tel: 457 60 00

Kavaklıdere

Restaurants

Aylak Madam

This bistro café is a regular hangout for artists and creative types. It's used as a meeting place and also a spot for working with one of their excellent coffees in the relaxed jazzy atmosphere. As well as the coffee, the simple but well-prepared menu offers options for breakfast, lunch and dinner.

Aylak Madam, Karanfil 2 Sokak No: 77/B Tel: 419 74 12
www.aylakmadam.com

Café des Cafés

This spot on Tunalı is, as the name suggests, a good place to go for a coffee. Many shoppers stop here for a hot drink, sandwich, cake or salad. It's an ideal place for refreshment and people-watching. The service is quick and friendly, and the tea is surprisingly excellent.

Café des Cafés, Tunalı Hilmi Caddesi No: 83/A
Tel: 426 55 11

La Gioia

La Gioia sits next to the Karum shopping mall at the corner of İran Caddesi and Tahran Caddesi. It's a modern, stylish restaurant with excellent Italian food.

La Gioia, Tahran Caddesi No: 2 Tel: 426 44 88

Kebab 49

Kebap 49 is a well-renowned chain of *kebap* restaurants, with other branches in Kızılay and Kavaklıdere. It's not a particularly fancy place but it serves decent typical Turkish food, with tasty *kebap* and *pide* headlining the reasonably priced menu. The staff is quick and friendly. A good place for lunch or dinner; for a bigger meal try one of the excellent *köfte* casseroles.

Kebab 49, Bülten Sokak No: 5 Tel: 467 48 49 www.kebab49.com.tr

Italic

This small trendy Italian restaurant serves great Italian food and wines out on its marvellous street-side terrace –an ideal spot to sit and people-watch. After dinner the restaurant changes tack into more of a bar, where you can continue drinking cocktails and good wines long into the night.

Italic, Bestekar Sokak No: 65/D Tel: 426 30 17

Café Sardunya

Café Sardunya is a charming little wine bar with a small garden in front. They serve a wide range of wines and light snacks. Their food menu is modest and the food itself rather ordinary, but the cosy setting with French music, candles, and helpful waiters, combined with the good selection of wines on offer, make it an enjoyable experience. A good place to go after dinner.

Cafe Sardunya, Bülten Sokak No: 21 Tel: 466 45 76

Café Botanica

This restaurant is hidden in one of the streets behind Hilton but worth to visit as the garden is a very relaxing place. It serves international as well as Turkish cuisine.

Café Botanica, Billur Sokak No: 5/1 Tel: 466 60 89

Café Lins

Café Lins has two branches: one near Tunalı Hilmi Caddesi and one near Filistin Sokak GOP. Both offer more or less the same food and atmosphere, with pleasant outside terraces. The menu offers pasta, chicken, fish dishes and such. They also offer light dishes like grilled vegetables, crêpes, sandwiches and quiche.

Café Lins, Bestekar Sokak No: 84 (Tunalı) Tel: 428 23 50 and Kader Sokak No: 9 (Filistin, GOP) Tel: 428 54 67 www.cafelins.com

Lo & Loud

This coffee shop and bakery, opposite Kuğulu Park and close to the D&R bookstore, is a nice spot for a quick lunch or cup of coffee. During summer they also serve excellent ice cream cones.

Lo & Loud, İran Caddesi No: 11/A Tunalı Hilmi Caddesi Tel: 466 03 33

Bars and Cafés

Tapa Tapa Tapas

The only tapas bar we've found in Ankara, although the tapas on offer are heavily influenced by local tastes. Nevertheless if you have a hankering for something a bit different it's a nice change. Besides the tapas, the restaurant also offers pasta dishes, salads, crêpes and the usual chicken, meat and fish dishes (reasonably priced).

Tapa Tapa Tapas, Tunalı Hilmi Caddesi No: 87 Tel: 428 35 62
www.tapas.com.tr

Golden Pub

Golden is a large basement venue, focusing on live televised sports and darts (playing, not watching). It's a popular spot for students and young expats and diplomats. Almost no wall-space is left uncovered by dartboards, and regular tournaments are held. International football and other sports deemed popular are shown on several big screen TVs. Despite being in a basement it has a large garden which is open all year round. Beside their focus on drinks, there's also a simple pub food menu. No frills, but a decent place to watch the game.

Golden Pub, Tunalı Hilmi Caddesi No: 112-D Tel: 427 15 25

Café Bien

This British style bar is a popular hangout for students, young professionals, diplomats and expats. The interior is possibly smaller than the garden out front, which is where everyone is anyway. At the weekends it tends to get very crowded, weekdays less so. It's a nice place to meet people and socialise with them, enjoy a drink or six, and dance to the (loud) music!

Café Bien, Bülten Sokak No: 4 Tel: 468 85 78

Dikmen

Recep Usta

In summertime this place has a glorious view over the Dikmen Valley. If you are early enough you can take your pick of the tables overlooking the gardens. On top of the lovely view it's also one of the best Turkish restaurants around, serving delicious *meze, kebap* dishes and other Turkish specialties. There is no alcohol, so try the *ayran* served in traditional bowls with a spoon. This is a good place to bring any out of town guests and give them a thoroughly Turkish experience.

Recep Usta, Dikmen Vadisi Hoşdere Girişi 5. Kapı
Tel: 442 29 45 and 442 26 42 www.tavacirecepusta.com

Keçiören

Wangcho Çin Lokantası

This Chinese restaurant is within Altınpark inside a wooden building, decorated in a fairly well dressed Chinese style. It offers good Chinese food for a reasonable price.

Wangcho Çin Lokantası, Altınpark, İrfan Baştuğ Caddesi No: 142
Tel: 318 14 07 and 318 12 07

Özbek Sofrası

This restaurant is housed in a nomad style tent next to the Estergon Kalesi. It has a nice view over Keçiören and offers Uzbekistani cuisine, which closely resembles the Turkish cuisine but with some little differences. The menu features soups, rice, *kebap, börek,* chicken and grilled meat, all prepared in an authentic Uzbekistani manner. The tent adds nicely to the atmosphere.

Özbek Sofrası, Fatih Caddesi, Estergon Kalesi Türk Dünyası Bahçesi
Tel: 360 28 29 www.samarkandsofrasi.com

The Suburbs

South: Çayyolu/Park Caddesi

To the south east of the main city, these new suburbs are on the rise. As the city expands (rapidly) towards these areas, many of the wealthier are moving out to get more space for less money while they still can. This exodus has brought many of the big restaurant and bar chains out to cater for the new inhabitants.

On Park Caddesi the restaurants line up next to each other. There is plenty of choice, but besides this row of eateries there's not much to do in this mostly residential area. Most restaurants here are from the same chains you'll find in Gaziosmanpaşa: Big Chefs, Quick China, Butcha Steakhouse are among others.

The kind of people who out live here tend to dictate the kind of menus you will find. Turkish dishes are always available, but "world dishes" feature prominently.

On the Way to the Airport

If you don't mind driving a little bit further for a good meal, or if you're already on your way to or from the airport, the Kav Club is a fine restaurant. It's located between the vineyards of the Kavaklıdere winery (see chapter *Kavaklıdere* for its history) so, as you would hope, you get plenty of choice when it comes to wine. A stylish restaurant, but with prices to match.

The Club also has a pool (only open during summer) as well as tennis and squash courts. These facilities are open to everyone –for the current fees take a look at their website.

Kav Club, Çankırı Bulvarı, Akyurt (close to Esenboğa Airport)
Tel: 847 52 62 www.kavclub.com

Hotels

Hotels

We offer only a few suggestions for the most favourite areas as there are many online services providing up to date hotel reviews, information and prices. For a more detailed description of the highlighted areas please check the chapter itself.

ULUS:

Divan Çukurhan

Tarihi Ankara Kalesi Necatibey Mahallesi, Depo Sokak No: 3
Altındağ-Ulus Tel: 306 64 00 *www.divan.com.tr*

AND

İçkale Mahallesi, İstek Sokak No: 2, next to the Alaaddin Camii,
Altındağ-Ulus Tel: 310 23 04 *e-mail: hoteland@scamv.com*

Angora House

Kalekapısı Sokak No: 16 Hisar-Ulus Tel: 309 83 80
www.boutiquesmallhotels.com/angoraevleri

KIZILAY:

Etap Mola

İzmir Caddesi No: 27 Kızılay Tel: 424 18 18
www.hoteletapmola.com.tr

Savis

Ziya Gökalp Caddesi No: 27/C Kızılay Tel: 432 31 31
www.savisotel.com

Rota Bulvar

Atatürk Bulvarı No: 63 Kızılay Tel: 431 80 02
www.rotabulvarhotel.com

KAVAKLIDERE:

Ankara Hilton

Tahran Caddesi No: 12 Kavaklıdere Tel: 455 00 00 *www.hilton.com*

Sheraton

Noktalı Sokak Kavaklıdere Tel: 457 60 00 *www.sheraton.com*

Divan

Güniz Sokak No: 42 Kavaklıdere Tel: 457 40 00
www.divan.com.tr

Rixos

Atatürk Bulvarı No: 183 Kavaklıdere Tel: 410 55 00 *www.rixos.com*

Gordion Hotel

Büklüm Sokak No: 59 Kavaklıdere Tel: 427 80 80
www.gordionhotel.com/en

Thanks!

Editors

Special thanks to our English editors, who made a great effort and read all chapters with incredible patience. The book is more fun because of them:

Tim Purkiss

Joanna Haydon

Advisors

We got help and advice from:

Pınar Alpay
Hülya Ateş
Ayla Aydoğmus
Mr. M. Başman
Nadia Hashmi
Anke Hoebers
Agnes van der Meij
Anna Molnar
Çiğdem Önal
Mehmet Gülerman
Filiz Güneş
Serkan Karaman
Saime Keser
Emine Torun

Also thanks to all others who told us stories or gave us tips about Ankara.

Photos

Besides our own photos we used photos from friends and family. Thanks:
Jak den Exter (Kızılcahamam)
Ciska Scheidel (hall of honour Anıtkabir)
Luc Scheidel (Samanpazarı, Pirinç Han)
Tamara Jaspers-van der Aa (Eymir Lake, Şengül Hamamı, castle)
Elidon Veshaj (soldiers Anıtkabir, author's photo)
Luc Scheidel: Zenger Paşa Konağı

In General

Family and friends for testing and commenting the book.
Rogier van der Pluijm and David Naves for their unconditional support and faith.

Sources

Books

Ankara Bağ Evi by the Vehbi Koç Foundation

Ankara City Map and Guide

Ankara Information Guide, Tatjana Vetter-Blanckenstein
Lonely Planet Turkey, 2009

Greater Ankara Municipality Guide 2011

Çankaya, Çankaya Municipality, Boyut Yayın Gurubu, 1992

Ankara The Professional's Business Reference by Ankara Business Centre, 2012

Ankara From the Past to the Present, Ankara Chamber of Commerce, 1998

Antik Ankara, Haluk Sargın, Arkadaş Yayınevi, 2012

Newspapers

Today's Zaman
Sunday's Zaman
Hürriyet Daily News
Sabah

Magazines

AnadoluJet Magazine – July 2012
Cornucopia Magazine, issues 39, 2002 and 47, 2012
Multicultural Guide editions 2011 and 2012

Websites

www.ankaratarihi.blogspot.com

www.mymerhaba.com

Ankara expat connection google mailgroup

www.ankaracityguide.com

www.wikipedia.com

www.academicjournals.org/ajar/pdf/pdf2012/26%20Feb/Ozdemir%20and%20Celik.pdf

www.archive.worldhistoria.com

www.agt.si.edu/cultural_history/turkey/recent_tr.html

www.ankara.bel.tr

www.cankaya.bel.tr

www.aoc.gov.tr

www.wowturkey.com

www.frommers.com/destinations/ankara/A43737.html#ixzz2Ach3EjTf

www.ankaram.net

www.ankararehberi.com

www.kenthaber.com

www.aev.org.tr

www.adventuresinankara.com

www.eng.koreanwar60.go.kr

www.kizilcahamamgezi.com/Historical_Buildings_in_Kizilcahamam.htm

www.kizilcahamampostasi.com.tr/sdetay.asp?did=34

www.kavaklidere.com

www.arber.com.tr

Dissertations

The relation between retail activity transformation and social sustainability. A case study of Bahçelievler 7th street, Ankara/Turkey by Özge Yalçıner Ercoşkun, Burcu Özüduru.

Cengizkan, Ali. 2002a. "Ankara 1924-25 Lörcher Plan: Bir Başkenti Tasarlamak ve Sonrası".

Modernin Saati, 37-59. Ankara: Mimarlar Derneği.

The Political Struggle on and at Kızılay Square with Respect to Perceived, Conceived and Lived Public Space before and after 1980 PhD seminar on Public space in Delft, Netherlands, Feb 2009, Middle East Technical University, Ankara, Yasemin Ilkay

Elif Ekin Akşit, "Women, Modern State and Religious Space" Mediations in Cultural Spaces: Structure, Sign, Body. John Wall (ed.), Newcastle: Cambridge Scholars Publishing, 2008, 154-169.

An Investigation of Water Supply in Roman Ankara, Thesis for the Middle East Technical University by Emre Katan, November 2008 (www.etd.lib.metu.edu.tr/upload/12610143/index.pdf)

Index

Notes

Notes

Notes